Communication and Writing for Paralegals

Ashlyn O'Mara

Helen Wilkie

John Roberts

emond ∎ Toronto, Canada ∎ 2018

Emond Montgomery Publications Limited
1 Eglinton Avenue East, Suite 600
Toronto ON M4T 1A3
http://www.emond.ca/highered

Printed in Canada.
Reprinted July 2021.

We acknowledge the financial support of the Government of Canada.   Canadä

Emond Montgomery Publications has no responsibility for the persistence or accuracy of URLs for external or third-party Internet websites referred to in this publication, and does not guarantee that any content on such websites is, or will remain, accurate or appropriate.

Vice president, publishing: Anthony Rezek
Publisher: Lindsay Sutherland
Director, development and production: Kelly Dickson
Developmental editor: Katherine Goodes
Production editor: Natalie Berchem
Copy editor: Sylvia Hunter
Typesetter: Tom Dart
Text designer: Tara Agnerian
Permissions editor: Monika Schurmann
Proofreader: Dancy Mason
Indexer: SPi Global
Cover image: Undrey/Shutterstock

Library and Archives Canada Cataloguing in Publication

O'Mara, Ashlyn, 1984-, author
    Communication and writing for paralegals / Ashlyn O'Mara,
    Helen Wilkie, John Roberts.

Includes index.
ISBN 978-1-77255-134-1 (softcover)

    1. Legal composition.   2. Communication in law.   3. Legal assistants—Canada.   I. Wilkie, Helen, 1943-, author   II. Roberts, John A., 1944-, author   III. Title.

KE265.O43 2018   808.06'634   C2017-906808-3
KF250.O43 2018

This book is dedicated to the following five friends whom I cherish deeply and who have always been there for me during the good times and the bad: Amanda, Christelle, Kal, Jeff, and Scott.

—AO

Brief Contents

Detailed Contents

1 Effective Legal Writing

2 Grammar Skills

7 Writing Memoranda

8 Email and Social Media Communication

9 Legal Forms

APPENDIXES

A Editing Checklist

B Proofreading Techniques and Exercises

C Speaking Effectively

D Readings

Preface

Communication and Writing for Paralegals is a complete communications program that enables paralegal students both to improve their writing skills and to become familiar with the various forms of communication required of practising paralegals.

The text covers the competencies required by the Law Society of Ontario in the communication and writing portion of an accredited paralegal education program. On November 2, 2017, Convocation of the Law Society of Upper Canada voted in favour of changing its name from the "Law Society of Upper Canada" to the "Law Society of Ontario," effective January 1, 2018. This book makes reference to the Law Society of Ontario to reflect the name under which the Law Society has been operating since January 1, 2018. Furthermore, while the book makes reference to various Ontario statutes and to Ontario rules of professional conduct, the broad principles of legal writing and communication apply generally in professional legal writing.

Beginning with an overview of the writing process, this text highlights the importance of proper writing in the legal profession. It then takes students through an analysis of grammar rules and good writing style. Chapters 2 and 3 contain exercises aimed at emphasizing the importance of proper grammar and style in legal communication.

Chapter 4 teaches students to develop their summarizing and paraphrasing skills, which are invaluable in the analysis of legal documents. It also teaches students to write a case brief and provides an example of one while including exercises that will assist students in writing case briefs. Chapter 5 looks at developing legal arguments, which will assist students in using the IRAC method to analyze and develop arguments in their writing.

Students are then introduced to the composition of letters, memoranda, and emails in Chapters 6, 7, and 8. These chapters explore various strategies for writing and formatting these documents in a paralegal practice, using law-related examples. Chapter 6 introduces students to the proper format and structure of letters, as well as the different kinds of letters a paralegal may write in practice. Chapter 7 includes a discussion on writing different kinds of memoranda and provides various exercises for students to develop the skills necessary to write a persuasive memorandum of law. This chapter also introduces students to the basic rules of legal citation. Chapter 8 covers email and social media communication, which are necessary to the modern-day paralegal practice.

Finally, Chapter 9 includes a discussion of different types of legal forms that a paralegal may need to draft. It canvasses the various types of legal forms in different areas of paralegal practice including landlord and tenant, human rights, and small claims court. This chapter presents scenarios in a variety of legal areas, followed by forms and scenario details that students can practice completing.

The text includes a multitude of examples and exercises to test students' mastery of the skills learned from previous chapters. It also includes a substantial appendix on proofreading skills and offers numerous exercises to improve students' proofreading skills. Perhaps one of the most useful features of this text is the inclusion of an editing checklist in Appendix A, which will assist students in developing an organized and detailed editing process.

Acknowledgments

I would like to thank Scott Tanaka, who kindly provided his time, expertise, and support in the writing and revision of this book. Thank you to my colleagues Camille Sherman, Kent Peel, JoAnn Kurtz, and Gilda Berger, each of whom provided invaluable support and answers to my questions. I would also like to acknowledge the generous and continuous support provided by my colleague Linda Pasternak.

—*Ashlyn O'Mara, BA, LLB, BCL*

From the Publisher and Author

We are grateful for the guidance of the following reviewers of the earlier versions of this text:

Mary Aroukatos, Durham College
Michelle Roy McSpurren, Mohawk College
Barbara Norell, Sheridan College
Leanne Smith, Humber College

About the Author

Ashlyn O'Mara, BA, LLB, BCL is a full-time professor in the School of Legal and Public Administration at Seneca College where she teaches a variety of subjects including Legal Drafting and Communication, Advocacy, Tribunal Practice and Procedure, and Computer Applications for Paralegals. Ashlyn also coaches Seneca's Paralegal Moot Team and helps paralegal students prepare for the Paralegal Cup Mooting Competition and the Osgoode Cup National Undergraduate Mooting Competition each year. For several years, Ashlyn worked as a practising lawyer in the areas of family law, estate planning and administration, estate litigation, and real estate law. She is a graduate of McGill University's Faculty of Law, having obtained degrees in both civil law and common law. She is also an author of *Advocacy for Paralegals*, 2nd edition, (Toronto: Emond, 2016). Connect with her on Twitter: @AshlynOMara.

Effective Legal Writing

1

LEARNING OUTCOMES

After reading this chapter, you should be able to:

- Explain the importance of proper writing.

- Describe the characteristics of effective legal writing.

- Identify and explain the five stages of the writing process.

- Describe the plain legal language movement.

- Understand the importance of point-first writing.

Introduction

The legal profession relies heavily on written communication. Paralegals provide legal representation to clients within limited areas of law as authorized by the **Law Society of Ontario**. Representing clients requires the ability to inform and persuade judges, colleagues, opposing advocates, clients, and other individuals through effective writing. This chapter discusses the importance of proper legal writing and the key considerations in developing effective legal writing skills.

The Importance of Proper Legal Writing

Proper legal writing is important for the individual paralegal, his or her clients, and the administration of justice. Paralegals have a duty to provide legal services to a standard of a competent paralegal, which includes proper writing and drafting skills.[1] In order to represent clients competently, paralegals need to use proper writing skills to communicate effectively. A paralegal who writes poorly risks falling below the standard of a reasonably competent paralegal, which may result in disciplinary proceedings by the Law Society of Ontario. It may also negatively affect a paralegal's reputation in the legal profession and his or her ability to build or maintain a profitable business.

When a paralegal sends correspondence to his or her client that is grammatically unintelligible, the client's confidence in the paralegal is shaken. Any client would question such a paralegal's ability to provide effective representation. Poorly written court documents can also result in rejected legal claims and the loss of a client's legal rights. For example, the rules regarding **pleadings** usually require the **plaintiff** to set out the **cause of action** clearly and concisely.[2] In other words, the document which commences a court proceeding must clearly identify the alleged facts that support the plaintiff's legal right to sue the defendant. If it does not, the court may **strike out** that document, thereby prohibiting the plaintiff from proceeding with his or her legal claim.[3]

Poorly written court documents also waste court time and resources. The court system relies heavily on written communication in the form of pleadings, affidavits, briefs, facta, and so on. When legal documents are confusing and unclear, judges, justices of the peace, adjudicators, and court clerks may spend unnecessary time trying to understand their substance.

Poor legal writing can also affect a paralegal's credibility with the court. If a paralegal is careless about his or her writing, the judge may conclude that the paralegal cares little about the substance of the client's case. Legal documents that are grammatically unintelligible, unclear, confusing, misleading, deceptive, or inflammatory will leave a negative impression on the judge. A paralegal should strive to make a good first impression with the judge or other decision maker through effective legal writing.

---

1 See *Paralegal Rules of Conduct*, Rule 3.01(4)(c)(iv), online: <http://www.lsuc.on.ca/list.aspx?id=1072> [Rules].

2 *Rules of the Small Claims Court*, O Reg 258/98, Rule 7.01(2), online: <https://www.canlii.org/en/on/laws/regu/o-reg-258-98/latest/>.

3 *Ibid*, Rule 12.02(1).

What Is Effective Legal Writing?

Paralegals who are effective legal writers convey meaning to their audience clearly and concisely. To do so, they need to follow the conventional rules of grammar and syntax. However, good grammar and syntax are not enough to make writing effective. Effective writers also know their audience and their purpose in writing each document. Is the document intended to inform, report, request, advise, persuade, or complain? Is the audience a judge, an employer, a client, an opposing advocate, or the public? The answers to these questions will set the stage for a paralegal and may affect his or her writing style.

The following are some examples of the different audiences a paralegal might write to, and the various reasons for doing so.

A paralegal might write a letter to his or her **client** to

- inform the client about a hearing date;
- inform the client about steps in the proceeding;
- request that the client produce documents;
- advise the client about his or her legal rights; or
- report to the client about the outcome of a meeting, hearing, or negotiation.

A paralegal might write a letter to **an opposing advocate** to

- request available dates for a hearing, mediation, or case conference;
- request disclosure;
- persuade the opposing advocate of a legal position; or
- propose a settlement.

A paralegal might write a memorandum to his or her employer to

- summarize the law on a particular issue;
- inform the senior lawyer or paralegal of the legal arguments in support of or against the client's position;
- inform the senior lawyer or paralegal of any developments on the file (e.g., a telephone call with the client); or
- instruct a process server to file legal documents with a court or tribunal.

A paralegal might draft a pleading or other court form to

- inform the judge, justice of the peace, or adjudicator of the alleged facts that support the client's cause of action or defence;
- advise the judge, justice of the peace, or adjudicator of the applicable legislation and case law; or
- persuade the judge, justice of the peace, or adjudicator to find in favour of his or her client.

Proper style is also necessary to ensure that a document is clear and concise. *Style* refers to how meaning is expressed through the use and arrangement of words, sentences, and numbers, as well as to the tone and organization of the document. In general, a paralegal can develop a good writing style by (1) simplifying his or her writing, (2) organizing his or her writing in an effective manner, and (3) ensuring the tone of the text is courteous and appropriate for the intended audience. Chapter 3 will teach you the tools necessary to accomplish these skills.

The Writing Process

Planning, outlining, writing, revising, editing—these are the components of the writing process. As mentioned above, effective writers know their audience and their purpose for writing each document. For example, you need to know why you are writing a letter to a client before you begin writing it. If you are writing an opinion letter to a landlord client to advise whether or not the landlord has to repair the rental unit, you should know the purpose of the letter—to answer the client's question. This is why it is easier to start writing after the legal research is complete: once you know the conclusion, an analysis and an introduction are much easier to develop.

Stage 1: Planning

The first stage of the writing process is the planning stage. This is the "why" of the document drafting. In the landlord client example above, the "why" of the letter is to advise the client about a course of action, based on your research and analysis of the law. When writing a research memorandum for an employer, the "why" might be to summarize and inform an employer about the state of the law on a particular issue. Prior to drafting the memorandum, you should conduct the necessary research as part of the planning stage.

The planning stage also involves **brainstorming**. After determining the "why" of the document and completing the research, you should start to write down ideas, facts, and information that the document will address. This is not the time to organize your ideas; rather, the focus should be on identifying all possible ideas, arguments, and so on.

Stage 2: Outlining

Preparing an outline involves logically organizing the information, facts, and ideas developed during the planning stage. This allows you to see the connections among different ideas and therefore is helpful in effectively organizing the substance of the document. There are different ways to prepare an outline. One way is to prepare a linear list of the points you would like to make or address, along with sub-points under each main point. You can then rearrange the points until you are satisfied with the organization and flow of information.

Stage 3: Writing/Drafting

Once the outline is complete, the next step is the writing/drafting stage. Completing a comprehensive outline makes drafting the document easy. The writing/drafting stage involves preparing the actual document in draft form—that is, drafting the text of the document in complete sentences, using the outline as a guide. When writing, you should always keep in mind the intended audience and the purpose of the document.

Stage 4: Revising

Revision is an essential stage in the writing process. After completing a draft of your document, you should spend time improving its content, rewriting to ensure that the information presented flows logically and coherently. At this point you should also revise the document to include missing information and remove unnecessary content.

Stage 5: Editing

The final stage of the writing process is editing the document for errors. You should devote significant time to correcting spelling mistakes, grammatical errors, and stylistic problems. It is not enough simply to read the document once to check for errors. Effective writers often read documents multiple times to identify errors. Appendix A provides a sample editing checklist that will help you with the editing stage.

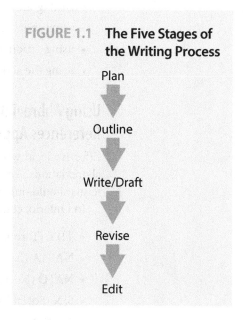

FIGURE 1.1   **The Five Stages of the Writing Process**

Plan
Outline
Write/Draft
Revise
Edit

The Plain Legal Language Movement

The use of legal jargon in written communication is a common critique of trained legal professionals. **Legal jargon** is specialized legal language that those who are not trained legal professionals find difficult to understand. In addition, legal professionals can produce written communications that are long, complex, and confusing. Many legal professionals do not write in language that clients or other readers can easily understand.

Over the years, there has been a movement towards encouraging legal professionals to embrace plain legal language communication. Cheryl M Stephens defines plain legal language as "language that is clear and comprehensible to its intended reader."[4] The goal of plain legal language writing is for people without legal training to understand legal documents. Those who do have legal training (such as judges, justices of the peace, and adjudicators) also commonly prefer reading documents written in plain language rather than obscure technical legal language. Using clear and simple language makes the concepts and issues clear to the reader, who can then understand the message without wondering what certain technical legal words or phrases mean.

Effective legal writers communicate in plain language, and paralegals can and should do the same. This book teaches you the tools necessary to write in plain, simple language, including:

---

4 Cheryl M Stephens, "Plain Language Legal Writing: Part 1—Writing as Process" (Canadian Bar Association, 4 March 2014), online: <https://www.cba.org/Publications-Resources/CBA-Practice-Link/Young-Lawyers/2014/Plain-Language-Legal-Writing-Part-I---Writing-as-a>.

- using short-form references appropriately,
- avoiding legal jargon,
- avoiding expressions (informal language and slang),
- cutting unnecessary words,
- using short sentences,
- using action verbs, and
- using the active voice.

Using Abbreviations, Acronyms, and Other Short-Form References Appropriately

Effective legal writers do not overuse short-form references, including acronyms and abbreviations. An **acronym** is a word formed from the initial letters of other words. Paralegals should only use acronyms that are commonly known.

In Ontario, commonly used acronyms include

- TIFF (Toronto International Film Festival),
- NAFTA (North American Free Trade Agreement),
- NATO (North Atlantic Treaty Organization),
- SIN (Social Insurance number), and
- MADD (Mothers Against Drunk Driving).

An **abbreviation** is a shortened version of a longer word or phrase. In Ontario, commonly used abbreviations include

- SCC (Supreme Court of Canada),
- LSO (Law Society of Ontario),
- CBC (Canadian Broadcasting Corporation),
- DOB (date of birth),
- ATM (automated teller machine), and
- OBA (Ontario Bar Association).

Paralegals should use acronyms, abbreviations, and other short-form references to shorten sentences and avoid overusing a long word or phrase. Some abbreviations and other short-form references are fine, as long as they are used appropriately, which includes not overusing them and being consistent in their use. Consider the following passage:

> The Applicant (A) and the Respondent (R) arrived at the Human Rights Tribunal of Ontario (HRT) on May 8, 2017 to attempt to resolve their dispute by negotiating a mediated agreement (MA) during mediation. A alleges R violated her human rights (HR) under section 5 of the Ontario *Human Rights Code* (OHRC) and requests monetary damages (MD) in the amount of $5,000.00. R does not believe he violated A's HR and he refuses to pay any MD under the OHRC. While A and R participated in the MS at the HRT, they did not reach a MA.

This passage contains eight different abbreviations, many of them uncommon and unnecessary. Towards the end of the passage, the reader becomes confused in trying to remember what each abbreviation stands for. Consider this revised passage, with the number of abbreviations minimized:

> The Applicant and the Respondent arrived at the Human Rights Tribunal of Ontario (HRT) on May 8, 2017 to negotiate a resolution of their dispute during a mediation session. The Applicant alleges that the Respondent violated her human rights under section 5 of the Ontario *Human Rights Code* (OHRC) and requests $5,000.00 in monetary damages. The Respondent does not believe he violated the Applicant's rights and he refuses to pay any damages under the OHRC. While the parties participated in the mediation session at the HRT, they did not reach a final resolution.

Good legal writers also use other kinds of short-form references in their writing, such as one or two words that represent a longer name or word.

Consider the following examples:

1. The Landlord applied to the Landlord and Tenant Board (the "Board") for an order evicting the tenant from his property. The Board held a hearing on May 29, 2017, and dismissed the Landlord's application.

2. In order to start an action in the Small Claims Court, the Rules of the Small Claims Court (the "Rules") require the plaintiff to file a plaintiff's claim (Form 7A) with the court clerk. You can access the Rules using the Canadian Legal Information Institute's website.

3. The paralegal appeared before the Ontario Court of Justice (the "Court") to request an adjournment of her client's trial. The Court adjourned the trial to September 12, 2017.

When using short-form references, including acronyms and abbreviations, always use the full name or phrase the first time and identify the short-form reference in parentheses. You can then refer to the short-form reference throughout the rest of the text. This helps you shorten your sentences and avoid using a long word or phrase repeatedly. Some people identify the short-form reference in quotation marks; some do not. Either way is acceptable, as long as you remain consistent.

Consider the following examples:

1. All members of the Law Society of Ontario ("LSO") are invited to attend the LSO Annual General Meeting on May 10, 2017. Please register with the LSO Equity Department via email.

2. An automated teller machine ("ATM") is a machine that performs various banking services electronically. There are 1,200 ATMs in the City of Oshawa.

3. The plaintiff attended the Toronto International Film Festival ("TIFF") on September 10, 2017. TIFF is one of the world's largest film festivals and features a number of films, lectures, and other events. The defendant worked as an event manager for TIFF in 2017.

Chapter 3 provides more examples of proper and improper uses of acronyms, abbreviations and other short-form references, as well as a number of practice exercises.

Avoiding Legal Jargon

Paralegals can develop their plain English written communication skills by avoiding the use of unnecessary legal jargon. This includes substituting plain English for Latin terms where possible, especially when writing an opinion or reporting letter to a client.

Common legal jargon words/phrases, with suggested alternatives, include the following:

- cause of action ⟶ set of facts that allows one person to pursue a legal claim against another
- conveyance ⟶ transfer
- forthwith ⟶ immediately
- herein ⟶ in this document/letter
- hereinafter ⟶ subsequently referred to as
- hereto ⟶ to this document/letter
- nil ⟶ nothing
- on the grounds of ⟶ because
- *prima facie* ⟶ on its face
- pursuant to ⟶ in accordance with
- subsequent to ⟶ following / after

Consider the following example:

> The Applicant filed a Form 1 Application with the Human Rights Tribunal of Ontario (hereinafter referred to as the "Tribunal") pursuant to the Ontario *Human Rights Code* (hereinafter referred to as the "Code"). Subsequent to the hearing, the Tribunal denied said Application on the grounds that the Applicant failed to establish a prima facie case of discrimination under section 5 of the Code. Attached hereto is a copy of the Tribunal's decision.

Now read the passage below, in which the legal jargon has been removed and replaced with plain English:

> The Applicant filed a Form 1 Application with the Human Rights Tribunal of Ontario (the "Tribunal") in accordance with the Ontario *Human Rights Code* (the "Code"). After the hearing, the Tribunal denied the Application because the Applicant failed to prove the necessary elements of the claim under section 5 of the Code. Attached is a copy of the Tribunal's decision.

The text is much easier to follow and understand, especially for a client or member of the public who is not legally trained.

In addition to avoiding legal jargon, effective legal writing includes simplifying the words used. Consider the following example:

> The paralegal engaged himself in an oral exchange with the prosecutor.

We can rewrite this sentence in plain English as follows:

> The paralegal spoke with the prosecutor.

Avoiding Informal Language and Expressions

While effective legal writers avoid legal jargon and use plain English, this does not mean they should write as they speak. There is a difference between oral communication and written communication, especially in the legal industry. Many informal words and expressions (also known as slang) are used in everyday spoken language but should not be used in written legal communication of any sort, including letters, emails, memoranda, and affidavits. When speaking, we use many informal words and expressions. Consider the following phrases and expressions common in spoken language:

> **I swear** I will attend the mediation tomorrow.
> **At the end of the day**, you need to file your claim before the limitation period expires.
> The Applicant decided to give the position **a shot** and started the job on April 5, 2017.
> There are **loads** of people who suffered as a result of the defendant's negligence.
> I am **gonna** schedule your appointment for May 8, 2017.

Good legal writers use simple, plain English *and* maintain a sense of formality and professionalism in the language they use. Consider how you can rewrite the above informal phrases and expressions in a professional and formal manner without changing the meaning:

> I confirm that I will attend the mediation tomorrow.
> It is important that you file your claim before the limitation period expires. If you do not, you may lose your right to pursue your claim.
> The Applicant decided to give the position a chance. She started the job on April 5, 2017.
> There are many people who suffered as a result of the defendant's negligence.
> I am going to schedule your appointment for May 8, 2017 / I will schedule your appointment for May 8, 2017.

Cutting Unnecessary Words and Using Short Sentences

Effective legal writers simplify their writing by cutting out unnecessary words and using short sentences. Doing so makes the text clearer and more persuasive.

It is usually when revising or editing a document that paralegals attempt to cut out unnecessary words or shorten sentences. When doing so, however, they must be careful not to change the meaning of a sentence or of the entire text.

Consider the following passage:

> It is absolutely necessary that the paralegal attend at the Ontario Court of Justice tomorrow to represent his client in this matter and make a formal request for an adjournment of the scheduled hearing. While the paralegal may put forward a request for an adjournment of the hearing, the prosecutor will oppose that request of the paralegal and will ask the justice of the peace to proceed with the hearing as scheduled.

This passage includes a number of unnecessary words that clouds the meaning of the passage. The sentences are also long. As a result, the passage is tiresome to read.

Clarity is improved when the passage is rewritten as follows:

> The paralegal must attend at the Ontario Court of Justice tomorrow on behalf of his client to request an adjournment of the hearing. The prosecutor will ask the justice of the peace to deny that request and proceed with the hearing instead.

The passage is reduced from 72 words to 42 words without changing the meaning of the text.

Chapter 3 provides a number of examples and practice exercises that will assist you in learning to cut out unnecessary words and using short sentences in your writing.

Using Action Verbs

Effective legal writers use strong action verbs in their writing and avoid using verb-noun combinations in sentences.

Consider the following example:

> The legislation offers protection to the workers.

We can simplify this sentence and make it more powerful by replacing the verb-noun combination *offers protection* with the verb *to protect* in the present tense, as follows:

> The legislation protects the workers.

Using the Active Voice

Voice refers to a type of sentence structure. There are two voices: active and passive. A sentence is in the active voice when the subject of the sentence performs the action of the verb. As such, the subject is usually at the beginning of the sentence.

Consider the following example:

> The paralegal filed the statement of defence.

The subject of the sentence is *the paralegal*. It is the paralegal who performs the action of filing the statement of defence.

A sentence is in the passive voice when what would normally be the object of the sentence becomes its subject. Passive voice shifts the focus of the sentence from the person or thing who acts to the person or thing acted upon.

Consider the following example:

> The statement of defence was filed by the paralegal.

The subject of the sentence is *the statement of defence*. It is the statement of defence that is being acted upon in this sentence.

Paralegals should write in the active voice whenever possible, both because it improves clarity and because using the active voice tends to simplify the writing for the reader. Writing a sentence in the active voice usually requires fewer words than writing it in the passive voice. It can also make the message stronger and more powerful than using the passive voice, producing a more persuasive message.

There are some situations in which a paralegal can use the passive voice. For example, the passive voice is useful when the action itself is most important, and the person initiating the action is less important or is not known. A paralegal can also use the passive voice to emphasize the receiver of the action in a sentence rather than the person carrying out the action.

Writers often struggle with identifying active and passive voice. Writing in the active voice can also be a challenge. Developing the habit of writing in the active voice takes time and practice. Chapter 2 explains the rules for identifying active and passive voice and includes a number of practice exercises.

The Importance of Point-First Writing

Point-first writing is exactly what it sounds like: writing that states the conclusion or point first, followed by an explanation or discussion of that point. Point-first writing requires beginning a document or paragraph by stating the demand or position, then following up with a supporting explanation. For example, if a paralegal is seeking the release of an opposing party's medical records, he or she should begin by stating that the release of the medical records is necessary and then explaining why the law and the facts support this conclusion.

Consider the following paragraphs:

Example 1

Pursuant to Rule 9.3(b) of the Licence Appeal Tribunal Rules of Practice and Procedure (the "Rules") a party may seek an order from the Tribunal at any stage of the proceeding ordering a party to disclose a list of witnesses whom the party may call to give evidence at the hearing and a brief description of each witness's intended testimony. Further, Rule 9.2(b) of the Rules requires a party to disclose a list of witnesses whom the party may call to give evidence at the hearing and a brief description of each witness' anticipated testimony at least 10 days before the hearing. The applicant made two written requests to the applicant to produce his list of witnesses; however to date the applicant has not produced it. The hearing is scheduled in five days and therefore the respondent seeks an order compelling the applicant to produce a list of witnesses he intends to call to give evidence at the hearing immediately.

This is the conclusion (or point)—the paralegal is asking the Tribunal to order the respondent to produce a list of witnesses.

Example 2

The respondent seeks an order compelling the applicant to produce a list of witnesses he intends to call to give evidence at the hearing immediately. Rule 9.3(b) of the Licence Appeal Tribunal Rules of Practice and Procedure (the "Rules") allows a party to seek such an order from the Tribunal at any stage of the proceeding. Rule 9.2(b) of the Rules requires a party to disclose a list of witnesses at least ten days before the hearing. The respondent made two written requests to the applicant to produce his list of witnesses. The hearing is scheduled in five days and to date the applicant has not produced the list.

Example 1 identifies what the paralegal is asking for at the end of the paragraph. The paralegal is requesting that the Tribunal order the applicant to produce a list of witnesses as required by the Tribunal's Rules of Practice and Procedure. As you can see, however, the paragraph reads a bit like a mystery novel: not until the very end of the paragraph do we learn what the paralegal wants the Tribunal to do.

Example 2 is the same paragraph as Example 1, rewritten using point-first writing. From the first sentence of the paragraph, it is clear what the paralegal wants: an order from the Tribunal compelling the applicant to produce a list of witnesses. The paragraph then goes on to explain why the Tribunal should make this order, providing the law (i.e., Rules of Practice and Procedure) and the facts that support what the paralegal wants.

Point-first writing is one of the most important skills of an effective legal writer, because it makes a document both clearer and more persuasive. This book teaches you a number of techniques that will help you develop your point-first writing skills.

Summary

Effective writers are not only good grammarians but also know their audience, avoid legal jargon, use plain language, and know why they are writing a document in order to write it well. This book will give you the tools you need to become an effective legal writer. The book starts with an overview of some important grammar skills. In order to be an effective legal writer, a paralegal must be able to write with proper grammar and identify various types of grammatical mistakes when editing documents. Chapters 2 and 3 introduce a number of techniques for improving writing style when drafting legal documents. Developing an effective legal writing style will help you make your writing clear, concise, and persuasive. Then, after an overview of how to summarize and develop written legal arguments, the book takes you through the different types of written communications, such as letters, memoranda, emails, and legal forms. You will not become an effective legal writer overnight. It will take lots of practice. This book provides numerous exercises for you to practise your legal writing skills.

REVIEW QUESTIONS

1. Why is proper writing important in the legal profession?

2. What is effective legal writing?

3. Describe the five stages of the writing process.

4. What is the plain legal language movement?

5. What is point-first writing? Explain why it is important for effective legal writing.

Grammar Skills

2

LEARNING OUTCOMES

After completing this chapter, you should be able to

- Identify parts of speech in a sentence.

- Identify the purpose of a sentence.

- Correct common grammar errors.

- Recognize different kinds of phrases and clauses.

- Identify common punctuation marks and their uses.

- Identify passive and active voice sentence constructions.

- Proofread legal documents to identify and correct grammatical errors.

Introduction

Correct grammar is important because it helps people understand each other. Conversely, poor grammar can be a significant barrier to communication, especially when it leads to misunderstanding and misinterpretation.

In the legal field, misunderstanding and misinterpretation must be avoided at all costs. Grammar is one of the essential tools of the trade for paralegals, whose ability and efficiency are directly related to their communicative competence. Lawyers, paralegals, clients, judges, and other decision makers will form an opinion of your professionalism on the basis of your use of language. As Chapter 1 explains, good grammar is a component of competent legal representation. Letters, memos, and forms can become legal documents, and errors in grammar and punctuation in these written communications can produce an entirely different meaning from the one intended.

Learn to use grammar and punctuation correctly. Misuse of language can have significant consequences for paralegals, their firm, and their clients.

To begin this chapter, complete the following pre-test to check your knowledge of grammar usage. The pre-test will help you locate your areas of weakness.

Grammar Pre-Test

Exercise 2.1

Finding Subjects and Verbs

Underline the subject with one line and the verb(s) with two lines in the following sentences:

1. Paralegals are becoming licensed at increasing rates.
2. In the modern law firm, the role of technology has evolved to a high level.
3. Many reasons are given for the fact that mainly baby boomers are retiring.
4. There has not been much attention given in the past to the impending personnel shortage.
5. Licensed paralegals can only practise law in the permitted areas of practice authorized by the Law Society of Ontario.

Exercise 2.2

Correcting Sentence Fragments

Change the following sentence fragments into complete sentences. One of the examples is already a complete sentence.

1. While preparing for her court appearance.
2. The partner's assistant received a call from the client about a problem with the contract.
3. A new property on the market.
4. At Osgoode Hall.
5. Was called to the Bar in 2013.
6. Received his paralegal diploma.

Exercise 2.3

Using Subordination and Coordination

Use subordination or coordination correctly to turn each of the following examples into one or more complete sentences. One of the examples is already correct.

1. In proofreading the contract. The assistant found a major error.
2. We all worked overtime on the document brief; the trial date was quickly approaching.
3. Many groups of lawyers are leaving big firms to start boutique firms, it seems to be a trend.
4. Sharon had been an assistant to many lawyers during her career; and was highly regarded by them all.
5. Working in a busy downtown law firm is exciting. And challenging too.
6. While appearing at the Ontario Court of Justice. The defendant fell ill.

Exercise 2.4

Recasting Run-On Sentences

Correct the following run-on sentences. One of the sentences is correct as it is.

1. I was asked to take photographs of striking workers, I decided to do so.
2. Strong competition exists, among small claims court litigation firms, they are each trying to build up their business.
3. Jessica wanted to become a paralegal, she did not realize how hard she would need to study.
4. It is important to address clients with respect it is their business that pays your salary.
5. The information you need to complete the offer to settle can be found using the firm's client database tools.
6. The witness appeared frustrated by the opposing paralegal's questions during cross-examination, the witness did not want to respond.

Exercise 2.5

Using Commas

Correctly punctuate the following sentences with commas. One of the sentences is correct as it is.

1. White-collar criminals dishonest employees and Internet scam artists are surfacing in growing numbers.
2. Recent arrests especially among technology manufacturers have been making headlines.
3. Even owners of sports franchises have been charged.
4. Small fines short prison terms or absolute discharges have not been effective.
5. Corruption reduces public trust in business corporations affects the stock market and has an overall negative effect on the economy.
6. A licensed paralegal can practise in limited areas of the law including small claims court provincial offences and residential tenancies.

Exercise 2.6

Using Other Punctuation Marks

Place punctuation marks (colons, semicolons, quotation marks) where they belong in the following sentences. One of the sentences is correct as it is.

1. He was advised to plead guilty the evidence was stacked against him.
2. The key term, say his lawyers, is plea bargain.
3. The *Highway Traffic Act* regulates the following motorists, passengers, and pedestrians.
4. There are three areas of specialty in the firm landlord and tenant, human rights, and accident benefits.
5. We do business according to the following rule: "The client's needs are paramount."
6. Kindly bring to our next meeting the following documents photographs, emails, and invoices.

Exercise 2.7

Ensuring Subject–Verb Agreement

Correct the errors in subject–verb agreement in the following sentences. One of the sentences is correct as it is.

1. The history of jurisprudence go back thousands of years.
2. Some writers from ancient Rome has described a system of law enforcement in that city.
3. Laws were modified so that the people could understand them.
4. Each group of explorers that went to America were surprised at the codification of laws in certain cultures.
5. The Iroquois Confederacy were able to formalize rules of behaviour.
6. The legal profession in Ontario have a long history.

Exercise 2.8

Establishing Parallel Structure

All but one of the following sentences lack parallel structure. Revise to create parallel structure.

1. In the early days of the profession, lawyers were expected to be male, have a university education, and well dressed.
2. Having women in the majority of law clerk positions offers many advantages, and to have them achieve senior positions is better yet.
3. With good planning and work hard, paralegals can establish and operate successful firms.
4. Report writing, research, and listening are more common activities than those depicted as occurring in the intrigue-filled law firms on television.
5. She was a good assistant, an intelligent woman, and she worked hard.
6. The memorandum should describe the facts, explain the law, and provide an identification of the parties.

Exercise 2.9

Identifying Active and Passive Voice

For each sentence below, identify if the sentence is written in active or passive voice.

1. The letter was sent by the court registrar to each party's advocate.
2. The senior lawyer spoke to the paralegal about completing a research memorandum.
3. The regulation of Uber in Toronto is planned by the City of Toronto next year.
4. New rules on advertising by lawyers and paralegals have been passed by the Law Society of Ontario.
5. All graduating students are invited by the College to attend Convocation.

Exercise 2.10

Editing Sentences for Errors

Each of the following examples contains an error in grammar or punctuation. Revise each example so that it is complete and correct.

1. These sort of experiences are helpful when applying for promotion.
2. No one wants to spend all their time writing reports.
3. I have not kept the record up to date however I know I am going to need it for court.
4. The Breathalyzer technician plan to come during the next shift.
5. All of my colleagues is very friendly.
6. The *Criminal Code* is long complicated and important.
7. Guns are dangerous they can cause a lot of trouble.
8. The siren wailed and we covered our ears loudly.
9. The files were lost for three weeks before the assistant found it.
10. Is a great advocate.
11. After the decision was released by the judge it was sent to the parties by the court clerk.
12. The affidavit was long, unclear, and was not completed.
13. The client claims that he did not do nothing.

Grammar Essentials: Sentences

A sentence is a group of words that contains a complete thought. Every sentence must contain a **subject** and a **verb**.

Subject

The subject of a sentence is the word or group of words that indicate who or what performs an action.

> Karen works as a paralegal.

The subject here is *Karen*. Karen is performing an action in the sentence. If you wrote *works as a paralegal*, you would not know that the sentence is about Karen. This type of subject is called a **simple subject**.

The simple subject may be a noun (Karen), a pronoun (she), or a word ending in *-ing*, also known as a *gerund* or *verbal noun*.

> Reading is her favourite hobby.

In this sentence, *reading* is the subject of this sentence.
The subjects in the following sentences are italicized.

> *I* am in my second semester at college.
> *Writing* is a skill.
> The *car* hit the pedestrian.
> The *store* was robbed last night.
> *She* became a licensed paralegal.
> *Bill* is in jail.

A subject can consist of more than one word, in which case it is called the **complete subject**. The complete subject contains the simple subject.

> The man on the jury seems to be asleep.

Here, *man* is the simple subject, and *the man on the jury* is the complete subject. The complete subject distinguishes this particular man from all other men in the courtroom. In the following sentences, the simple subject is italicized, and the complete subject appears in parentheses:

> (*Pat* and *René*) are partners.
> (*Lawyers* and *paralegals*) attended the seminar.
> (The *people* who live at the top of the hill) run a restaurant.
> (All the *students* wearing green shirts) want to join the hockey team.
> (*To run or to surrender*) are his only options.
> (*Meeting new clients* and *representing them in court*) are my favourite parts of my job as a paralegal.

In every case, remember that in order to be complete, a sentence must have a subject or subjects. Without a subject, a sentence is called a sentence fragment, which will be discussed later in this chapter.

Exercise 2.11

Adding Complete Subjects

Add complete subjects to turn the following fragments into sentences:

1. is responsible for court documentation.
2. were my favourite courses at college.
3. teaches advocacy and practice management courses at the college.
4. takes emergency calls from the public.
5. manages the accounting department.
6. passes federal legislation.

Verb

The verb is the action word in a sentence. Every sentence must have a verb; otherwise, like a sentence without a subject, it is not a sentence but a sentence fragment, which is a grammar error.

The verb in the following sentence is italicized:

> The lawyer *impresses* the jury with her argument.

The subject of this sentence (*the lawyer*) does something, or causes an action to take place (*impresses*). Therefore, *impresses* is the verb.

> Ming *operated* the radio.
> She *arrested* the offender.
> Jane *questioned* witnesses on the stand.
> The lawyer *mentors* the paralegal field placement students.

The **tense** of a verb indicates whether the action took place (past), is taking place (present), or will take place (future).

> *Past:*   I *walked* to work every day.
> *Present:* I *walk* to work every day.
> *Future:*   I *will walk* to work every day.

Many verbs in the English language are what are known as **regular verbs**; these can be changed from present to past tense by adding *-ed* to the present form of the verb. This is not true of **irregular verbs**, which this chapter deals with below.

Changing the present tense to the future tense usually involves adding a word such as *will* or *shall* to the verb:

> I *will apply* to a small law firm.
> She *shall obtain* her diploma.

There are some verbs that do not appear to be "action" words; the action is not obvious. These verbs are called **linking verbs** because they link subjects to other parts of the sentence. They are as much verbs as any action word, however. The most common linking verbs are various forms of the verb *to be*: *is, am, are, was,* and *were*.

> The lawyer *is* efficient.
> I *am* an employee of a human resources department.
> They *are* guilty as charged.
> The officers *were* on patrol.

The verb *to be* is known as an *irregular verb* because it does not follow the same forms as most regular action verbs. For instance, instead of adding *-ed* to the present form of *to be* to form the past tense, use the following forms:

Present	Past
I *am*	I *was*
You *are*	You *were*
He, she, it *is*	He, she, it *was*
We, you, they *are*	We, you, they *were*

The various tenses of the irregular verb *to be* may combine with an *-ing* word, or present participle, to produce the progressive verb tense:

I *am* running.
He *was* training.
They *will be* exercising.

These present participles, ending in *-ing*, form part of the complete verb; in the examples above, *am running, was training*, and *will be exercising* are complete verbs.

Another irregular verb is *to have*. Note that *to be* and *to have* are called **infinitives**. The infinitive is the "to" form of the word—the basic verb form, without conjugations to show person, number, or tense.

Present	Past
I *have*	I *had*
You *have*	You *had*
He, she, it *has*	He, she, it *had*
We, you, they *have*	We, you, they *had*

Below are some irregular verbs in their infinitive, present tense, and past tense forms.

Infinitive	Present	Past
to break	break	broke
to catch	catch	caught
to do	do	did
to drive	drive	drove
to eat	eat	ate
to give	give	gave
to go	go	went
to know	know	knew
to see	see	saw
to sit	sit	sat
to speak	speak	spoke
to take	take	took
to write	write	wrote

A final point to keep in mind is that there can be more than one verb in a sentence.

Exercise 2.12

Changing Verb Tense

Underline the complete verbs in the following passage. Then rewrite the passage, changing the verbs from the present to the past tense.

The injury occurs on November 3, 2017, at the Plaintiff's property located at 123 Manchester Avenue, Anytown, Ontario. The Plaintiff is using an electric device to trim the hedge at the front of his garden when the Defendant walks past with his dog. The dog, a large German shepherd, suddenly leaps toward the Plaintiff, who is startled. His grip loosens and the machine slips and severs the Plaintiff's left thumb. The Defendant claims it is not his responsibility, as the dog is on a short leash and cannot possibly reach the Plaintiff, so the Plaintiff is in no danger from the Defendant's dog.

Subject–Verb Agreement

Subjects and verbs must agree in both person and their number. Follow the "rule of *s*." As a general rule, put an *s* on the end of either the subject or the verb, but not both at once:

> Car**s** speed.
> A car speed**s**.

> Paralegal**s** advocate
> A paralegal advocate**s**.

When trying to ensure that your subjects and verbs agree, take particular care in the following situations:

1. *Words intervening between simple subject and verb.*

   One of the pictures *shows* the firm's founding partner.
   The *suspect* in the robberies *was* arrested yesterday.

2. *Subject following verb.*

   Have John and Heather started a new firm?
   Around the corner *ride* the cyclists.

3. *Two or more singular subjects joined by* or *or* nor.

   John *and* Bill *work* in litigation. [Compound subject takes plural.]
   John *or* Bill *works* in litigation. [Either John or Bill, but not both, works there.]

4. *Collective noun (group word) subject.*

   The jury *is* ready with its verdict. [The entity is acting as a single unit.]
   The jury *were* not in agreement. [Individual actions within the whole entity are meant to be considered.]

5. *Nouns plural in form but singular in meaning.*

   The news *is* reporting that the bank was robbed.
   The West Indies *is* a group of islands.
   Politics *is* of no concern to the law.

6. *Periods of time, fractions, weights, amounts of money.*

   Three days *is* a long time to spend on a cross-examination.
   Three-quarters of the stash *was* seized.
   Fifty pounds of contraband *is* in that car.
   A hundred dollars *is* the fine for the bylaw infraction.

If a fraction refers to a quantity ("three-quarters of the membership"), it is treated as singular; if it refers to a number, it is treated as plural ("three-quarters of the pencils").

7. *Relative pronouns.* These pronouns (*who, which, that*) agree with their antecedent (the word to which they refer or the word that they replace) in number.

   These are the *employees who are* always reliable. [The antecedent of *who* is *employees*.]

Bill is one of the *employees who are* always reliable. [*Employees* is the antecedent of *who*, requiring the plural verb *are*.]

George is the *only one* of the legal assistants *who is* on vacation. [*Only one* is the antecedent of *who*, requiring the singular verb *is*.]

Lian is one of the *women who work* in the firm's library. [*Women* is the antecedent of *who*.]

8. *Indefinite pronouns.* The following indefinite pronouns are always singular: *one, each, anybody, anyone, somebody, someone, everybody, everyone, nobody, no one, either*, and *neither*.

One *is* not obliged to purchase a raffle ticket.
Each of the students *has* an assignment.
Anybody who works with him *knows* he could not have done it.
Anyone who *wants* to join may do so.
Somebody up there *likes* me.
Someone *is* following them.
Everybody *is* going to the staff picnic.
Everyone in the room *is* dancing.
Nobody *cares* about that.
No one *has* a salary increase.
Either suspect *fits* the description.
Neither Joe nor Dave *has* a girlfriend.

The following indefinite pronouns are always plural: *both, many, few*, and *several*.

Both of the cars *were* blue.
Many of the students *speak* French.
A few of the officers *are* at the scene.
Several of the people *were* victims of the scam.

The following indefinite pronouns are singular for quantity and plural for number: *all, any, most, none*, and *some*.

Quantity (Singular)	**Number (Plural)**
All of the parking lot *was* full.	All of the parking spots *were* taken.
Any time *is* good for me.	Any days *are* good for me.
Most of the audience *likes* the show.	Most of the people *like* the show.
None of the laundry *feels* dry.	None of the clothes *feel* dry.
Some of the food *was* spoiled.	Some of the eggs *were* spoiled.

9. *Compound subjects that do not agree in number.* In a compound subject, where one subject is singular and one is plural, make the verb agree with the *nearest* subject.

Either the manager or the *assistants are* at the workshop.
Either the assistants or the *manager is* at the workshop.

Exercise 2.13

Revising: Subject–Verb Agreement and Pronouns

1. Correct the errors in subject–verb agreement and any pronoun errors in the following passage:

The correspondence in my files indicate that Joan Bennett has liabilities of approximately $10,000.00. These amounts include an estimated additional accruals of rental to my client of approximately $5,000.00. Ms. Bennett also have realizable assets of less than $25,000.00, which mean that a division of sale of her assets among her creditors result in a realization of less than four cents on the dollar. From this amount also comes the fees of a trustee and other realization costs.

2. Complete the following sentences, using the correct present tense of the verb *to be*:
   a. Anyone _____ .
   b. Each _____ .
   c. Somebody _____ .
   d. Neither _____ .
   e. Either _____ .
   f. No one _____ .
   g. Something _____ .
   h. Much _____ .
   i. Anybody _____ .
   j. Everyone _____ .

Sentence Fragments

Since every complete sentence must have a subject, must have a verb, and must make a complete thought, any group of words without one of these three characteristics is a **sentence fragment**.

> She reads a textbook.

This is a complete sentence: It has a subject (*she*) and a verb (*reads*), and it is a complete thought; it makes sense, and it's understandable. However, without the subject in the sentence, the remaining words would be

> Reads a textbook.

This is a sentence fragment, because the sentence now has no subject. Who or what reads a textbook? The sentence requires a subject.

Examples of different kinds of sentence fragments are set out below.

> Parked at the court house. [What or who parked at the court house?]
> My memorandum of law on my boss's desk. [What about the memorandum of law on the desk?]
> With only my briefcase. [What happened with the briefcase?]
> Waiting for the courier. [Who is or was waiting?]

Adding a subject and verb to these fragments makes them into complete thoughts:

> I parked at the court house.
> My memorandum of law is on my boss's desk.
> With only my briefcase, I fought off a swarm of bees.
> The law clerk was waiting for the courier.

Any group of words that contains a subject and a verb is called a **clause**. A sentence is a clause in most cases, but not always. There are two types of clauses: independent and dependent.

An **independent clause** contains a subject, a verb, and a complete thought; therefore, independent clauses are also sentences.

> He will answer for his crimes.

A **dependent clause** contains a subject and a verb, but it does not express a complete thought. It is a fragment that needs something else to complete it.

> Because he was caught.

He is the subject, *was caught* is the verb, but the clause does not explain what happened because he was caught. Therefore, this group of words does not contain a complete thought and is a sentence fragment.

> Because he was caught, he will answer for his crimes.

As shown here, a dependent clause at the beginning of a sentence must be followed by a comma. No comma is needed if the dependent clause falls at the end of a sentence.

> He will have to answer for his crimes because he was caught.

Another type of sentence fragment to be considered is the "list" fragment.

> Paralegals must be. Intelligent, resourceful, and diligent.

Both of these fragments are dependent. The first fragment has a subject and a verb, but it needs the list ("intelligent, resourceful, and diligent") to complete its meaning. The list does not have a subject or a verb. The straightforward solution is to combine the two:

> Paralegals must be intelligent, resourceful, and diligent.

Two further examples of common sentence-fragment errors are set out below, along with their corrected forms:

> *Fragment:*   I like card games. Such as euchre, poker, and blackjack.
> *Complete:*   I like card games, such as euchre, poker, and blackjack.
> *Fragment:*   We went to court. Saw the judge, the bailiff, and the lawyer.
> *Complete:*   We went to court, where we saw the judge, the bailiff, and the lawyer.

Finally, you should be aware that commands, brief though they usually are, do not qualify as sentence fragments.

> Stop!

The subject *you* is implied here, so the sentence is complete.

Remember, too, that an *-ing* word, also known as a present participle (e.g., *running, shooting*), can never be the complete verb in a sentence.

> *Fragment:*   I running to keep in shape.
> *Complete:*   I am running to keep in shape.

Exercise 2.14

Correcting Fragments

Form the following fragments into complete sentences:

1. I worked hard. So that I could get a promotion.
2. We went into law. Because we love advocating for people's rights.
3. Tell me the truth. If you know it.
4. The police officer arrested him; because he was drinking and driving.
5. I love to travel. Wherever I go.
6. You will find your shirt. In the drawer. Where you keep your socks.
7. Because the traffic was heavy.
8. If they get their act together.
9. While running for the bus.
10. Human rights, landlord tenant, social benefits law.

Run-On Sentences

The **run-on sentence** is the opposite of the sentence fragment. While the fragment is part of a sentence, the run-on occurs when two complete sentences or independent clauses are joined together in an inappropriate way.

> I always stop here for coffee it is my favourite place.

You can correct the above sentence in four ways. First, you could use two sentences:

> I always stop here for coffee. It is my favourite place.

Second, you could use a conjunction:

> I always stop here for coffee because it is my favourite place.

Third, you could use a semicolon:

> I always stop here for coffee; it is my favourite place.

And, fourth, you could use a dependent clause:

> Since this is my favourite place, I always stop here for coffee.

Keep in mind that an independent clause contains a complete thought, but only one complete thought. The run-on expresses more than one thought, with no division between the thoughts.

Another type of run-on is the **comma splice**.

> There is a leash law, no one obeys it.

In this case, the comma is misplaced; two independent clauses cannot be separated by a comma without a conjunction or linking word. A comma splice can be corrected in the same four ways as any other run-on. You can use two sentences:

> There is a leash law. No one obeys it.

You can use a conjunction:

> There is a leash law, but no one obeys it.

You can use a semicolon:

> There is a leash law; no one obeys it.

You can use a dependent clause:

> Although there is a leash law, no one obeys it.

Exercise 2.15

Correcting Run-Ons

1. Correct the following run-on sentences:
   a. Just let me do the talking you will get us a ticket if you do not keep quiet.
   b. The cabin was cold however it had a wood stove.
   c. A strong wind was blowing the boat from the yacht club nearly sank.
   d. Most people have $^{20}/_{20}$ vision that is a requirement for a job here.
   e. There are different career opportunities for students in the paralegal program many employers demand experience.
2. Remove the run-on sentences from the following paragraph:

Thank you for your attention to this matter if I can be of any assistance to you in collecting the necessary documents please contact me I will do what I can to expedite the process it is important that you complete this as soon as possible if any of the documents are missing the court may dismiss your case you would still be liable for court costs.

Modifiers

A modifier is a word or phrase that refers to, describes, or explains another word in a sentence. You must place modifiers as close as possible to the word or words they modify. There are two types of sentence errors involving modifiers: **misplaced modifiers** and **dangling modifiers**.

Misplaced Modifiers

Misplaced modifiers are modifiers that are placed in such a way that it is unclear which word or words in a sentence they apply to.

> The audience cheered when we graduated from college excitedly.

The modifier *excitedly* is misplaced here because it is unclear whether it modifies *graduated* or *cheered*.

Consider these other examples, in which the misplaced modifiers are italicized:

> He protested at the noise of the siren wailing *angrily*.
> The police officer approached the hostile-looking dog *with a hockey glove on*.
> Our lawyer rated our chances of winning *without much enthusiasm*.

To correct the sentences, place the modifiers closer to the words they modify.

> He angrily protested at the noise of the siren wailing.
> With a hockey glove on, the police officer approached the hostile-looking dog.
> Without much enthusiasm, our lawyer rated our chances of winning.

Exercise 2.16

Correcting Misplaced Modifiers

Correct the misplaced modifiers in the following sentences:

1. The woman was stopped for speeding with the hat.
2. He made cookies for his friends with chocolate chips in them.
3. The police chief led the parade in full dress uniform.
4. Customs officers intercepted the smugglers guarding the coast line.
5. The criminal laughed when she was almost convicted maliciously.
6. The man escaped before the fire spread barely.
7. We planned to start work early Christmas Eve a long time ago.
8. The defendant stood in the dock without any signs of cracking.
9. The suspect said he was at home with a bow tie.

Dangling Modifiers

The other form of modifier fault is the dangling modifier. A dangling modifier is one that does not logically modify anything in its sentence.

> Crossing the border, my bags were searched.
> Expecting a lot of work, extra help was requested.
> Demanding an answer, a meeting was called.

In these sentences, the modifier is dangling. In the first sentence, who was crossing the border? *My bags*? In the second sentence, who is expecting a lot of work? In the third sentence, who is demanding an answer? These sentences can be corrected as follows:

> When I was crossing the border, my bags were searched.
> Expecting a lot of work, we requested extra help.
> Demanding an answer, my manager called a meeting.

To fix a dangling modifier, add a word to which the modifier refers, and put the modifier as close to that word as possible.

Exercise 2.17

Correcting Dangling Modifiers

Correct the dangling modifiers in the following sentences:

1. Risking her life, the accident victims were rescued by the lifeguard.
2. Crossing the street, my hat blew away.
3. To pass the Advocacy course, participation in a mock trial is required.
4. Driving through the suburbs, several luxury vehicles were seen.
5. Jogging through the park, a dog bit me.
6. On receiving an offer of employment, tears filled his mother's eyes.
7. When learning legal terminology, memorizing is often used.
8. Driving at night, his mind began to wander.
9. Being a licensed paralegal, a framed certificate was proudly displayed.
10. While attending the theatre, the apartment was looted.

Pronoun References

A pronoun is a word that replaces a noun. It may be used as the subject of a sentence (the word that indicates who or what performs an action).

Noun:	Roy works in Toronto.
Pronoun:	*He* works in Toronto.

Noun:	Kiran always travels with her laptop.
Pronoun:	*She* always travels with her laptop.

A pronoun may also be the object of a sentence (the word that indicates upon whom or what an action is performed).

Noun:	Sylvie and Randi handle complete mediation files.
Pronoun:	Sylvie and Randi handle *them*.

Pronouns may also be used as both the subject and the object of a single sentence.

Nouns:	Joe writes his report.
Pronouns:	*He* writes *it*.

Joe is the subject of the sentence, which is replaced with the pronoun *he*; the thing being written, *his report*, is the object of the sentence, which is replaced with the pronoun *it*.

When replacing a subject, use the following personal pronouns:

Singular	Plural
I	we
you	you
he, she, it	they

When replacing an object, use the following personal pronouns:

Singular	Plural
me	us
you	you
him, her, it	them

Note the use of both subjective and objective personal pronouns in the following examples:

Nouns:	Rex ran away from the intruders.
Pronouns:	*He* ran away from *them*.
Nouns:	The police officer told Fred to move the van.
Pronouns:	*She* told *him* to move *it*.
Nouns:	The paralegal questioned the witnesses.
Pronouns:	*She* questioned *them*.
Nouns:	The students graduated from college.
Pronouns:	*They* graduated from college.

Pronouns and Case

The *case* (subjective, objective, or possessive) of a personal pronoun is determined by the function it serves in a sentence. Pronouns can be subjects or subject complements (subjective case); they can be direct objects, indirect objects, or objects of prepositions (objective case); or they can indicate ownership (possessive case).

Subjective pronouns	Objective pronouns	Possessive pronouns
I	me	my (mine)
you	you	your (yours)
he	him	his
she	her	her (hers)
it	it	its
who	whom	whose
we	us	our (ours)
they	them	their (theirs)

He (*subject*) made the donation for me (*object*).
With whom (*object*) did I (*subject*) see you (*object*) last night?
Her (*possessive*) litigation caseload is much heavier than his (*possessive*).

A subject complement following a linking verb (*to be* [am, is, are, was, were, have been], *to act, to appear, to become, to feel, to grow, to seem, to look, to taste*) takes the subjective case; for example, "It was I who opened the file."

Exercise 2.18

Using Pronouns

Underline the correct pronoun in parentheses in each of the following sentences:

1. We expect you and (they, them) at the meeting.
2. Wait for my partner and (I, me).
3. (He, Him) and Ahmad worked together.
4. The receptionist told you and (her, she) to stay here.
5. Everyone was at the party except (we, us).
6. You and (I, me) are both in line for promotion.
7. Professionals such as you and (he, him) should help younger employees.
8. Was it (she, her) that you saw?
9. I think that the shoplifter was (he, him).
10. It could have been (they, them) who won the race.

Ambiguous and Indefinite Pronoun References

It is important to eliminate ambiguity in pronoun references.

> When Rebecca saw Jane, she was angry.

Which of the two was angry? To indicate that Rebecca and not Jane was angry, the sentence can be recast as follows:

> Rebecca was angry when she saw Jane.

To indicate that Jane was the angry one, recast the sentence as follows:

> Jane was angry when Rebecca saw her.

Use a pronoun to refer to a single noun, not a group of words.

> He admitted that he defrauded the client. This was welcome news.

Does *this* refer to the fact that he defrauded the client, or to his admission of the fact? Rewrite the sentence to remove this ambiguity:

> He admitted that he defrauded the client. His admission was welcome news.

Avoid the indefinite use of *it* and *they*.

> They say automation is a growing factor in legal proceedings.

Who is *they*? Rewrite the sentence to give *they* a face:

> The Law Society says that automation is a growing factor in legal proceedings.

> The judge ruled that it was not enough to prove the Plaintiff's case.

What is *it*? Rewrite the sentence to give *it* a face:

> The judge ruled that *the evidence* was not enough to prove the Plaintiff's case.

Exercise 2.19

Removing Ambiguous and Indefinite Pronoun References

Correct the pronoun errors in the following sentences:

1. They did not see the Smiths arrive because they were having lunch.
2. I do not know what he said to him, but he was angry.
3. The girl's mother studied law, and she is going to be one when she grows up.
4. He began his career as a private investigator, which was terminated by his death.
5. In my first job, I learned to change a toner cartridge without getting it all over me.
6. I let my relatives help me with the new cars although they were rather dirty.
7. The assistant told her manager that whatever she did she could not please her.
8. They say that crime is decreasing in the city.
9. He fell while addressing the jury, which was embarrassing.
10. They have good traffic laws in Ontario.

Parallel Structure

Parallel structure involves joining similar structures together in a sentence. When creating lists, for example, a paralegal should balance the sentence by ensuring that each idea matches the others in grammatical form.

> Francis likes reading, writing, and speaking.

These *-ing* words all refer to forms of communication, and they are parallel in structure because they all end in *–ing* and are verbs.

Incorrect parallel structure joins structures that are not in the same form. For example,

> Kevin is a teacher, a paralegal, and trains people in hockey.

This sentence does not have parallel structure because "teacher", "paralegal" and "trains" are different parts of speech. "Teacher" and "paralegal" are both nouns, but "trains people in hockey" is a verb phrase, led by the present tense of the verb "to train" (*trains*). Therefore, this sentence contains a noun–noun–verb list. To correct the parallel structure, the list should be recast with three nouns or three verbs.
The sentence can be rewritten with correct parallel structure as follows:

> Kevin is a teacher, paralegal, and hockey trainer.

The list in this sentence now consists of three ideas expressed as nouns (*teacher, paralegal*, and *hockey trainer*).

> Svetlana is intelligent, witty, and charms people.

The list in this sentence consists of two adjectives and a verb phrase. Correcting the parallel structure requires rewriting the sentence so that all three ideas are adjectives:

> Svetlana is intelligent, witty, and charming.

Parallel structure should be used when phrases, clauses, or infinitives are connected by conjunctions:

Two phrases:	up the hill and down the valley
Two clauses:	that he is a thief and that he is in jail
Two infinitives:	to go or to stay

Correlatives

Correlative conjunctions are specific sets of words that require parallel structure when used together. Some common correlative conjunctions are the following:

either ... or
neither ... nor
not ... but
not only ... but also
both ... and

Consider the following example:

The paralegal not only advocates in court but also writes scholarly articles.

This sentence uses the correlative conjunction *not only ... but also* and therefore requires parallel structure. It is in proper parallel form because it uses a verb after *not only* and after *but also*. *Advocates* is the present tense of the verb *to advocate*, and *writes* is the present tense of the verb *to write*.

Consider the following example:

The paralegal is both confident and has experience.

This sentence is not in proper parallel form because it uses an adjective–verb construction. The adjective *confident* follows *both*; therefore, an adjective should also follow *and*. Instead, the present tense of the verb *to have* follows *and*. To correct the parallel structure, rewrite the sentence as follows:

The paralegal is both confident and experienced.
The paralegal has both confidence and experience.

Exercise 2.20

Using Parallel Structure
Rewrite the following sentences so that they use correct parallel structure:

1. Fish or a steak meal is fine by me.
2. I do not enjoy jogging when it is raining or it snows.
3. He learned juggling and to type.
4. I knew all the dangerous areas of the city and to avoid them.
5. He did not know the bylaw or the *Highway Traffic Act*.
6. Catherine taught us minute taking, writing reports, and how to do summaries.
7. Every paralegal is taught the value of conducting research and how to analyze case law.
8. The supervisor is influential and a popular person.
9. He is not happy nor satisfied with his job.
10. The witness testified voluntarily, honestly, and was clear.

Grammar Essentials: Punctuation and Capitalization

Commas

As a general rule, fewer commas are better than many. Do not use a comma if you are not sure you need one. However, there are certain rules for comma use that you should follow.

1. Use a comma to separate three or more items in a series.

   The warrant was signed, sealed, and delivered.

   Some people prefer not to use a comma before the word *and* in a series. The only firm rule is be consistent.

2. Use a comma between two independent clauses separated by the coordinate conjunctions *and, but, or, nor, yet,* and *so,* especially if the subject changes in the second clause.

   He was a strong advocate, and his successful career was an inspiration to many young professionals.

3. Use a comma after a long introductory element.

   After 10 years with the firm, Tom became a partner.

4. Do not use a comma if such an expression is put at the end of the sentence.

   Tom became a partner after 10 years with the firm.

5. Use commas to separate "interrupters" from the rest of the sentence. Interrupters are words or phrases that are not essential to the meaning of the sentence and can be removed without changing its meaning.

   I knew, *of course*, that I would be caught.
   The judge, *on the other hand*, did not agree with the Defendant's advocate.
   The professor scheduled the final exam. The exam, *in fact*, will cover chapters 1 to 5.

   You should use interrupters sparingly in legal documents, because they can affect the clarity of the text. Using interrupters can also be seen as informal and unprofessional.

6. Use commas to surround material that is not essential to the sentence. The difference between this rule and the preceding one is that, in this case, the information surrounded by commas adds some substance to the meaning of the sentence.

   Lawyers, no matter how talented, cannot function without efficient assistants.
   The client told his lawyer, in confidence, that he committed the crime.
   The paralegal scope of practice, with some exceptions, could be expanded within the next few years.

7. Use a comma to separate different parts of addresses and dates.

   198 Queen Street South, Hamilton, Ontario L8P 3S7 [Do not use a comma between the province and the postal code.]
   November 10, 2002

8. Do not use commas unnecessarily in addresses and dates.

    Incorrect: 198 Queen Street South, Hamilton, ON, L8P 3S7 [Do not place a comma between the province and postal code]
    Correct: 198 Queen Street South, Hamilton, ON L8P 3S7
    Incorrect: 10 November, 2002
    Correct: 10 November 2002 *or* November 10, 2002

9. Do not use commas with the 24-hour clock or when dates are written as numerals.

    1320 (1:20 p.m.)
    44.05.31 (31 May 1944)

10. Use commas before or after a direct quotation.

    She said, "I am here for the written communication test."
    "I am here for the written communication test," she said.
    He answered, "You must be joking!"

Exercise 2.21

Using Commas

Insert commas where necessary in the following sentences:

1. Her excuse of course was completely ridiculous.
2. Please take note you have been promoted.
3. The elderly man coughed staggered and fell to the ground.
4. She smuggled drugs was caught as she left the plane and now has to pay for the crime.
5. The court date is set for August 8 2018.
6. I live at apartment 5 216 Bold Street Toronto Ontario.
7. Tomorrow July 31 is my birthday.
8. That is the best way I think to take creases out of your uniform.
9. I said "Your last statement isn't the truth."
10. You have to comply with the court order or you will be arrested.

Apostrophes

The apostrophe shows possession. It is also used in contractions.

Possession:	John's [belonging to John]
Contraction:	Didn't [did not]

Possessives

The possessive indicates ownership or affiliation. Most possessives can be written by adding an apostrophe and an *s* to a singular noun.

Possession:	Theo's whistle [Theo owns the whistle.]
Affiliation:	Mao's club [Mao is a member of the club.]

In determining possessives, it is often helpful to rephrase a sentence using the word *of* to show possession:

> The whistle of Theo.
>
> The club of Mao.

When forming the possessive of plural nouns ending in *s*, add the apostrophe after the noun.

> The cars' noise [More than one car is making noise.]

Compare this to the singular possessive:

> The car's noise [One car is making noise.]

A review of various forms of the word *car* is provided below.

Word	Part of speech
car	singular noun
car's	possessive singular noun [belonging to one car]
cars	plural noun
cars'	possessive plural noun [belonging to more than one car]

The following rules will help you in creating possessive nouns:

1. If a singular word ends in *s*, add an apostrophe and an *s* to the final letter.
   My boss's office [There is one boss with one office.]

2. Words that are already plural take an apostrophe followed by an *s*.
   My children's toys

3. Statements relating to time need apostrophes in certain situations.
   I am eligible for a week's vacation [a vacation of one week].
   I am eligible for three weeks' vacation [a vacation of three weeks].

4. Never use an apostrophe with the following pronouns:

my	your	yours	his
whose	their	theirs	her
its	our	ours	hers

Note that *it's* is a contraction meaning "it is"; it does not show ownership or affiliation.

Contractions

Contractions are formed from a combination of two words. Both contractions and possessives use apostrophes, but contractions do not show ownership or affiliation. The contraction is formed by replacing a letter or group of letters with an apostrophe.

> *I am* becomes *I'm.*
> *You are* becomes *you're.*
> *It is* becomes *it's.*
> *We have* becomes *we've.*

Common contractions include:

I'm (I am)	they're (they are)
I'd (I had/I would)	they'd (they had/they would)
I'll (I will)	they'll (they will)
I've (I have)	we're (we are)
you're (you are)	we'd (we had/we would)
you'd (you had/you would)	we'll (we will)
you'll (you will)	who're (who are)
you've (you have)	who'd (who had/who would)
he's (he is/he has)	who'll (who will)
he'd (he had/he would)	it's (it is)
he'll (he will)	it'd (it had/it would)
she's (she is/she has)	it'll (it will)
she'd (she had/she would)	let's (let us)
she'll (she will)	isn't (is not)
aren't (are not)	hadn't (had not)
wasn't (was not)	wouldn't (would not)
weren't (were not)	would've (would have)
don't (do not)	couldn't (could not)
doesn't (does not)	could've (could have)
didn't (did not)	shouldn't (should not)
hasn't (has not)	should've (should have)
haven't (have not)	

Paralegals should use contractions carefully. While contractions are acceptable in certain types of communications, such as emails and social media, using them in legal writing can sometimes signal unprofessionalism and laziness. Chapter 3 will further address the use of contractions as part of a paralegal's writing style.

Exercise 2.22

Using Apostrophes

Use apostrophes correctly in the following sentences:

1. Junes mother works for the Ministry of the Attorney General.
2. Those are the employees [plural] records we seized.
3. The clerks salaries were up for review.
4. The rooftops slant made it difficult to repair the tiles.
5. Is that Carlos desk?
6. We will be there in about a minutes time.
7. The ropes mark on the corpse was a clue.
8. Jeff Wongs daughters will be married next week.
9. The lawyers offices had to be cleaned.
10. Tobaccos high cost is leading to more smuggling.

Periods

The period has several functions, including signalling the end of a sentence. Note the following guidelines for the use of periods:

1. Use a period at the end of a sentence.

   The process server arrived at the court house to file the statement of defence. He waited two hours to speak to the court clerk.

2. Use a period after most **abbreviations**.

   Mr. (Mister)
   Dr. (Doctor)
   Oct. (October)

4. Note that certain organizations do not use periods in their abbreviated names. Acronyms and initialisms usually do not have periods.

   RCMP (Royal Canadian Mounted Police)
   CSIS (Canadian Security Intelligence Service)

5. Note that the names of most provinces have alternative abbreviations, some of which do not contain periods.

   Ont. or ON (Ontario)
   Alta. or AB (Alberta)

Question Marks

A question mark is used to indicate that a question is being asked. Note the following guidelines for the use of question marks:

1. Use a question mark after a direct question.

   She asked, "Are you writing the legal research examination?"

2. Do not use a question mark in an indirect question.

> She asked whether I was writing the legal research examination.

Exclamation Points

Use an exclamation point after an emphatic statement or command.

> Stop, or you'll go off the road!

Quotation Marks

Quotation marks (informally known as "quotes") are most often used to indicate that the exact words of a speaker or material from another document is being reproduced word for word. The correct use of quotation marks is particularly important in legal writing, where they are often used when reproducing text word for word from a piece of legislation or a court decision. Citing the source of the reproduced text is also important, and Chapter 7 will teach you some of the rules for proper citation.

Note the following guidelines for the use of quotation marks:

1. Use quotation marks to enclose the exact words of a speaker.

> I said, "I am going on vacation next week."
> The defendant yelled, "I took your dog and will not give him back."

2. Do not use quotation marks around an indirect quotation.

> I said that I am going on vacation next week.
> The defendant yelled that he took my dog and would not give him back.

3. After quotation marks, use a capital letter unless the quotation is split.

> I said, "My vacation begins next week." Then I left the office.
> "My vacation begins," I said, "next week."

4. Use quotation marks to enclose the titles of short works, including poems, essays, articles, short stories, songs, and radio or television programs. (Longer works, such as books or movies, are underlined or italicized.)

> I read the pamphlet "Better Reports" before my test.
> I watch the television show "Suits" on a regular basis.

5. Use quotation marks to enclose a short-form reference in a sentence. As discussed in Chapter 1, short-form references are one or two words that represent a longer name or word. Always use the full name or phrase the first time, then immediately identify the short form in parentheses (mandatory) and quotation marks (optional). Remain consistent in your choice of whether to use quotation marks or not.

> The paralegal attended at the Landlord and Tenant Board (the "Board") last week. The Board adjourned the hearing until further notice.
> The Law Society of Ontario (the "Law Society") is considering amendments to the paralegal licensing process. The Law Society invites all members of the public to provide feedback about the proposals.

Semicolons

A semicolon is commonly used to separate two independent clauses. Note the following guidelines on the use of semicolons:

1. Use a semicolon to indicate connection between two independent clauses. In the following example, the two independent clauses can be either separated by a period or, if you want to stress the connection between the two statements, joined with a semicolon:

    I witnessed the accident. I will testify in court.
    I witnessed the accident; I will testify in court.

2. Certain conjunctions usually need to be preceded by a semicolon and followed by a comma:

however	otherwise	nevertheless
moreover	therefore	nonetheless

    I did not see the accident; however, I was asked to testify in court.
    He was not happy with his allocation; nonetheless, he stayed with the firm.

3. Do not use a semicolon with the coordinate conjunctions *and, but, or, nor, yet,* and *so*. When these coordinate conjunctions separate two independent clauses, a comma is used in preference to a semicolon.

    I witnessed the accident, but you will testify in court.

4. Use semicolons in pleadings or other legal documents to make lists of complete sentences. Legal professionals often do this to organize facts or arguments in a clear and logical manner. If the sentence introducing a numbered or bulleted list ends with a colon, then the clauses in the list should be separated by semicolons.

    The defendant failed to provide the following documents:

    1. The contract dated May 15, 2017;
    2. All receipts for materials purchased; and
    3. All invoices for services rendered between May 15, 2017 and June 15, 2017.

Colons

A colon is used after an independent complete sentence to introduce a list of items.

I have three favourite career choices: lawyer, paralegal, and court clerk.

The introductory clause may often conclude with *the following* or *as follows*.

The thieves stole the following: a camera, a television, and a computer.
Kindly provide me with the following documents: contracts, receipts, and invoices.

Exercise 2.23

Using Punctuation

The following confidentiality clause has been stripped of all punctuation, including paragraph breaks. Read the passage carefully until you are sure you understand it, then punctuate the passage so that the sentence structure is correct and the meaning is as clear as possible.

Passage from a Confidentiality Agreement

This agreement constitutes the entire agreement between the two parties hereto with respect to the subject matter hereof and cancels and supersedes any prior understandings and agreements between the parties hereto with respect thereto if in any jurisdiction any provision of this agreement or its application to any party or circumstance is restricted prohibited or unenforceable such provision shall as to such jurisdiction be ineffective only to the extent of such restriction prohibition or unenforceability without invalidating the remaining provisions of this agreement and without affecting the validity or enforceability of such provisions in any other jurisdiction or without affecting its application to other parties or circumstances

Capital Letters

Capital letters are also known as large or upper-case letters (as opposed to small, or lower-case, letters). Note the following guidelines on the use of capital letters:

1. Capitalize the first word in a sentence.

   The letter arrived at the office today.

2. Capitalize the first word, last word, and all nouns, verbs, adjectives, and adverbs in a title.

   Communication and Writing for Paralegals

3. Capitalize the names of specific persons, places, languages, nations, and nationalities.

Mayor Huang	Hamilton
French	Canada
Canadian	Ontario

4. Capitalize the names of specific organizations, institutions, departments, ministries, agencies, tribunals, and courts. Note that when used in a sentence, "the" is not capitalized.

   The Law Society of Ontario
   The Ontario Paralegal Association
   The Ontario Court of Justice
   The Social Benefits Tribunal
   The Human Rights Tribunal of Ontario
   The Ministry of Education

5. Capitalize the titles of statutes, regulations, rules, etc.

     The Courts of Justice Act
     The Law Society Act
     The Paralegal Rules of Conduct
     The Statutory Powers of Procedure Act
     The Rules of Civil Procedure

     Chapter 7 further discusses guidelines for citing statutes, regulations, and rules.

6. Capitalize the names of days, months, and holidays. **Do not capitalize the seasons.**

     Monday
     November
     Labour Day
     summer

7. Capitalize the first word in a direct quotation.

     I told her, "There is no charge for these services."

8. Capitalize the word *I*.

     I mean what I say.

9. *Capitalize the names of specific academic courses.* Do not capitalize general words that refer to a course.

     I am taking Communications I.
     I am taking a communications course.

Exercise 2.24

Applying Grammar Rules

Correct the punctuation and capitalization errors in the following sentences. Not all examples contain errors.

1. Mrs Ames appeared to be ready to settle her lawsuit.
2. Get away from me he yelled.
3. I warned my sister to "drive slowly on icy roads."
4. Stop you are going to hit that pole.
5. The first chapter of this book is entitled effective legal writing.
6. I have read: a book, a poem, and a short story.
7. I lost the following from my wallet; my money, my identification, and my credit cards.
8. There are 200 students enrolled in the paralegal program.
9. Dr Reagan is the coordinator of the paralegal program at simpson college.
10. He failed the grammar, and the spelling part of the communications course.
11. The instructor said both him and I should pass the course.

12. The hearing was supposed to begin at noon however the witness had not arrived.
13. She was employed by a woman who owned a van named Mary.
14. They are the children who were called to the principals office.
15. That is the forth traffic ticket I've received.
16. Each of the lawyers owns their own house.
17. Neither the Defendant nor the witness impress the inspector.
18. I do not mind postponing the trial. Because that is my time for vacation.
19. The Law society of ontario is located at 130 Queen Street West, Toronto, ON, M5H 2N6.

Voice

Voice is the form of a verb that indicates whether the subject of a sentence performs or receives the action of the verb. There are two voices: active and passive. A sentence is in the active voice when the subject of the sentence initiates the action.

> He *sued* his former employer.
> Our client *cannot sell* his property because of liens against it.

A sentence is in the passive voice when the subject receives the action. When an active verb is made passive, a form of the verb *to be* is used.

> He *was sued* by his former employer.
> Property with liens against it *cannot be sold*.

The active voice is more forceful and direct than the passive voice, and should be used in most legal writing when possible. Using the active voice also simplifies the writing for the reader, because it usually requires fewer words than writing in the passive voice. However, when the action itself is more important than the person performing the action, when the person performing the action is indefinite or unknown, or when you wish to emphasize the receiver rather than the performer of the action, use the passive voice.

As discussed in Chapter 1, developing the habit of writing in the active voice takes time and practice. A key to developing this skill is to practice identifying active and passive voice sentence constructions. Here are some tips that will help you identify whether a sentence is written in the active or passive voice:

1. Identify the subject of the sentence.
2. Determine whether the subject is acting (i.e., doing something) or being acted upon (i.e., having something done to him, her, or it). If the subject is being acted upon, the sentence is likely passive.

In this example, the mediation (subject) is being acted upon (completed). It is also unclear who cannot complete the mediation. The sentence can be reworded in the active voice as follows:

Here, the parties (subject) are the instigators of the action—they are the ones who cannot complete the mediation.

3. Look for a form of the verb *to be* (*am, are, is, was,* or *were*) followed by the past participle of another verb; this construction often signals passive voice.
    For example,

- The law was passed.
- They were informed.
- The case was dismissed.

Consider the following example:

To be verb   past tense of the verb *to complete*

The case brief was completed at the office.

Exercise 2.25

Voice

For each sentence below, identify whether the sentence is written in the active or in the passive voice. Revise passive voice to active voice.
1. The plaintiff's case was dismissed by the court.
2. Research was conducted by the paralegal.
3. The paralegal's request for an adjournment of the trial will be determined by the Justice of the Peace.
4. The adjudicator awarded damages to the Applicant in the amount of $5,000.00.
5. Bill C-25 was passed by the Ontario Legislature on Friday, May 19, 2017.

Exercise 2.26

Voice

Read the following draft letter from a paralegal to her client. Identify all uses of passive voice in the letter, then rewrite the letter in the active voice.

Letter from Paralegal to Client

June 19, 2017

BY REGULAR MAIL

Mr. Kegan Wright
210 Sullivan Boulevard
Toronto, Ontario M8A 7M5

Dear Mr. Wright:

RE: WRIGHT V VINCE

I confirm that an appointment has been scheduled for June 15, 2017.

During our meeting, the upcoming settlement conference will be discussed.
Mr. Stevens, paralegal for the defendant, was advised of the settlement conference date.

Please note that my office policies were changed and 24 hours' notice is required for any cancellations.

I look forward to meeting with you.

Yours truly,

Sindi Lin
Licensed Paralegal

Editing/Proofreading Documents for Grammatical Errors

As discussed in Chapter 1, editing is an important part of the writing process. Paralegals need to develop excellent proofreading skills in order to identify and correct grammatical errors in various kinds of documents, including correspondence, pleadings, and other legal forms.

Paralegals must be able to identify and correct mistakes in their own writing, but they should also be able to identify and correct mistakes in documents prepared by others, such as a senior lawyer, law clerk, or legal assistant. Strong attention to detail is a critical skill to have as a legal professional; employers value it.

Using the grammar skills you have learned throughout this chapter, identify and correct the errors in the following documents. Ignore all formatting errors.

Exercise 2.27: Proofreading Exercise

Identify and correct the errors in the following letter. You must identify and correct at least 12 errors.

Brison Bean
Licensed Paralegal
150-3567 Law Street,
Toronto, Ontario
M6Y 9R2

19, January, 2017

Dr. Norman Wattingford
207-2100 Robinson Boulevard
Toronto, Ontario, M8A 7M5

Dear Dr Wattingford:

RE: DOROTHY LANGHAM V BIG BAD MACHINERY COMPANY

I am a licensed paralegal Ms. Dorothy Langham is represented by myself in the above noted matter; Ms. Langham is a chiropractic patient at your clinic. It is our understanding from our discussions with Ms. Langham that he had a accident on the factory floor of Bianto Machinery Company on December 20, 2015. As a result of the accident Ms. Langham injuring her big toe. The accident was caused by a big heavy piece of machinery falling on Ms. Langhams toe. Ms. Langham has been experiencing great pain since the accident thus she has been unable to work.

You agree that Ms. Langham is unable to return to work in the event that she reinjures her big toe. Ms. Langham has been experiencing problems with walking, lifting, and is unable to carry goods.

I understand that Ms. Langham has complained about anxiety, so she has been advised by you to consult a psychologist.

Please send us all of Ms. Langhams medical records. So that compensation can be obtained from Bianto Machinery Company. An authorization and direction from Ms. Langham has been enclosed.

Sincerely,

Brison Bean

Brison Bean
Licensed Paralegal

Encl.

*This passage has been adapted from H Wilkie & J Roberts, *Communication for Legal Professionals* (Toronto: Emond Montgomery, 2006) at 121.

Exercise 2.28: Proofreading Exercise

Identify and correct the errors in the Offer to Settle below. There are eight errors to correct.

The plaintiff offers to settle this action on the following terms

1. The defedants will pay to the plaintiff the sum of $15,000.00 for damages.
2. The defendants will paid the plaintiff prejudgment interest according to the *Courts of justice act*, RSO 1990, c C43, as amended
3. The defendants will pay special damages in the amount of $1,125.14; representing the amount paid for treatment to the Ministry of health under the Ontario Hospital Insurance plan.
4. The four defendants will pay costs to the Plaintiff as agreed between themselves.

---

*This passage has been adapted from H Wilkie & J Roberts, *Communication for Legal Professionals* (Toronto: Emond Montgomery, 2006) at 192.

Exercise 2.29

Edit the following defence for all typing and grammar mistakes, including punctuation, capitalization, and unnecessary use of passive voice.

ONTARIO
Superior Court of Justice

Defence
Form 9A Ont. Reg. No.: 258/98

ontario
Small Claims Court

SC-17-1029
Claim No.

**47 Sheppard Avenue East
Toronto, Ontario, M2N 5N1**
Address

416-326-3554
Phone number

Plaintiff No. 1   ☐ Additional plaintiff(s) listed on attached Form 1A.   ☐ Under 18 years of age.

Last name, or name of company		
Drew		
First name	Second name	Also known as
Anthony		
Address (street number, apt., unit)		
60 Hazelon Lane		
City/Town	Province	Phone no.
Toronto	**Ontario**	**416-888-9999**
Postal code		Fax no.
M2P 4H3		
Representative		LSUC #
Lee Jyson		**P2934F**
Address (street number, apt., unit)		
99 Brooke Avenue, Suote 209		
City/Town	Province	Phone no.
Toronto	**Ontario**	**416-222-3434**
Postal code		Fax no.
M3P 1P9		

Defendant No. 1   ☐ Additional defendant(s) listed on attached Form 1A.   ☐ Under 18 years of age.

Last name, or name of company		
Carson		
First name	Second name	Also known as
David		
Address (street number, apt., unit)		
299 Victoria Street		
City/Town	Province	Phone no.
toronto	**Ontario**	**647-222-2121**
Postal code		Fax no.
M6P 2H2		
Representative		LSUC #
Sarah Hughes		**P1423Y**
Address (street number, apt., unit)		
12 Midlane Avenue		
City/Town	Province	Phone no.
Toronto	**Ontario**	**416-234-4543**
Postal code		Fax no.
M9P 2G2		

Les formules des tribunaux sont affichées en anglais et en français sur le site www.ontariocourtforms.on.ca. Visitez ce site pour des renseignements sur des formats accessibles.

SCR 9.01-10.03-9A (January 23, 2014) CSD

FORM 9A   PAGE 2   SC-17-1029
                                                                  Claim No.

THIS DEFENCE IS BEING FILED ON BEHALF OF: (Name(s) of defendant(s))

Dave Carson

and I/we: (Check as many as apply)

☒   Dispute the claim made against me/us.

☐   Admit the full claim and propose the following terms of payment:

$_____ per _____ commencing _____ , 20 ____ .
       (Amount)   (Week/month)

☐   Admit part of the claim in the amount of $_____ and propose the following terms of payment:
                                                        (Amount)

$_____ per _____ commencing _____ , 20 ____ .
       (Amount)   (Week/month)

REASONS FOR DISPUTING THE CLAIM AND DETAILS:

Explain what happened, including where and when. Explain why you do not agree with the claim made against you.

If you are relying on any documents, you **MUST** attach copies to the Defence. If evidence is lost or unavailable, you **MUST** explain why it is not attached.

What happened?
Where?
When?

1. The defendant David Carson (the defendant) and the plaintiff Anothony Drew (the plaintiff) worked together at victoria park hotel in toronto, Ontario from june 8, 2009 to November 8 2014.

2. The defendant and the plaintiff were friends for approximately five years.

3. In June 2011, when the defendant's sister died in a car accident the defendant became distraught, depressed, and lost his job suddenly.

4. The defendant communicated his feelings of dispair to the plainitiff from June 2011 to November 2011.

5. On November 12, 2011, a desire was expressed to buy a golden retriver dog to help the defendant overcome his grief.

6. $1,000.00 was gifted to the plainitff by the defendant to purchase the dog on November 22, 2012.

7. The defendant was not required to repay the plaintiff. The parties did not sign a loan agreement and no demands for repayment were made by the plaintiff until July 1, 2014

8. The defendant relies on the limitations act, 2002. The plaintiff's claim was issued on September 1, 2017, over three years after the first demand for payment was made.

9. The defendant requests that the claim be dismissed with costs.

SCR 9.01-10.03-9A (January 23, 2014) CSD

Continued on next page

FORM 9A   **PAGE 3**   SC-17-1029
_____
Claim No.

**Why I/we disagree
with all or part of
the claim:**

☐ **ADDITIONAL PAGES ARE ATTACHED BECAUSE MORE ROOM WAS NEEDED.**

Prepared on: **September 5**   , 20 **17**   _____
                                                          (Signature of defendant or representative)

NOTE:	Within seven (7) calendar days of changing your address for service, notify the court and all other parties in writing.

CAUTION TO PLAINTIFF(S):	If this Defence contains a proposal of terms of payment, you are deemed to have accepted the terms **unless** you file with the clerk and serve on the defendant(s) a Request to Clerk (Form 9B) for a terms of payment hearing **WITHIN TWENTY (20) CALENDAR DAYS** of service of this Defence [R. 9.03(3)].

SCR 9.01-10.03-9A (January 23, 2014) CSD

Summary

Studying grammar will help you understand that there are different ways of expressing yourself. While there may be more than one correct method of writing, grammar rules must be followed. Using correct grammar helps you to write clearly and to eliminate potential misunderstandings and ambiguities. Continue developing your grammar skills by completing the additional practise exercises available online at <http://emond.ca/CWPL>

Once you have honed your grammar skills, you can turn your attention towards developing a good writing style. Style is different from grammar. Style includes the use and arrangement of words, sentences, and numbers, as well as the document's tone and organization. Appropriate writing style for paralegals is the subject of Chapter 3.

Writing with Style

3

LEARNING OUTCOMES

After completing this chapter, you should be able to

- Demonstrate appropriate use of abbreviations, acronyms, and other short-form references.

- Avoid using legal jargon, expressions, and contractions in written legal communication.

- Understand how to express numbers properly in written communication.

- Avoid using redundant synonyms.

- Practise simplifying and shortening your writing.

- Use topic sentences, transitional words, and headings to organize your writing effectively.

- Identify appropriate and inappropriate tone in written legal communication.

Introduction

Good writing style is important because it increases the clarity of the document. The term *style* refers to how the writer expresses meaning through the use and arrangement of words, sentences, and numbers, as well as to the tone and organization of a document.

Correct grammar and syntax are not enough to make writing effective. Paralegals must spend time developing a good writing style by simplifying their writing, organizing their writing effectively, and using the appropriate tone. This chapter will give you the tools you need to develop a good writing style.

Abbreviations, Acronyms, and Other Short-Form References

Chapter 1 introduced you to the use of abbreviations, acronyms, and other short-form references. Use **abbreviations**, **acronyms**, and other short-form references to shorten sentences and increase the readability of your document. Legal writing often uses long words or phrases repeatedly. Using abbreviations and other short-form references will simplify your writing.

When using short-form references, always use the full name or phrase the first time and identify the abbreviation, acronym, or other short-form reference in parentheses. Some people identify the short-form reference in quotation marks; some do not. You can then use the short form on its own throughout the rest of the text. Do not use short-form references for words or phrases that appear only once in your text.

For example:

> According to the local newspaper, our government will attempt to renegotiate the terms of the North American Free Trade Agreement ("NAFTA"). NAFTA is an agreement between Canada, the United States of America, and Mexico regarding free trade between these countries. The Canadian Broadcasting Corporation will likely report on the NAFTA negotiations.

It is important to always be consistent in your use of short-form references. In other words, once you identify the short form you will use, use it consistently throughout the rest of the text. Do not switch back and forth from the short form to the complete word or phrase, and do not use different short forms for the same word or phrase.

Consider the following passage:

> The Supreme Court of Canada ("SCC") will hear an appeal of the Court of Appeal for Ontario ("Court of Appeal") decision of *Joseph Groia v The Law Society of Upper Canada* 2016 ONCA 471. The ONCA dismissed an appeal by Mr. Groia after the Law Society Tribunal found that he breached the rules of civility under the *Rules of Professional Conduct*. A number of organizations are seeking leave to intervene in the case before the Supreme Court, including the CBA.

This passage uses abbreviations, acronyms, and other short-form references inconsistently. For example, in the first sentence the abbreviation "SCC" is used for "the Supreme Court of Canada," but the last sentence uses "the Supreme Court" rather than "SCC." The passage also uses two different short-form references—"Court of Appeal" and "ONCA"— to identify the Court of Appeal for Ontario. Finally, it is not clear what the abbreviation "CBA" in the last sentence stands for.

You should only use acronyms and abbreviations that are common and generally known. Otherwise, you will confuse the reader. Refer to Chapter 1 for a list of abbreviations, acronyms, and other short forms commonly used in Ontario. Consider the following example:

> The defendant ("D") was charged with careless driving ("CD") under the *Highway Traffic Act.* D hired a paralegal to represent her on her CD charge. Paralegals can practise in the area of provincial offences ("PO") including charges under the *Highway Traffic Act.*

This passage uses uncommon short forms such as

- "D" for defendant,
- "PO" for provincial offences, and
- "CD" for careless driving.

Exercise 3.1

Rewrite the following passage using the appropriate abbreviations, acronyms, and/or short-form references:

> Sarah Jones hired the Respondent, Karen Greene, as her paralegal in June 2016 to represent her in a provincial offences matter. The court scheduled a hearing on February 15, 2017; however, the Respondent, Karen Greene, did not show up at the hearing. Sarah Jones tried to contact the Respondent, Karen Greene, on several occasions after the hearing, but she received no response from the Respondent, Karen Greene. Sarah Jones complained to the Law Society of Ontario in May 2017 about the Respondent's conduct. The Law Society of Ontario conducted an investigation over three months. A hearing took place before the Law Society Tribunal on October 5, 2017 to determine whether the Respondent, Karen Greene, breached the *Paralegal Rules of Conduct.* The Law Society Tribunal examined the *Paralegal Rules of Conduct* and found that the Respondent, Karen Greene, breached Rule 3.01 of the *Paralegal Rules of Conduct.*

Exercise 3.2

Read the following letter from a paralegal to his client. Identify the improper use of abbreviations, acronyms, and other short-form references by circling or highlighting each one. Rewrite the letter using abbreviations, acronyms, and/or other short-form references appropriately.

Dear Mr. Landon:

It was a pleasure meeting with you yesterday.

I confirm that I will represent you with respect to your human rights (HR) claim under the Ontario *Human Rights Code* (the "Code"). As I explained to you, section 5 of the OHRC prohibits discrimination in employment because of a disability.

The Code defines disability to include a mental disorder (MD). An MD can include schizophrenia, bipolar disorder, depression, and in your case, an anxiety disorder.

Over the next week, I will prepare an Application on your behalf, which outlines the facts that support your HR claim. Once you review the Application, I will file it with the Tribunal. Your employer will likely file a response to your Application and the Tribunal will schedule a hearing to determine the claim.

I will prepare your draft Application for your review this week. Please contact me if you have any questions or concerns.

Yours truly,

Aaron Lee
Licensed Paralegal

Legal Jargon, Expressions, and Contractions

Good legal writers find a proper balance between using plain English and maintaining a sense of formality and professionalism in their writing. Using unnecessary legal jargon in written communication can make the text formal and difficult to understand. On the other hand, this does not mean that paralegals should be too informal, using everyday spoken words and expressions (also known as **slang**), in their written communication. Inappropriate informal writing suggests that the paralegal writer may be lazy and unprofessional.

Legal Jargon

As discussed in Chapter 1, **legal jargon** is specialized legal language that people who are not legal professionals find difficult to understand. While paralegals will come across a lot of legal jargon in their studies and practice, they should avoid using it where possible. As discussed in Chapter 1, this includes avoiding the use of Latin words where possible. When a paralegal can use plain English instead of a Latin term, he or she should do so.

Figure 3.1 below reproduces a list of common legal jargon words and phrases from Chapter 1.

FIGURE 3.1 Common Legal Jargon, with Preferred Alternatives

• Cause of action	set of facts that allows one person to pursue a legal claim against another
• Conveyance	transfer
• Forthwith	immediately
• Herein	in this document/letter
• Hereinafter	subsequently referred to
• Hereto	to this document/letter
• Nil	nothing
• On the grounds of	because
• Prima facie	on its face
• Pursuant to	in accordance with
• Subsequent to	following

Exercise 3.3

Rewrite the following passages to remove the legal jargon:

1. The plaintiff conveyed her car to the defendant on September 1, 2017. The defendant agreed to pay the plaintiff $5,500.00 for the car; however, the defendant paid nil. The plaintiff herein states that she has a cause of action in contract law pursuant to the common law principles of breach of contract. The plaintiff demands that the defendant pay her $5,500.00 plus interest forthwith.

2. Mr. Smith signed up for dance lessons with Neon Dance Studios and paid a $200.00 deposit. Five days subsequent to Mr. Smith signing the contract, Mr. Smith changed his mind on the grounds of negative internet reviews about the dance studio. Pursuant to the *Consumer Protection Act, 2002,* revocation of the contract is permitted and the continued holding of Mr. Smith's deposit is unlawful.

3. The defendant must serve and file his Statement of Defence within the prescribed time.

Exercise 3.4

Rewrite the following letter from a paralegal to a client to remove any legal jargon:

Dear Ms. Little:

It was a pleasure meeting with you yesterday.

You will recall that we discussed your upcoming trial in the Ontario Court of Justice (the "Court") on November 15, 2017. At the trial, the Court will resolve the facts and the evidence to determine your culpability under the *Highway Traffic Act*, RSO 1990, c H.8 (the "Act") for careless driving.

Please note that the prosecutor or I may take issue with the admissibility of some forms of evidence. The court will decide on any challenges to the admissibility of evidence. I reviewed a number of precedent cases on careless driving charges under the Act and I am confident that you will be acquitted.

Prior to the trial, we should meet to review your case and discuss any questions or concerns you may have.

Yours truly,

Aneeta Liam
Licensed Paralegal

Expressions

Paralegals should avoid using slang—words or phrases usually used in informal speech—in any type of legal communication, including emails, letters, briefs, and affidavits.

When speaking, people often use informal words and expressions such as the following:

- My client is **miffed** about the damage to the car.
- The police officer **busted** the windshield when arresting the defendant.
- Do you **wanna** schedule a phone call next week?
- **It's cool**; I will agree to your adjournment request.

These informal phrases and expressions can be replaced by more professional and formal language without changing the meaning:

- My client is **annoyed** about the damage to the car.
- The police officer **broke** the windshield when arresting the defendant.
- Do you **want to** schedule a phone call next week?
- **It is not a problem**; I will agree to your adjournment request.

Exercise 3.5

Rewrite the following sentences in a professional and formal manner without changing the meaning:

1. Sam was fuming when his friend refused to pay him.
2. The employee believed that her boss always had a beef with her during the time she worked for him.
3. You can catch me in my office from 9:00 a.m. to 5:00 p.m.
4. There were tons of complaints against her.
5. The court dealt a big blow to Ms. Wong when dismissing her case.
6. You can cancel your contract with no strings attached.

Exercise 3.6

With two or three classmates, make a list of words and expressions commonly used in oral communication that are inappropriate for use in written legal communication.

Contractions

Chapter 2 introduced the proper use of contractions in the context of punctuation. **Contractions** are formed by replacing a letter or group of letters with an apostrophe.

There is a lot of debate about whether lawyers and paralegals should use contractions in their writing. In the past, contractions had no place in legal writing; the profession overwhelmingly opposed their use. More recently, there has been a move towards accepting the use of contractions in legal writing because it helps to simplify documents for readers. The plain legal language movement, discussed in Chapter 1, supports this argument.

Paralegals should use contractions carefully, since their use in legal writing can sometimes signal unprofessionalism and laziness. Using contractions in legal writing is a personal style choice. This author suggests avoiding contractions in formal legal documents and communications such as formal letters, pleadings, offers to settle, and legal forms, but using contractions in certain types of written communication, such as emails and social media, is acceptable.

Numbers

There are several different rules for expressing numbers in writing. Numbers can be written in words or in numerals. Determining when to write out a number (e.g., *seven*) and when to use a figure (e.g., *7*) depends on many factors, including the industry, country, publication, type of document, or style guide the writer is adhering to.

Rules on expressing numbers are often determined by a style guide. Different organizations and industries have developed their own style guides for writing. Some examples that address how to express numbers are the *Publication Manual of the American Psychological Association* ("APA style")[1] and the *MLA Handbook*, published by the Modern Language Association.[2] The *Queen's Law Journal* recently prepared a legal style guide, titled *Canadian Guide to Legal Style*, for Canadian legal practitioners, academics, and students.[3] Whatever guide or rule is used when expressing numbers in a document, you should follow it consistently throughout.

Some general rules to follow when expressing numbers in writing include:

1. Write out numbers one to nine and use numerals for numbers 10 and above.

   There are three issues in this case.
   The defendant made 25 attempts to contact the plaintiff.

2. When starting a sentence with a number, write it out.

   Thirty-four people witnessed the accident.

3. Use numerals when writing a percentage.

   According to the report, approximately 45 per cent of licensed lawyers in Ontario are women.

4. Express monetary amounts in numerals and use decimal points.

   The Applicant seeks $15,000.00 in damages.
   Robin paid Liam $945.80.

Simplify Your Writing

Effective legal communication involves using simple and clear language. Chapter 1 introduced the importance of plain legal language and the tools you can use to simplify your writing. You can develop a good writing style by using the suggestions discussed below.

Avoid Redundant Synonyms

One element of good writing style is avoiding the use of **redundant synonyms**—that is, using two or more words together that mean the same thing. Avoiding redundant synonyms will help you to simplify your writing so that it is clear and concise.

The following sentences use redundant synonyms:

- The contract must be in the **proper, correct, and appropriate** form.
- The President has **sole and exclusive** authority to bind the corporation.
- That was my **last and final** offer.
- Sam and Lilly **separated and divided** their household contents.

---

1 American Psychological Association, *Publication Manual of the American Psychological Association*, 6th ed (Washington, DC: American Psychological Association, 2009) at 111-14.
2 Modern Language Association, *MLA Handbook*, 8th ed (New York: Modern Language Association, 2016) at 92.
3 Queen's Law Journal, *Canadian Guide to Legal Style* (Toronto: Carswell, 2014).

You can rewrite the above sentences to eliminate redundant synonyms as follows:

- The contract must be in the proper form.
- The President has exclusive authority to bind the corporation.
- That was my final offer.
- Sam and Lilly divided their household contents.

While you should be able to identify redundant synonyms, you should also be cautious when rewording them. Make sure that the words used together really do mean the same thing in the context of a particular sentence or document, so that your revisions do not change the meaning of the sentence.

Exercise 3.7

Rewrite the following passage to remove the redundant synonyms without changing the meaning:

> On November 5, 2017, Brendan agreed to paint Jeffrey's house. After Brendan finished the paint job, Jeffrey transferred and conveyed the sum of $2,000.00 to Brendan for the work. Brendan argues that this amount does not cover all of the costs and expenses of painting the house. Jeffrey believes he is free and clear from any liability towards Brendan because they agreed to the amount of $2,000.00 and that is what Jeffrey paid him.

Cut Unnecessary Words and Use Short Sentences

Effective legal writers simplify their writing by cutting out unnecessary words and sentences, which increases the text's clarity and persuasiveness. Many legal professionals are guilty of producing documents that are long, complex, and confusing. Legal professionals often use long, wordy sentences rather than short, simple ones. If a paralegal can express the same message in three 30-word sentences rather than ten 90-word sentences, he or she should do so.

Cutting unnecessary words and shortening sentences takes practice. It also takes time. A reasonable amount of editing time is required to identify unnecessary words and eliminate them without changing the meaning of a sentence or an entire text.

Cutting unnecessary words involves identifying wordy phrases and run-on sentences. Chapter 2 discusses run-on sentences in the context of grammar skills. A run-on sentence consists of two or more complete sentences or independent clauses that have been joined together in an inappropriate way. It can be simplified by omitting unnecessary words or by breaking it up into independent short sentences.

Consider the following passage:

> The Defendant is of the opinion that the Plaintiff's claim should never have been filed on the basis of the fact that the Plaintiff has absolutely no single basis in law to pursue her claim. While the Defendant prepared a defence to the claim, he does not want to continue litigating this matter and prefers to attempt negotiation at this point in time but he wants to find representation for himself.

The passage includes both unnecessary words and run-on sentences. You can simplify the passage by rewriting it as follows:

> The Defendant believes the Plaintiff should not have filed her claim because it has no basis in law. The Defendant has prepared a defence, but he does not want to continue with the litigation. He prefers to negotiate with the Plaintiff; however, he wants to find himself a representative first.

The passage is reduced from 71 words to 49 words. The sentences are also shorter than in the original.

Read the following letter from a paralegal to opposing counsel:

Dear Sir:

I am writing to confirm that I am not available for our telephone conference currently scheduled for June 27, 2017, at 1:00 p.m. and would like to reschedule for another time when I am available.

Please note that my client does acknowledge receipt of your client's offer to settle and I have reviewed it with her and have discussed the various options going forward and would like to discuss the case further with you during our telephone call before I do respond to your offer in writing.

Please contact my office to speak to my clerk who will advise you of my available dates for a rescheduled telephone conference and provide me with an update regarding your communications with the court about the scheduled settlement conference and whether you have obtained a date for the settlement conference.

Sincerely,

Liam Brown
Licensed Paralegal

Here is the same letter in a simpler form:

Dear Sir:

I write to confirm that I am unavailable for our telephone conference scheduled for June 27, 2017, at 1:00 p.m. Please contact my office to reschedule our conference to a mutually agreeable time.

Please note that my client received your client's offer to settle. I reviewed it with her and discussed the options going forward. I would like to discuss the case with you before I respond to your offer in writing.

Also, kindly advise whether you have obtained a date for the settlement conference.

Sincerely,

Liam Brown
Licensed Paralegal

Identify and Replace Wordy Phrases

You can shorten sentences by identifying wordy phrases whose message can be expressed in one or two words.

Consider the following sentence:

> **In the event that** the Respondent fails to attend the mediation session, the mediator will cancel the session.

The phrase *in the event that* is unnecessary. You can say the same thing using one word rather than four:

> **If** the Respondent fails to attend the mediation session, the mediator will cancel the session.

Figure 3.2 is a list of common wordy phrases and the simple words that can replace them.

Consider the following passage:

> Rachel Lynn attended the settlement conference **on the basis that** the Rules of the Small Claims Court required her to. **Prior to** her attendance, she met with her legal representative to prepare for the conference. There were only **a limited number of** issues to discuss **due to the fact that** this is a simple case. **Over the course of** the conference, the parties discussed the issues but they each made only **a limited number of** substantive offers.

You can rewrite this passage to remove the wordy phrases and replace each one with a single word:

> Rachel Lynn attended the settlement conference because the Rules of the Small Claims Court required her to. Before attending, she met with her legal representative to prepare for the conference. There were only a few issues to discuss because this is a simple case. Throughout the conference, the parties discussed the issues, but they each made only a few substantive offers.

FIGURE 3.2   Simplifying Phrases

Wordy Phrase	Simple Word
In connection with	With
For the purpose of	Because
On the basis that	Because
Due to the fact	Because
In reference to	About
In regards to	About/regarding
A limited number of	Few
A limited amount of	Little
In the absence of	Without
In the course of	During
Over the course of	Throughout
In the event that	If

Exercise 3.8

With two or three classmates, make a list of other wordy phrases and simpler words to replace them, adding to the list in Figure 3.2.

Exercise 3.9

Identify the wordy phrases in the passage below, then rewrite the passage to simplify it.

> The Applicant worked as a police officer for the Respondent, the Royal Canadian Mounted Police ("RCMP"). After her hiring, the Applicant refused to wear the RCMP uniform on the basis that it was made of leather and fur. The Applicant is an ethical vegan and believes that exploiting non-human animals for the benefit of humans is morally wrong. This includes wearing any type of fur or leather in clothing. The RCMP fired the Applicant for failure to follow instructions in regards to the wearing of the RCMP uniform. The Applicant filed this Application on the basis of section 5 of the *Ontario Human Rights Code* and for the purpose of getting her job back.

Use Affirmatives and Avoid Negatives

Using affirmatives rather than negatives usually simplifies a text and increases its clarity; it also makes sentences more direct and forceful. An **affirmative sentence** is a sentence that is in positive form. A **negative sentence** is one that is in negative form.

Figure 3.3 gives examples of sentences written in negative form and their corresponding affirmative form.

FIGURE 3.3   Negative and Affirmative Sentences

Negative	Affirmative
The evidence was not insufficient to establish cause.	The evidence was sufficient to establish cause.
The judge did not fail to consider all of the evidence.	The judge considered all of the evidence.
The plaintiff established that he did not fail the test for default judgment against the defendant.	The plaintiff established that he met the test for default judgment against the defendant.
The article did not fail the test for publication.	The article passed the test for publication.
No person is permitted to board an aircraft unless he or she passes a security check.	A person is permitted to board an aircraft only if he or she passes a security check.

Overusing negatives in a sentence can also confuse a reader. Paralegals should practise spotting the overuse of negatives in a document when editing it, then revise each one into affirmative form without changing the meaning of the sentence.

For example:

> No party shall refuse to attend a settlement conference unless a judge orders him or her not to attend.

This sentence contains multiple negatives and confuses the reader. It can be rewritten in a more affirmative form as follows:

> A party must attend a settlement conference unless the court orders otherwise.

Exercise 3.10

Rewrite the following sentences in affirmative form:

1. No Simpson College paralegal graduate has not passed the paralegal licensing exam.
2. The professor is never late to class.
3. No student shall refuse to sign the Student Code of Conduct.
4. The judge decided not to refuse to adjourn the hearing.

Use Action Verbs

Using strong action verbs and replacing nouns with verbs where possible can increase the clarity and simplicity of legal writing. You will recall from Chapter 2 that a verb is the action word in a sentence. Every sentence must have a verb; otherwise it is a sentence fragment, which is grammatically incorrect. Refer to Chapter 2 for a discussion on using verbs in sentences.

Using strong action verbs increases the persuasiveness and impact of your writing. In general, using strong action verbs means minimizing your use of *to be*. This will also help you avoid writing in the passive voice. Refer to Chapter 2 for a discussion of voice. Recall that the verb *to be* can take the forms *am, are, is, was, were,* or *will be*.

Consider the following example:

> The victim was injured by the defendant.

You can rewrite this sentence to use a strong action verb and eliminate *was*. In doing so, you also change the sentence from passive voice to active voice:

> The defendant injured the victim.

When possible, you should try to replace a verb–noun combination in a sentence with a strong action verb. For example:

> The paralegal had an argument with the judge → The paralegal argued with the judge

> The adjudicator should take into consideration all of the evidence → The adjudicator should consider all of the evidence

> The police officer provided a description of the suspect → The police officer described the suspect

Exercise 3.11

Rewrite the following passage to replace any verb–noun combinations with strong action verbs, as necessary:

> The judge was of the opinion that the case should be dismissed. The judge provided communication of the decision to the parties in writing. The Plaintiff made an objection to the decision but it did not matter. The Plaintiff's lawyer said the Plaintiff must make a decision whether to appeal the decision or not. If the Plaintiff appeals, he must make an application to the Court.

Organize Your Writing Effectively

Good style in legal writing also requires effective organization. How a document is organized will depend on the document's audience and purpose.

Chapter 1 identified the different audiences a paralegal might write for and the various purposes for doing so. For example, a paralegal might write a letter to his or her client to advise the client about his or her legal rights or to report the outcome of a court hearing. A paralegal might write a letter to opposing counsel to persuade him or her of a legal position or to propose a settlement. A paralegal might also draft pleadings or other court forms to inform the judge, justice of the peace, or adjudicator of the alleged facts that support the client's cause of action or defence or to advise the decision maker about the applicable law.

Regardless of the audience and purpose of the document, you should always spend time organizing your writing to ensure that it is easy for the reader to follow and understand. As discussed in Chapter 1, organizing your writing is part of the revision stage of the writing process.

There are a number of things you can do to improve the organization of your writing.

Use Topic Sentences

A **topic sentence** introduces the reader to the substance of a paragraph by summarizing the main idea of that paragraph. Topic sentences are very important in legal writing because using them improves clarity for the reader.

While a topic sentence can often appear in the middle or at the end of a paragraph, effective legal writing requires point-first writing (see Chapter 1). This means that you should use topic sentences to begin your paragraphs.

Consider the following paragraph:

> In 2017, the Ontario Legislature passed the *Rental Fairness Act, 2017*, SO 2017, c 13 (the "Act"). The Act amends the *Residential Tenancies Act, 2006*, SO 2006, c 17, to provide new protections for tenants in Ontario. These protections include introducing rent control for all residential rental units and protecting tenants from unauthorized evictions. The changes come after many people voiced concern over large rent increases for units built after 1991.

This paragraph lacks a good topic sentence. The first sentence does not summarize the main idea of the paragraph; it simply introduces the statute discussed in the paragraph. Reread the paragraph and ask yourself: What is the main point of this paragraph? Is it that the Ontario government introduced changes to the *Residential Tenancies Act, 2006,* to ensure people in Ontario have stability in their living arrangements?

Consider the same paragraph with an effective topic sentence as the first sentence:

> **The Ontario government recently made changes to the residential tenancies regime in Ontario in an effort to ensure people have stability in their living arrangements.** In 2017, the Ontario Legislature passed the *Rental Fairness Act, 2017*, SO 2017, c 13 (the "Act"). The Act amends the *Residential Tenancies Act, 2006,* to provide new protections for tenants in Ontario. These protections include introducing rent control for all residential rental units and protecting tenants from unauthorized evictions. The changes come after many people voiced concern over huge rent increases for units built after 1991.

Consider the following paragraph:

> In the case of *R v Jordan*, 2016 SCC 27, the Supreme Court of Canada (the "Court") allowed an appeal from the British Columbia Court of Appeal resulting in charges against the accused being stayed. The Court found that the trial delay in this case violated the accused's right to be tried within a reasonable period of time under section 11(b) of the *Canadian Charter of Rights and Freedoms*. The Court introduced a new framework for determining if a person has been tried within a reasonable time. According to the majority, if it takes a person more than 18 months to get to trial in provincial court, the delay will be "presumptively unreasonable."

Again, the paragraph lacks a good topic sentence. The first paragraph simply introduces the outcome of the Supreme Court of Canada decision in *R v Jordan*.

Consider the same paragraph with an effective topic sentence as the first sentence:

> **To determine unreasonable delay in criminal trials, a court must follow the time limits set out by the Supreme Court of Canada (the "Court") in *R v Jordan*, 2016 SCC 27.** According to the majority, if it takes a person more than 18 months to get to trial in provincial court, the delay will be "presumptively unreasonable." In this case, the Court introduced a new framework for determining if a person has been tried within a reasonable time under section 11(b) of the *Charter of Rights and Freedoms* (the "Charter"). The Court found that the trial delay in this case violated the accused's right to be tried within a reasonable period of time under the *Charter*. The Court therefore allowed the appeal from the British Columbia Court of Appeal and stayed the charges against the accused.

Exercise 3.12

Find a recent Supreme Court of Canada decision. Read the decision and identify topic sentences in the various paragraphs of the decision.

Use Transitional Words and Phrases

Transitional words and phrases help the reader to understand the connection between various ideas and arguments. They also help guide the reader smoothly from one point to another in a paragraph or between paragraphs.

Figure 3.4 includes a list of common transitional words and phrases.

FIGURE 3.4   Common Transitional Words and Phrases

Concluding	Contrasting
• In conclusion • Therefore • As a result • To conclude • Thus	• In contrast to • As opposed to • However • But • Rather
Comparing	**Using Examples**
• Similarly	• For example • For instance • Such as
Adding Additional Points	
• Moreover • In addition • First… Second… Third • Furthermore	

It is helpful to use these words in your writing, whether you are writing to a client, opposing counsel, a decision maker, or your employer. They will improve clarity and comprehension.

You can also improve the clarity and flow of your writing by using numbered lists. A numbered list signals to the reader up front how many issues, points, arguments, and so on there are. You can use numbered lists directly in the text or as an indented point-form list.

Consider the following example:

> The contract has three main elements: (1) the identity of the parties; (2) the value of the work; and (3) the deadline to complete the work.

The above sentence can also be written as follows:

> The contract has three main elements:
> 1) the identity of the parties;
> 2) the value of the work; and
> 3) the deadline to complete the work.

Consider the following letter from a paralegal to a client and note the transitional words:

Dear Mr. Jones:

I write regarding your settlement conference scheduled for May 1, 2017, at the Ontario Small Claims Court.

There are several purposes for holding a settlement conference. **First**, it can assist the parties in settling the case. **Second**, it can allow for full disclosure between the parties. **Third**, it can assist the parties in preparing for trial. **Finally**, it can narrow the issues in the proceeding and speed up the trial process.

Kindly contact my office to schedule an appointment to meet with me to prepare for the conference.

Yours truly,

Lianne Smith
Licensed Paralegal

The use of the words *first, second, third,* and *finally* identify each point for the reader clearly and concisely.

Exercise 3.13

Read the following passage and identify all the transitional words and phrases:

> The Applicant applied to the Law Society of Ontario ("LSO") for an L1 licence. Upon review of his Application, the Law Society Tribunal (the "Tribunal") held a good character hearing and determined the Applicant was not of good character as required by section 27(2) of the *Law Society Act,* RSO 1990, c L.8.
>
> The Tribunal deemed the Applicant not of good character for two reasons. First, the Applicant acted aggressively and violently towards his neighbours, resulting in a criminal charge. Second, the Applicant showed little remorse for his actions. For example, he refused to write an apology letter to the victims of his behaviour. Similarly, he did not apologize to the Tribunal for his behaviour.
>
> The Tribunal recognizes that the Applicant attempted to rehabilitate himself. For example, he attended anger management classes for a period of six months. However, this is insufficient for a finding of good character in this case. The gravity of the Applicant's actions is too great. In addition, a significant period of time has not passed since the incident. The incident occurred only eight months ago.

Use Headings and Sub-headings

Using headings and sub-headings can help organize a document; it can also assist the reader by signalling a transition to a new topic or idea.

The use of headings and sub-headings in a document is a personal preference. Many lawyers and paralegals use headings in their documents, but many do not. Judges often use headings and sub-headings in their written decisions.

Using headings involves breaking a piece of writing into separate parts, then giving each part a title and using formatting such as bold or underlining to set it off from the text.

For example, assume you are writing a memorandum (see Chapter 7) on whether the Law Society Tribunal is likely to find your firm's client to be of good character under the *Law Society Act*.[4] Figure 3.5 is an example of such a memorandum, showing how you might use headings and sub-headings to organize it.

FIGURE 3.5   Sample Memorandum

MEMORANDUM

TO: File
FROM: Lianne Smith
DATE: September 1, 2017
RE: Buttle v The Law Society of Upper Canada

Ms. Buttle is likely to show that she meets the test for good character under the *Law Society Act*, RSO 1990, c L.8 and therefore should receive her P1 licence. A determination of good character requires considering five factors: (1) the nature and duration of the misconduct; (2) whether the applicant is remorseful; (3) what rehabilitative efforts, if any, have been taken, and the success of such efforts; (4) the applicant's conduct since the misconduct; and (5) the passage of time since the misconduct.[1]

The Nature and Duration of the Misconduct
Ms. Buttle's misconduct was minor. It was also an isolated incident.

....

The Applicant's Remorse
Ms. Buttle showed remorse for her behavior in a number of ways. First...

...

The Applicant's Rehabilitation
Ms. Buttle has spent a significant amount of time rehabilitating herself.

...

The Applicant's Conduct
Ms. Buttle took a leave of absence from her part-time job after the incident. She also agreed to a mentorship arrangement with a lawyer in good standing with the Law Society of Ontario.

...

The Passage of Time
The incident occurred two years ago. This is a significant amount of time.

...

LJ

---

4   RSO 1990, c L.8.

You can use headings and sub-headings in most types of documents, including correspondence, memoranda, affidavits, facta, case briefs, and pleadings. Chapter 4 introduces the topic of case briefs. A case brief is a concise summary of a court decision. The sample case brief in Chapter 4, Figure 4.3, uses basic headings to organize the summary. More uses of headings in sample legal documents appear throughout the remainder of this book.

Tone and Civility in Legal Writing

An important element of effective legal writing style is using an appropriate tone. **Tone** refers to the attitude conveyed by the writer. In legal writing, the tone of a document is just as important as its content.

The tone used depends on the audience and purpose of the communication. A paralegal's tone in a letter to an opposing advocate persuading the advocate to accept a legal position may be different from the tone used in a letter from a paralegal to a client.

Regardless of the audience or purpose of the communication, however, a paralegal must always communicate in a professional, civil, and respectful tone; as Figure 3.6 shows, the *Paralegal Rules of Conduct* (the "Rules") require it.

FIGURE 3.6   Rule 2.01

Rule 2   Professionalism

2.01   Integrity and Civility

(1)   A paralegal has a duty to provide legal services and discharge all responsibilities to clients, tribunals, the public and other members of the legal professions honourably and with integrity.

(2)   A paralegal has a duty to uphold the standards and reputation of the paralegal profession and to assist in the advancement of its goals, organizations and institutions.

(3)   A paralegal shall be courteous and civil, and shall act in good faith with all persons with whom he or she has dealings in the course of his or her practice.

Source: Law Society of Ontario, *Paralegal Rules of Conduct* (1 October 2014; amendments current to 29 June 2017), online: <http://www.lsuc.on.ca/paralegal-conduct-rules/>.

Rule 7.01, shown in Figure 3.7, prohibits paralegals from corresponding with others in an abusive or offensive manner, or in a tone that is inconsistent with professional communication. It also prohibits paralegals from engaging in ill-considered criticism of the competence, conduct, or advice of other licensees.

FIGURE 3.7   Rule 7.01

Rule 7   Duty to Licensees and Others

7.01   Courtesy and Good Faith

(1)   A paralegal shall avoid sharp practice and shall not take advantage of or act without fair warning on slips, irregularities or mistakes on the part of other licensees not going to the merits or involving the sacrifice of a client's rights.

(2)   A paralegal shall agree to reasonable requests concerning trial dates, adjournments, waiver of procedural formalities and similar matters that do not prejudice the rights of the client.

(3)   A paralegal shall not, in the course of providing legal services, communicate, in writing or otherwise, with a client, another licensee, or any other person in a manner that is abusive, offensive, or otherwise inconsistent with the proper tone of a professional communication from a paralegal.

(4)   A paralegal shall not engage in ill-considered or uninformed criticism of the competence, conduct, advice or charges of other licensees, but should be prepared, when requested, to represent a client in a complaint involving another licensee.

(5)   A paralegal shall answer, with reasonable promptness, all professional letters and communications from other licensees that require an answer, and a paralegal shall be punctual in fulfilling all commitments.

(6)   A paralegal shall not use any device to record a conversation between the paralegal and a client or another licensee, even if lawful, without first informing the other person of the intention to do so.

(7)   A paralegal who receives a document relating to the representation of the paralegal's client and knows or reasonably should know that the document was inadvertently sent shall promptly notify the sender.

Source: Law Society of Ontario, *Paralegal Rules of Conduct* (1 October 2014; amendments current to 29 June 2017), online: <http://www.lsuc.on.ca/paralegal-conduct-rules/>.

As the Rules affirm, a paralegal has a duty to communicate in a respectful, courteous, and professional manner with all people he or she deals with in the course of his or her practice. Failure to do so may result in disciplinary action by the Law Society of Ontario. This duty arises when a paralegal deals with *any* third party in the course of his or her practice, including a client, a legal assistant, opposing party or advocate, a judge, a justice of the peace or other decision maker, a court clerk, etc. Examples of uncivil, disrespectful, and unprofessional communication include threats, aggressive tone, swearing, name-calling, and personal insults.

Even when a paralegal disagrees with the approach or position of another licensee or party, he or she can express that disagreement in a respectful and professional manner. Figure 3.8 is an example of a letter from a paralegal to an opposing advocate written using appropriate tone.

FIGURE 3.8 **Letter to Opposing Advocate Using an Appropriate Tone**

Dear Sir:

I refer to your letter dated June 5, 2017.

With respect, I disagree with your client's position. The *Consumer Protection Act, 2002*, SO 2002, c 30, Sch A, requires a consumer to provide notice of his or her intention to cancel the contract within 10 days of receiving a copy of the contract. It does not require written notice. My client provided the required notice by telephone within that 10-day period.

Kindly advise whether your client will cancel the contract and refund my client's deposit. Otherwise, I will consult with my client regarding next steps.

Sincerely,

Marco Fiano
Licensed Paralegal

In contrast, Figure 3.9 is an example of a letter from a paralegal to an opposing advocate written using uncivil, rude, and disrespectful language.

FIGURE 3.9 **Letter to Opposing Advocate Using an Inappropriate Tone**

Dear Sir:

I refer to your letter dated June 5, 2017.

Your client's position is outrageous. You appear to have no understanding of the applicable law whatsoever. How did you pass the LSO licensing exam? You shouldn't be practising law. If you don't get your client to cancel the contract and refund my client's deposit, your client will pay dearly.

Now do your job or I'll see you in court!

Marco Fiano
Licensed Paralegal

An appropriate tone is also necessary when communicating with clients. Sometimes clients can be difficult or demanding; however, a paralegal must never respond in a disrespectful manner.

In addition to corresponding with people in a civil, courteous, and professional way, paralegals must also strike the right balance between formal and informal tone in their written communication. Expressions, slang, and contractions are examples of informal language discussed at the beginning of this chapter. Using them can create an informal tone in a written document, which may signal unprofessionalism and laziness. It may also signal to the client that the paralegal is incompetent to handle the client's case. Figures 3.10 and 3.11 are examples of letters from a paralegal to a client written in an inappropriately informal tone.

FIGURE 3.10   Informal Letter A

Hey Sarah!

Don't worry about the hearing tomorrow. I've got it all covered. The law's on your side and I've done my research. The law says you can cancel the contract. Period! You gave the notice as required. I don't think the lawyer for the defendant knows what he's doing either. I'll catch you at the courthouse at 10:00 a.m.

Marco

FIGURE 3.11   Informal Letter B

To Sarah:

I don't appreciate you missing your appointment with me today. I have a busy practice and your missed appointment caused me a headache. I could have been doing something else. If you are going to continue missing our scheduled meetings then you will have to find another paralegal to help you. I frankly do not have time for this. I may consider rescheduling if you contact my office by Monday morning.

Allan

Chapter 6 addresses how to draft different kinds of letters and provides more letter-writing examples and exercises. When reading Chapter 6 and completing the exercises, remember the importance of proper tone.

Summary

Effective legal writing requires more than following the rules of grammar; it also requires using proper style to ensure that documents are clear and concise. A paralegal can develop a good writing style by using abbreviations, acronyms, and short-form references properly, avoiding legal jargon and informal expressions, and expressing numbers appropriately. Paralegals also need to practice simplifying their writing by avoiding redundant synonyms, cutting unnecessary words and using short sentences, replacing wordy phrases with single words, using affirmative rather than negative sentences, and using strong action verbs (instead of nouns) when possible.

Good writing style also involves organizing content effectively by using topic sentences, transitional words and phrases, and headings.

Finally, a paralegal must always consider the tone of his or her message when drafting a document. Regardless of the audience or purpose of the document, the tone of the document must be civil, courteous, and professional.

This chapter teaches the skills needed to develop a good writing style. You will use these skills in the various drafting exercises contained in Chapters 4 through 9.

Review Exercise

Below is a letter from one paralegal to another paralegal who represents the opposing party in a case. Identify the types of stylistic problems in the letter, then rewrite it in appropriate style using the skills developed throughout Chapter 3.

July 11, 2017

Dear Ms. Lai:

RE: Krall v Daniels
          File No. 17-1043

I don't know who you think you are. Where did you go to law school? The circus? Your client's offer to settle (OTS) sent with your letter of June 30, 2017, is outrageous. Stop beating around the bush and make a decent OTS or we'll see you in court. Ms. Lai, this is the last straw. My client provided an indication that she was open to negotiation, but your OTS is insulting. If this is your client's last and final OTS, then we'll see you in court. I'm more than capable of arguing a good trial while word on the street is that you, my friend, aren't. At the end of the day, you need to realize that the ball is in your court.

Yours truly,

Victor Sears
Licensed Paralegal

Summary and Paraphrase

4

LEARNING OUTCOMES

After completing this chapter, you should be able to

- Write summaries that contain the main ideas of the original works.

- Paraphrase for understanding.

- Detect bias in reporting.

- Write a case brief.

Introduction

There are two different methods of shortening a piece of writing while keeping its main points: the **summary** and the **paraphrase**. Each is written differently, and with a different emphasis.

When summarizing, the writer puts other people's words, substantially reduced, into his or her own words while retaining the meaning of the original. When paraphrasing, the writer demonstrates his or her understanding of a speaker's or writer's expressed meaning.

Writing a case brief is a form of summarizing. A case brief is a concise summary of a court decision that briefly describes the facts, the legal issues, the decision, and the court's reasoning for its decision. In practice, paralegals may write case briefs for themselves or for an employer.

Writing a Summary

Paralegals often need to summarize material. A summary allows a reader to understand the contents of an original piece of writing without having to read the entire original. When summarizing, paralegals must break down legal documents into their essentials and analyze important information. It is important for paralegals to be able to summarize effectively.

A summary can also be called a *synopsis* or an *abstract*. Its demands are threefold: it requires reading carefully, selecting wisely, and writing concisely. Summarizing is a valuable skill to develop. In addition to its legal applications, learning to summarize can help paralegals to take better notes and to listen more effectively. The ability to summarize is also useful in legal research.

The purpose of the summary is to condense an original piece of writing and give the reader the main ideas of the original, allowing him or her to understand the facts contained in the original without reading the entire passage.

A number of rules apply to summary writing:

1. *Read the document carefully several times.* As you do so, note the **thesis** and any bias in the original.

2. *Underline the main ideas.* Eliminate anything that is not essential to the meaning.

3. *Count the words in the original.* The summary should be about one-third or one-quarter the length of the original. The summary may consist of one sentence, one paragraph, or several paragraphs, depending on the length of the original. It should not be written in **point form**.

4. *Prepare a basic outline.* Outlining is a key stage in the writing process. Preparing an outline in point form will help you remember key points from the original document and organize your writing effectively. (Chapter 1 discusses outlining as part of the writing process.)

5. *Without looking at the original document, use the outline to write a draft summary.* Be sure that the essential points from the original appear in the summary. Although you should use your own words, the summary must reflect the intent

of the original passage. It should follow the order of the original and contain a number of supporting examples.

6. *Substitute single words for clauses and phrases.* Whenever possible, you should summarize details with generalizations. Following are some means of doing this:

   a. Change direct speech to indirect speech.

   b. Write in the third person if possible.

   c. Do not make critical comments or state personal opinions; report the facts.

   d. Do not lift passages verbatim; you should not use more than three words at a time from the original.

   e. The amount of textual space given to the summarized ideas should be proportional to the amount they receive in the original.

   f. Identify and eliminate minor supporting details.

   g. Simplify sentences. In Chapter 3, you learned how to simplify writing by cutting unnecessary words, using short sentences, re-wording wordy phrases, and avoiding compound constructions. For example, change *as a result of* to *because* and *in the end* to *finally*.

   h. Identify and eliminate unimportant modifiers such as *extremely*, *huge*, and *friendly*.

6. *Look again at the original.* Check that you

   a. have not quoted from the original,

   b. have covered all the main points,

   c. have excluded all non-essential material, and

   d. have not included your personal point of view.

7. *Edit your summary for spelling, grammar, and style.* Recall the grammar and style skills you learned in Chapters 2 and 3 respectively.

Changing Direct Speech to Indirect Speech

The general procedures for changing direct speech to indirect speech are set out below.

1. *Direct words become an indirect statement, question, or command.* Eliminate quotation marks.

   Direct: "I finished that file yesterday," she said.
   Indirect: She said she finished that file yesterday.

   Direct: "Where are you going?" he asked me.
   Indirect: He asked me where I was going.

   Direct: "Have all of the documents ready for the next hearing," the judge told me.
   Indirect: The judge told me to have all of the documents ready for the next hearing.

2. *Pronouns usually change from first to third person.* For example, *I* changes to *he*, *she*, or *it*.

3. *Verbs in the present tense usually change to some form of the past tense.*

Counting Words

Your summary should contain one-third or one-quarter as many words as the original, depending on the instructions given. Count the words in the original, then count the words in the completed summary. When counting words, observe the following rules:

1. Articles (*a, an, the*) count as one word.
2. Abbreviations count as one word.
3. Numbers count as one word.
4. Dates (23 October 2017) count as three words.
5. Compound words (e.g., *first-rate*) count as one word.
6. Words separated by a slash (e.g., *either/or*) count as one word.

Exercise 4.1

Removing Wordy Expressions

Find single words to replace the following phrases:
- conduct a discussion of
- give consideration to
- perform an analysis of
- make an assumption of
- create a reduction in
- is of the opinion that
- make a discovery of
- on account of the fact that
- engage in the preparation of
- carry out an investigation of

Sample Summaries

Compare the following passage with the summarized version below it:

> We wish to acknowledge receipt of your letter dated September 22, 2017. We regret to inform you that we cannot fulfill your request at this point in time to bring a group of paralegal students to tour our law office because the building is undergoing renovation. Within the next three months, we expect renovations to be complete and we will again allow visitors in the facility.
>
> We do not usually book appointments for tours this far in advance, but under the circumstances, if you are still interested in a tour when renovations are complete, we would be happy to book an appointment with you immediately. I enclose a brochure about our law firm with pertinent telephone numbers.
>
> We hope that this arrangement will meet with your satisfaction. (127 words)

> Concerning your letter dated September 22, 2017, we cannot meet your request, since the building is undergoing renovation and will not be ready for three months. However, we will book an appointment for a student tour when renovations are complete. We enclose a brochure for your information. (47 words)

Exercise 4.2

Practising Summarizing

1. Summarize each of the following paragraphs into no more than two sentences.
   a. Gossip is a message that is not factual. It is not acceptable to consider gossip as fact. There may be several reasons for gossip: mischief, misunderstanding, boredom, or inattention by the person who is passing on the gossip. On the other hand, gossip may be offered as fact because people are in a rush, are busy, or simply don't get the message straight.
   b. It seems as if busy people attract business. There is always more to do for the busy person and more responsibility to accept. It is important that a law clerk keep active and busy when not on the job. The more a person becomes involved with things outside of work, the more that person learns. At the same time, one should not neglect other important things in life such as family and friends.
   c. Every paralegal is faced with problems that need solving. He or she can take the easy way out by reporting each and every problem to a supervisor, if any, and then simply following instructions. A better idea, however, is to take some initiative and attempt to solve a problem before it has to be taken to a supervisor.
2. Summarize the two readings, "Clients without Lawyers Disturb Chief Justice" and "Report Recommends Paralegals Provide Services in Some Family Law Matters," from Appendix D.
3. Summarize opinion-based newspaper articles on legal issues. It will be especially informative to find articles that consider an issue from different points of view. Articles should be at least 300 words in length.
4. Summarize the article "By the Book," which begins below. The original article is 935 words long.

By the Book

Tara Schauerte

When people think of law, most think only of the work done by lawyers and judges and their related careers. Campus Starter took a closer look at a few of the many other professional careers associated with the administration of justice. While these careers may not be profiled in television courtroom dramas or legal thriller novels, they are just as essential for keeping the justice system running *by the book*.

In the Office

Public agencies, private law firms and corporations all seek the expertise of a variety of professionals in their legal departments. For example, law secretaries handle the firm's correspondence, law librarians provide supporting research for key cases and abstractors summarise pertinent legal or insurance details. Among the many careers at a law office is that of a paralegal (sometimes called a legal assistant) who assists lawyers with a range of administrative legal work.

Lynn Dechaine is a paralegal with the law firm of McLennan Ross, a large firm with over 50 lawyers and numerous support staff. As one of eight paralegals in a Litigation Support department, Lynn is charged with maintaining and organising large files, assembling briefing materials for the lawyers in the firm and preparing undertakings, transcripts, research and appeal books.

To get where she is today, Lynn obtained a Diploma from the Legal Assistant Program at Grant MacEwan College and worked for both a sole practising lawyer and in the legal department of a small software company before joining the firm. "Both positions gave me experience in the various administrative and legal procedures that I now use in my current job," says Lynn. "I also volunteered on various committees that gave me experience in dealing with many different people on one particular matter—a valuable asset now that I work in a larger firm."

"If you have an interest in law and are an organised person (organisation is a key quality in this field), and enjoy working in a very professional environment, then a job as a legal assistant or paralegal may just be the position for you," adds Lynn.

In Court

On the other side of the legal field, the court systems also offer a diverse range of employment opportunities beyond just judges and crown attorneys (the lawyers who prosecute cases). Bailiffs supervise prisoners and keep order in court, court stenographers record the proceedings and court clerks review and file the legal documents that arrive, and then act as an assistant to the judge.

One such court clerk is Rachel Yakimchuk with the Alberta Court of Queen's Bench. Her job as a court clerk is twofold. Part of her time is at a front counter in a team setting, helping the public and judiciary file legal documents correctly. These documents can include payments for fines and Rachel also helps individuals through the steps required to collect on or appeal their judgements. The second part of her job is in the court room—assisting the judge by opening court, swearing in witnesses and interpreters, reading the charge in criminal cases, handling the exhibits assisting the jury, monitoring digital recording equipment and keeping log notes.

Rachel started with a Bachelor of Arts (Criminology) from the University of Alberta and also worked for Campus Security while completing her degree. "Having experience in other areas of the justice system is not required but is a bonus in joining the court clerks—management also looks favourably on any experience in public service or community programs," says Rachel. "The fact that I came from a background in criminology definitely helped me because of its focus on the operation of the justice system. Also, my previous experience in law enforcement and community service with Campus Security was specifically mentioned to me as a reason for a higher pay scale."

"The best advice I could give if you're interested in this career is to speak to someone who works in the field. There are so many areas that use people with legal backgrounds that you never hear about. I would also suggest to think about the importance of a second language as any language abilities outside of English that staff can provide are always an asset."

On Campus

Research is another area within the field of law that is often overlooked but offers a wealth of opportunities individualized to your area of interest. Researchers studying in the fields of criminology, sociology, psychology and anthropology offer insight into criminal behaviour and corrections. They research trends and publish their findings, offer counselling services, make recommendations for changes within the justice system, provide expert testimony in cases before the courts and often also teach at university campuses. Dr. E. Andreas Tomaszewski, an Assistant Professor in the Department of Sociology, Anthropology and Criminology at Eastern Michigan University is an example of one such researcher. He specialises in topics such as Criminology, Deviance, Street Crime and White Collar & Corporate Crime—all with a focus on Canadian Studies.

While completing his Masters in Canadian Studies, Dr. Tomaszewski interned with the International Council for Canadian Studies (funded by the Department of Foreign Affairs) to study Canadian issues and wrote his thesis on "Rethinking Crime and Criminal Justice in Nunavut." This was soon followed by graduate research in Sociology at Carleton University on crime in public housing and led to the publication of refereed articles and a book. Dr. Tomaszewski then took a lecturer position at Ohio University for one year followed by a tenure-track position as an Assistant Professor at EMU. "Due to the university's location [Ypsilanti is near the border with Windsor, Ontario], I can take advantage of my expertise on Canadian issues and incorporate that in all of my classes, which students appear to appreciate," he says.

When asked for his advice for Canadian students interested in research, Dr. Tomaszewski recommended taking courses at your college or university like the ones he teaches—courses where your professor has a background in Canadian issues. "Also," he adds, "schools can help students get excellent internships that are extremely helpful in securing jobs after, and sometimes even before, graduation."

Source: Campus Starter. Reprinted by permission of the EI Group.

Writing a Paraphrase

The terms *paraphrase* and *summary* are often used interchangeably. It is true that both are summaries, but there is a key difference. The main point of a summary is to condense the basic concepts of a longer passage into a specific number of words. The summary is true to the meaning and tone of the original, but significantly shorter.

A paraphrase, on the other hand, translates a written passage or discussion into simpler terms; paraphrasing is a more radical rewording of the original. It need not be true to the tone or mood of the original, and *it need not be shorter*, but it should offer the reader or listener a clearer understanding of the original.

When you are trying to understand what someone is saying, you may use a paraphrase to show the speaker how you are interpreting what has been said. For example, if you ask a person for a telephone number, that person might say, "The number is 905-555-1111." Your response might be, "Did you say 905-555-1111?" The reply might be, "Yes, that's right."

If you state in your own way what another person has said, that person can determine whether or not the message was received as intended. If the speaker thinks you have misunderstood the message, he or she can provide clarity by rewording or repeating the information.

Paraphrasing has two additional benefits: it lets the other person know that you are interested in what he or she said and, since you appear to be interested in the other person's views, that person may accept your own views more willingly.

Keep in mind that paraphrasing is not merely a rearranging of words; it is an attempt to reach understanding. The following example shows how a cursory attempt at paraphrasing may produce no further understanding.

JOAN: John should train to become a licensed paralegal.
SANJIT: You mean the legal field is the right career for him?
JOAN: Exactly! The legal field is the right career for him.

No understanding is achieved in this exchange. Compare it with the following example, where the speakers use paraphrase to reach a higher level of understanding.

JOAN: John should have become a licensed paralegal.
SANJIT: Do you mean his skills are suited for the job?
JOAN: I mean that he is interested in the law, he works well in an office environment, and he is very good at detail work.
SANJIT: Oh, I see. He should have gone into a career where he can enjoy what he is doing.
JOAN: Exactly. Being a paralegal is the career for him.

Keep in mind that the paraphrase is not an exercise in mind reading. As the receiver of a message, you are repeating what the message means *to you* in order to establish the speaker's intended meaning.

Methods of Paraphrasing

There are several ways to paraphrase successfully:

1. Use the speaker's own words in your restatement.

    ORIGINAL: "I hate paperwork!"
    PARAPHRASE: "You say you hate paperwork?"

2. Restate the speaker's ideas in your own words.

    ORIGINAL: "I hate paperwork!"
    PARAPHRASE: "You have some really negative feelings about paperwork."

3. Talk about an experience of your own that is similar to the speaker's. This self-reference shows the speaker that you understand.

    ORIGINAL: "I hate paperwork!"
    RESPONSE: "I know what you mean. When I used to do a lot of paperwork, I had trouble keeping everything straight, and I always seemed to be confused."

4. Identify the underlying implications of the message. This might lead to a deeper understanding of the speaker's message.

    ORIGINAL: "I hate paperwork!"
    RESPONSE: "Are you concerned that you will not be able to do your job properly?"

Since the function of paraphrase is to explain what someone has said and to demonstrate that you understand the speaker's or writer's message, it is important to check that your interpretation is correct.

Exercise 4.3

Paraphrasing

Working in groups of three, select one of the legal topics listed below and ask the members of your group their opinion on that topic. Paraphrase what the other people have said in an attempt to reach understanding.

- Physician-assisted dying
- Animal rights
- Compensated surrogacy
- Guaranteed minimum income
- Carbon tax

Bias in Reporting

You are likely aware by now that not everyone agrees with everyone else all the time. In fact, you can have as many different points of view as there are topics to discuss. Most people have a particular point of view because they are biased about certain things or have strong opinions that they cannot easily change.

A bias does not necessarily involve a prejudice. The statement "I do not like people with brown hair" expresses a prejudice, defined as an unfavourable opinion or feeling formed beforehand, without knowledge, thought, or reason. A bias, on the other hand, can be favourable or unfavourable, but it indicates a strong opinion one way or the other, often based on experience.

The following example, taken from a local newspaper, shows two opposite biases on a single subject: dogs running free in local parks.

Dear Editor:
There are too many dogs running free in local parks while their owners just stand there and watch. This is against the law. Parks are for people. The by-law states quite clearly that dogs are supposed to be on leashes, and people are supposed to "stoop and scoop" when dogs leave their droppings. Just the other day, I stepped in a pile of droppings that some ignorant owner didn't bother to pick up. Enforce the law! Leash your dogs, or lose them.
—An unhappy taxpayer

Dear Editor:
Why can't parks be leash-free? Most dog owners, like parents of children, are very responsible and take care of their pets, picking up after them and keeping them under control. The animal shelter sells us stray and unwanted pets, but doesn't give us a place to exercise them. Then, Animal Control comes around to the parks and issues tickets to owners of dogs not on leashes. How hypocritical! We're taxpayers too. Give us a place to exercise our pets. Parks are for everyone, including dog owners.
—An unhappy taxpayer

Both letter writers are unhappy taxpayers, but each looks at the issue of dogs in parks from a different point of view. Both appear biased: the first writer wants dogs leashed, while the second writer does not. Each writer seems to base his or her opinion on an experience. The first writer had a negative experience stepping in dog droppings. The second writer appears to be a dog owner who feels he or she acts responsibly with pets. Who is right? It likely depends on whether or not you own a dog, and whether or not you decide to obey local bylaws.

Paralegals should be aware of bias in writing and communication. They should practise spotting bias in other people's writing as well as their own.

Exercise 4.4

Understanding Bias

In addition to the leash law mentioned above, there are numerous by-laws that cause controversy. Research some of your local by-laws and try to imagine the biases that might result from their enforcement or their neglect. What might be the reasons for the different points of view?

Exercise 4.5

Understanding Bias

The possible expansion of the paralegal scope of practice to include certain areas of family law, such as child custody, access, and child support, is a very controversial topic. Judges, lawyers, paralegals, and the public all have different points of view on this issue. Write one page explaining the possible reasons for these different points of view.

Writing a Case Brief

Paralegals will often write case briefs in the context of the practice of law. A **case brief** is a concise summary of a court decision. It summarizes the facts, legal issues, decision, and reasoning for the decision. The brief is the same as a summary of any other text or document in that it does not provide any new information; its purpose is to summarize the essential components of a court decision using one's own words.

As a paralegal, you may write a case brief for yourself or for a senior lawyer or paralegal to summarize the application of a complicated legal test or rule by a court. Writing a case brief helps the writer to spot legal issues, distinguish important facts from unimportant facts, and understand the logic of legal tests and rules. For the reader, a case brief can save time—it means the difference between reading a succinct three-page summary of a 40-page court decision and reading the decision itself.

As a paralegal, you will need to read a case a few times to understand it well. After reading a case, it is easy to identify most of its parts. Some judges use headings in their decisions, which can make the cases easier to understand, but many do not. Highlighting and labelling the case will make it easier to summarize. Case briefs should be short, so identifying the most relevant information matters. Preparing an outline before drafting the brief will help with this.

Case briefs can follow several different formats. Essentially, the structure of a case brief should address the relevant parts of a court decision in an organized manner. This text will focus on the following case brief format outlined in Figure 4.1.

Title of Proceeding/Case Citation

The first part of a case brief identifies the court decision that is the subject of the brief. This is the formal **title of proceeding**, or case citation. The title of proceeding identifies important information about the case, including the parties, the year of the decision, and the court level. It should enable the reader to find the case easily. Chapter 7 addresses how to properly cite a case.

Judge(s)/Adjudicator(s)

The second part of a case brief identifies the judge or other decision maker who handed down the decision; there may be one or several. If the case is an **appellate decision**, there may be more than one written opinion. For example, in addition to the **majority decision of a court**, there may be a **concurring decision** and/or a **dissenting opinion**.

History of Proceedings

The third part of the case brief is an overview of the history of proceedings, if any. This section is necessary only if the decision you are summarizing is an appeal from a lower decision or a judicial review of an administrative decision, which would mean there were one or more lower-level decisions prior to the decision you are summarizing. For example, if you are summarizing a Supreme Court of Canada decision, then there should be several lower court decisions, including a decision from a provincial court of appeal such as the Court of Appeal for Ontario; you should briefly summarize these decisions. Similarly, if you are summarizing a decision of the Ontario Superior Court of Justice—Divisional Court involving a **judicial review** of a tribunal's decision, you should briefly state what that tribunal decided.

For example:

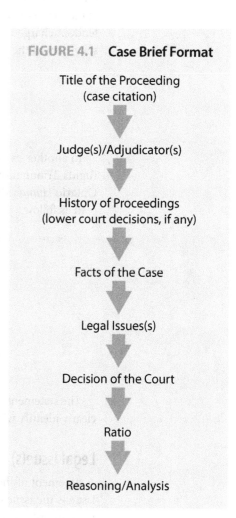

FIGURE 4.1   **Case Brief Format**

Title of the Proceeding
(case citation)

Judge(s)/Adjudicator(s)

History of Proceedings
(lower court decisions, if any)

Facts of the Case

Legal Issues(s)

Decision of the Court

Ratio

Reasoning/Analysis

> The trial judge found that the defendant failed to prove an infringement of his section 11(b) Charter right and refused to enter a stay of proceedings. The defendant was subsequently convicted of wilfully obstructing a peace officer contrary to section 129(a) of the *Criminal Code*, RSC 1985, c C-46. The defendant appealed his conviction to the Court of Appeal for Ontario, which agreed with the trial judge and dismissed the appeal.

Facts of the Case

The fourth part of the case brief involves writing a brief statement of the essential facts of the case. You should summarize only the basic facts that led up to the commencement of the legal proceeding, as reported in the decision itself. This is the "what happened" part of the case. For example, perhaps a case before the Ontario Court of Justice involves a defendant charged with careless driving under section 130 of the *Highway Traffic Act*.[1] A statement of the facts might read as follows:

> Facts: On November 2, 2016, Ashton Sears (the "defendant") was driving a motor vehicle westbound along Eglinton Avenue West in Toronto, Ontario, when he hit and injured a pedestrian. The defendant was charged with careless driving under section 130 of the *Highway Traffic Act*, RSO 1990, c H.8.

In another example, suppose you are drafting a case brief of a decision of the Human Rights Tribunal of Ontario involving a claim of employment discrimination under the Ontario *Human Rights Code*, RSO 1990, c H.19. A statement of the facts of the case might read as follows:

> Facts: In November 2016, Hi-Ten Manufacturers (the "Respondent") fired Sara Jenkins (the "Applicant") from her position as a manager. The Respondent is a firm owned by two brothers, Karl Smith and Dan Smith. The Applicant's mother was charged with murder and was found guilty in August 2016 while the Applicant was working for the Respondent. Shortly after the conviction, Mr. Smith fired the Applicant. The Applicant filed an Application with the Human Rights Tribunal of Ontario claiming that her termination constituted employment discrimination on the ground of family status under section 5 of the Ontario *Human Rights Code*, RSO 1990, c H.19.

The statement of facts should be very brief—no longer than five sentences—and should clearly identify who the parties are (plaintiff, applicant, defendant, respondent, etc.).

Legal Issue(s)

A statement of the legal issue(s) of the case is always necessary in a case brief. The legal issue is the issue or question raised by the facts that the court must deal with or determine in order to decide the case.

Spotting the issue takes practice. The legal issue of a case is not simply whether the defendant is guilty or not guilty in a criminal or provincial offences case, or whether the respondent discriminated against the applicant in a human rights case. The legal issue is usually much narrower than that.

In a case brief, the legal issue should be written in the form of a question. For example, the legal issue in the human rights case example above might be:

> Issue: Whether the respondent discriminated against the applicant on the basis of family status under section 5 of the Ontario *Human Rights Code* upon terminating the Applicant's employment.

---

1 RSO 1990, c H.8

The legal issue in the careless driving case example above might be written as follows:

Issue: Whether the defendant's driving prior to and in relation to the accident constitutes careless driving within the meaning of section 130 of the *Highway Traffic Act*, RSO c H.8.

There can also be more than one legal issue in a case. You should be aware of multiple legal issues in a case when writing a case brief. When there is more than one legal issue, you should clearly numerate each issue. For example:

Issue: (1)   Did the installation of an infrared camera on the meter outside the defendant's house without judicial authorization constitute a violation of the defendant's right to be secure from unreasonable search and seizure under section 8 of the *Charter of Rights and Freedoms* (the "Charter").
         (2)   If so, was the search warrant obtained to search the defendant's house valid.
         (3)   If the defendant's section 8 Charter right was violated, should the evidence obtained in breach of his right be excluded from trial under section 24(2) of the Charter.

The legal issue of a case also depends on the level of court deciding the matter. Appellate courts usually determine whether a lower court erred in its application of the law. For example, in the human rights example above, suppose the Human Rights Tribunal of Ontario decided that the respondent did not discriminate against the applicant on the basis of family status under section 5 of the Ontario *Human Rights Code* because the definition of family status does not include the particular identity of a family member. In other words, the Ontario *Human Rights Code* protects people against discrimination on the basis of simply having (or not having) a family, not on the basis of the identity of a particular family member. On review, the issue before the reviewing court might be as follows:

Issue: Did the Tribunal err in finding that the definition of family status does not include the identity of a particular family member?

Decision of the Court

This part of the case brief summarizes the court's final decision in the case. What did the court decide? The answer to this question should correspond to the legal issue you identified in the previous section. You should now answer each issue with *yes* or *no*. You must also identify the **disposition of the case**. For example, did the court dismiss the action or application? Did the court find the defendant liable for the plaintiff's injuries? If the case is an appeal from a lower-level decision, the court will either dismiss the appeal or allow the appeal.

Ratio

The word *ratio* is a short form for the Latin phrase ***ratio decidendi***, which means "reason for the decision." You should practise identifying the ratio of court decisions, as it is not easy to do. Many experienced lawyers and other legal professionals have trouble finding the ratio in a case. You should think of the ratio as the principle of law for which the judicial decision stands.

Reasoning/Analysis

This part of the case brief summarizes the court's rationale for its decision. It involves summarizing the court's application of the law (legislation, case law, rule, etc.) to the facts of the case. This section is the most important and the lengthiest section of the brief; therefore, you may wish to use headings and sub-headings to help organize this section. This can be especially helpful when the decision deals with more than one issue. See Chapter 3 for a discussion of using headings and sub-headings to improve your writing style.

You should not simply copy the section of the legislation, rule, or legal test that applies in the case; instead, summarize in your own words how the court has interpreted and applied it to the facts of the case. To do this you have to identify the relevant rule(s) the court relied on to make its decision and understand the relevant facts that the court relied on to interpret and apply the law in a particular way.

Remember that the goal is to summarize clearly and concisely the court's reasoning for deciding the way it did. You must not include your personal opinions about the decision or the court's reasoning. You should also avoid including lengthy, verbatim sentences from the decision.

After drafting the case brief, recall the other stages of the writing process discussed in Chapter 1: revising and editing. You should spend time improving the content of the case brief to ensure that the summarized information flows logically and coherently. Finally, always proofread your case brief to identify and correct spelling and grammar errors.

Exercise 4.6

Summarizing

Read the decision of Justice Marshall of the Ontario Small Claims Court in *Liang v Brock University*, 2015 CanLII 31300 (Ont Sup Ct J (Sm Cl Ct)), which appears in Figure 4.2. After you read the case, compare it to the sample case brief summarizing the decision in Figure 4.3.

FIGURE 4.2   *Liang v Brock University,* **2015 CanLII 31300 (Ont Sup Ct J (Sm Cl Ct))**

ONTARIO SUPERIOR COURT OF JUSTICE 1072/15
(ST CATHARINES SMALL CLAIMS COURT)

BETWEEN:

XIYING LIANG
Plaintiff

-and-

BROCK UNIVERSITY
Defendant

Before: Marshall Deputy Judge

Heard: June 5, 2015

Released: June 9, 2015

Plaintiff: E. Shi, paralegal

Defendant: S. McHugh, counsel

ENDORSEMENT

[1]   The Plaintiff enrolled in the Professional Masters Preparation Certificate Program ["PMPCP"] at the Defendant for the 2014-2015 academic year. There were complaints about the quality of teaching of course instructor Brenda Rose ["Rose"] and how the Defendant handled the complaints. Matters were not resolved to the satisfaction of the Plaintiff. She advised the Defendant she was leaving the program and sought reimbursement of tuition and rent expenses. The Defendant refused to do so.

[2]   The Plaintiff's Claim was issued on February 9, 2015. A Defence was filed on March 16, 2015. A settlement conference on April 9, 2015 was unsuccessful. The matter is presently listed for trial on July 15, 2015. The Defendant has brought a motion to dismiss the action under various aspects of Rule 12 of the *Rules of the Small Claims Court*:

> "12.02   (1)   The court may, on motion, strike out or amend all or part of any document that,
> (a)   discloses no reasonable cause of action or defence;
> (b)   is inflammatory, a waste of time, a nuisance or an abuse of the court's process.
> 12.02   (2)   In connection with an order striking out or amending a document under subrule (1), the court may do one or more of the following:
> 1.   in the case of a claim, order that the action be stayed or dismissed."

FIGURE 4.2   **Continued**

PLAINTIFF'S CLAIM

[3]   A fair reading of the pleading outlines what was the underlying source of the action. The pleading is less successful in clearly articulating a cause of action.

[4]   As is stated in para 1, "The Plaintiff brought this action against the Defendant after experiencing deficiency and inadequacy of teaching and learning among her scheduled classes. The Plaintiff expressed her dissatisfaction towards the quality [of the] program; no rectification of performance was made."

[5]   The Plaintiff came from China to attend school at the Defendant. She had received her admission into the PMPCP on June 10, 2014. Her tuition was paid in due course. She arrived in Canada via Toronto on August 23, 2014. Classes commenced on September 3, 2014.

[6]   Rose was an instructor in three of the six courses the Plaintiff took the first term. On four occasions over the next two months, lectures conducted by Rose were cancelled. Quite apart from the lack of timely notice—if any notice at all—of these cancelled lectures, the Plaintiff's real worry was the effect on "the quality of teaching and learning" in the PMPCP [para 10].

[7]   Things got worse. The third impacted lecture was when Rose forgot her textbooks and audio CDs at home and had to "wing it" [my phrasing] in class. The presentation was inadequate, again impacting the quality of teaching [para 11]. The fourth lecture that went awry was a cancellation due to Rose purportedly being ill [para 14].

[8]   Rose's quality of teaching was addressed in other English as a second language classes [para 13] and with a professor in the program [para 16].

[9]   At an unspecified date, the Plaintiff advised the Defendant since nothing was being done she would have to go to another academic institution "to seek a better teaching and learning environment" [para 20].

[10]   Under a section called "Issue(s)," most of the nine listed items relate to Rose's performance. There are references to a duty of care and a standard of care. The word "contract" is used once, more in the context of a suggestion there should be some pro rata refund [para 27].

BASIS OF THE MOTION OF THE DEFENDANT

[11]   Program dissatisfaction is not a proper basis for a cause of action in either contract or tort. Internal academic issues are within the discretion of a university.

[12]   The Defendant's offer of admission to the PMPCP speaks about when tuition is to be paid but does not deal with any possible tuition refund scenarios.

[13]   Two different versions of a document entitled "Tuition Refund Policy" for the PMPCP were before me. That included in the motion materials noted it was revised in March, 2015[,] so it could not possibly have been relevant. That contained as part of the Plaintiff's Claim was revised in January, 2010. The substance of the two versions appears to be the same. Both documents suggest a refund only if a student did not get a student visa or was too ill to remain in Canada to complete their studies. On the facts, neither exception would appear relevant.

RESPONSE OF THE PLAINTIFF TO THE MOTION

[14]   The responding affidavit was in the name of Emrick Shi, the paralegal acting for the Plaintiff. He attended on the motion. He did not appear to realize he could not appear and argue on his own affidavit. After advising the parties I was prepared to adjourn the motion if the issue could not be resolved, Ms McHugh advised the Defendant was nevertheless prepared to proceed notwithstanding this impropriety. The affidavit was part of the responding argument.

[15]   The affidavit listed twenty-seven "causes of action" against Rose [10], the Defendant [7], inexplicably the Plaintiff [9] and the tuition refund policy [1]. Suffice to say the argument by the Defendant about no reasonable cause of action was not adequately understood. The responding affidavit does make reference to contract matters at [4] 3) and 4). On a very generous reading of things, the "high-handed purposes" at [5] re the tuition refund policy might be considered tortious.

[16]   One area of agreement amongst the parties is the Plaintiff left the PMPCP after two months, in early November, 2014.

CASE LAW PROVIDED BY THE DEFENDANT

[17]   The tension in this action is the scope of a claim in the civil courts where the underlying issue involves academic issues between a student and a university. It is at times not a clearly defined line. If such a claim exists in the civil courts, there is the issue of pleading proper causes of action in contract and/or tort.

[18]   In *Gauthier v Saint-Germain* 2010 ONCA 309 (CanLII), the Court of Appeal reviewed principles arising out of the case law. While the Defendant referenced just para 47, I find it useful to set out paras 45 to 50:

> "[45]   It would therefore appear that no precedent dictates that the court does not have jurisdiction to hear cases for the sole reason that the tort or related breach of contract arises from a scholastic dispute.

> [46]   In my opinion, in order to determine whether the court has jurisdiction, it is more helpful to focus on the remedy being claimed by the plaintiff. When a party seeks to overturn an internal academic decision made by a university, the appropriate route is judicial review. However, if the plaintiff alleges the constituent elements of a cause of action based in tort or breach of contract, while claiming damages, the court will have jurisdiction even if the dispute stems from the scholastic or academic activities of the university in question.

> [47]   Moreover, when a student enrols in a university, it is understood that the student will be subject to the discretion of that institution when it comes to resolving academic issues, whether in the evaluation of the quality of the student's work, the structure and implementation of university programs, or the identification of the skills required to serve as a professor or thesis supervisor. This discretion is very broad. Thus, claiming that a grade is incorrect or that a professor is incompetent, without more, will not normally be sufficient grounds on which to base a cause of action in breach of contract or tort.

FIGURE 4.2 Continued

[48] In order to establish a cause of action for breach of contract, the student must demonstrate that the university failed to fulfil an express or tacit obligation to which this institution had committed by accepting the student's registration. In *Wong*, the statement of claim was struck out because the plaintiff was unable to demonstrate that the university had agreed to assign him a specific supervisor. In the same vein, *Zabo* shows that a university can require changes to a thesis unless the relationship extant between the university and the student implied otherwise.

[49] In regards to allegations of negligence, *Young* confirms that a university indeed owes a duty of care to its students. Nonetheless, in order to establish a cause of action based on negligence, the student must do more than merely state that a professor was too exacting in his evaluations or demonstrate his or her incompetence. In order to establish that the university breached its duty of care, the student must plead specific facts tending to show that the conduct of the university or professor in question constituted an intentional tort, as in *Zabo*, or was outside the broad margin of discretion that the university and its professors enjoy.

[50] Thus, even if the court has jurisdiction, *Dawson* and *Zabo* nonetheless demonstrate that it is prepared to strike out the cause of action under rule 21.01 (1) or, in exceptional circumstances, under rule 25.11 when it appears that the cause of action is untenable or could not succeed. The circumstances in which the court will exercise its discretion to strike a cause of action fall into one of two categories. First, if the action in tort or breach of contract is but an indirect attempt to appeal an internal academic decision when the appropriate approach would be judicial review (for example, the decision to give a certain grade, to require certain work, to refuse admission to a program or to not award a diploma), the court can strike it out. Second, if the pleadings do not provide the necessary information to demonstrate that the university or its employees have exceeded their broad discretion, the court could also strike out the cause of action."

While the Court found there were issues outside the "broad discretion granted to universities in the design and implementation of their academic programs" [para 57], it also found "a bare allegation that a professor is not competent is insufficient to support a valid cause of action" [para 59]. The plaintiff was granted leave to amend the pleading.

[19] *Jaffer v York University* 2010 ONCA 654 (CanLII) alleged failure to accommodate the disabilities of a student. Karakatsanis JA [as she then was] cited *Gauthier*, decided just five months before, in particular para 47 thereof:

"[27] ... it is understood that the student agrees to be subject to the institution's discretion in resolving academic matters, including the assessment of the quality of the student's work and the organization and implementation of university programs."

The Court also confirmed contractual and tortious claims can be advanced if it is pleaded obligations were owed by a university to a student and the failure to meet such obligations caused the student to sustain damages: para 29. The Court in *Jaffer* framed the matter in the following terms:

> "[30]   There is no dispute that the relationship between a student and a university has a contractual foundation, giving rise to duties in both contract and tort: *Young v Bella*, 2006 SCC 3 (CanLII), [2006] 1 S.C.R. 108, at para 31.
>
> [31]   The real issue is this case is not whether the dispute is academic in nature, but rather whether the pleadings support a cause of action in either contract or tort."

That is equally the issue I ultimately have to address.

[20]   The Court in *Jaffer* noted there was but a "bald statement" about any duty to accommodate [para 46] and a duty of good faith was not a stand alone duty [para 49]. Notwithstanding the deficiencies in pleading, leave was granted to amend the Statement of Claim.

[21]   *King v Sly* 2015 ONSC 584 (CanLII) involved claims of verbal harassment by the defendant professor. An original pleading had been struck out with leave to amend. The defendants moved to strike the Fresh as Amended Statement of Claim. C.J. Brown J found it contained no discernable cause of action nor material facts in support thereof: para 5. The issue of the underlying academic dispute was considered:

> "[10]   As regards her claim for damages relating to an academic dispute, these appear to relate to improperly administered exams and failure to respond to questions regarding essay exams, which, pursuant to the jurisprudence, the courts have repeatedly declined to inquire into and pass judgment upon….
>
> [11]   In the present case, the plaintiff's claim would require the court to inquire into and assess the correctness of academic decisions made by the defendants regarding the administration of an exam, the plaintiff's grades and Ryerson's conduct in handling the plaintiff's complaints about her grades. In other words, the court would be asked to assess decisions made by the defendants surrounding the 'organization and implementation of university programs,' a matter clearly within the discretion of the University and not appropriate for a tort or a breach of contract claim."

The claim was struck out without leave to amend.

ADDITIONAL LEGAL PRECEDENTS

[22]   The courts have continued to wrestle with the extent of jurisdiction in the civil courts involving university issues after *Gauthier* and *Jaffe*. The key factor in each decision is the pleading. I note in passing no precedents were provided on behalf of the Plaintiff.

FIGURE 4.2 Continued

[23]   In *Murray v Lakehead University*, 2011 ONSC 5319 (CanLII), the plaintiff sought damages due to inadequate oversight by his thesis supervisor. Pierce RSJ struck the Statement of Claim:

"[8]   Here, the plaintiff has not pleaded a duty of care between the plaintiff and the defendant. He has not identified the alleged negligence of the university. Particularly, he has not named the thesis supervisor; he has not indicated whether he requested an alternative supervisor; he has not indicated whether he asked to remain in the program or what alternatives were available to him; he has not pleaded the defendant breached its duty of care to him; nor has he established a causal connection between the damages suffered and the alleged negligence of the university....

[9]   Thus, the pleading is bad and must be struck.

[10]   It is common for pleadings to be struck with leave to amend granted to correct the deficiencies. I am of the view that leave should not be granted here on the ground that even a corrected pleading would disclose no reasonable cause of action.

[11]   The claim arises out of an academic dispute with the university. The jurisprudence establishes that the courts will defer to universities in matters of academic disputes except in narrow circumstances.

. . .

[13]   Here, the pleadings do not disclose a factual basis to establish that the conduct of the university goes beyond the broad discretion that the courts have recognized is the province of the university.

[14]   Courts are not well-positioned to oversee academic issues at universities. The deference of the courts to universities in such disputes is well-established in the case law. The rationale is articulated in *Blasser v Royal Institution for Advancement of Learning*, (1985) 1985 CanLII 3061 (QC CA), 24 D.L.R. (4th) 507, (Q.C.A.), para. 40:

'In any university, ... there are certain internal matters and disputes that are best decided within the academic community rather than by the Courts. This is so, not only because the Courts are not as well equipped as the universities to decide matters such as academic qualifications, grades, the conferring of degrees and so on, but also because these matters ought to be able to be decided more conveniently, more quickly, more economically and at least as accurately by those who are specialized in educational questions of that kind. In addition, of course, there is very good reason not to risk compromising the essential independence of universities by undue interference in their academic affairs.'"

[24]   In *Lobo v Carleton University*, 2012 ONSC 254 (CanLII), Toscano Roccamo J dealt with in part negligence claims involving discrimination, holding the necessary elements of a cause of action in negligence had been properly pleaded. Further, intentional conduct was potentially found to fall outside the *Gauthier* parameters about the normal broad discretion enjoyed by a university.

[25]   The 'broad discretion' reference is from *Gauthier* at para 47, cited by Ms McHugh in support of this motion. *Lobo* involved facts that at least at the pleadings' stage successfully advanced a cause of action in tort. The appeal of the decision did not address this issue: 2012 ONCA 498 (CanLII).

[26]   *Turner v York University*, 2012 ONSC 4272 (CanLII) is a Divisional Court decision dealing with refusal of certification of a class proceeding concerning disrupted classes and exams from a 2008 strike. Cunningham ACJ upheld the refusal to certify any class proceeding, dealing with *Gauthier* and *Jaffer* in the following paragraphs in holding the pleadings did not disclose a cause of action:

> "[31]   … *Gauthier* and *Jaffer* … are entirely unhelpful to the appellant. While it is *possible* for a student to enter into a contract with a university, that is not to be confused with the academic relationship between a student and his or her university. *Gauthier* enunciates, and *Jaffer* confirms that the contract must be pleaded and there must be particulars given that the university has gone beyond its broad academic discretion.

> [32]   For a court to consider the claim as argued by the appellant, a court would have to inquire into whether York's decisions in dealing with the strike were right, as measured against a standard of academic integrity. This is exactly the kind of discretion the courts ought not to review, as it falls within the purview of a university's ability to make decisions concerning academic integrity.

> [33]   The appellant has failed to demonstrate that Cullity J erred in his application of the law as it relates to the relationship between the parties. At issue is whether the university, in modifying the academic schedule to accommodate the strike's disruption, was within its discretion over 'the organizing and carrying out the university programs,' as noted in *Gauthier*. The appellant's statement of the existence of a contractual relationship is insufficient on its own, and moreover is not distinguished from the academic discretion described in *Gauthier* and *Jaffer*." [emphasis in original]

[27]   *Turner* holds the likes of scheduling are within the exclusive ambit of a university.

[28]   *Thode v University of Ottawa*, 2012 ONSC 7284 (CanLII) involved claims against a university that included negligence in the handling of a defamatory statement made by a co-defendant. In finding it was not plain and obvious the court did not have jurisdiction, McNamara J found as follows:

> "[10]   The defendants argue firstly that this court does not have jurisdiction because this matter is of an academic nature. They submit that where the essence of a dispute is in respect of academic matters which are internal to the university and within its internal code, the court should not intervene because of the special relationship of member of a university, the importance of academic independence, and the special ability of university tribunals to fairly consider their internal procedures and customs. (See *Gauthier* …).

FIGURE 4.2 Continued

[11] Generally speaking, while that statement is accurate, the cases make it clear that whether a dispute is an academic dispute is a question of fact. The only document before me on this motion relative to that issue is the Statement of Claim. There is nothing in that document that would lead to a conclusion that the dispute between these parties arises out of the academic decisions and procedures of the University. Rather the remedy claimed is for defamation and negligence. It does not seek, for example, to have an internal academic decision of the University reversed or anything else of that nature. There is nothing before the court about any internal codes of the University, nor the availability of university tribunals to consider problems of this nature." [underlining in original]

[29] *Thode* suggests the avenue by which a defendant university seeks to strike such a claim is important, i.e., internal codes and the availability of university tribunals could have been incorporated into a Rule 20 summary judgment motion, quite apart from not finding defamation to be an internal academic issue.

[30] *Mortazavi v University of Toronto* was before the Court of Appeal on two occasions: 2013 ONCA 66 (CanLII) before Laskin JA in chambers on a procedural matter and 2013 ONCA 655 (CanLII) before a panel on the merits.

[31] Mortazavi was married to the co-plaintiff. Both were doctoral students from Iran. When Mortazavi's father became ill, they sought some accommodation to return to Iran to care for him. They received failing grades and paid tuition for classes they did not attend. All internal academic appeals were exhausted. No judicial review was sought but a Statement of Claim was issued. Belobaba J struck out the claim without leave to amend. Mortazavi appealed. Before Laskin JA, an extension of time was sought to perfect the appeal. That decision depended on whether there was any merit in the appeal. One of the issues was tuition fees.

[32] Laskin JA granted an extension to perfect the appeal, holding the Statement of Claim disclosed a reasonable cause of action in contract and negligence [para 29]. At the same time, he noted, per *Gauthier*, the limited scope of causes of action in contract and negligence against universities. A breach of contract claim has to involve an express or implicit obligation of the university in approving the student's attendance, in essence a quid pro quo. A negligence claim is limited to an intentional tort or facts pleaded beyond the normal discretion a university has to deal with academic matters.

[33] The actual appeal was summarily dismissed:

"[4] ... what is left is an attack on a series of academic decisions relating to admission, enrolment, leave of absence, grades, and appeals. In these circumstances, the motion judge had ample justification to conclude, as he did, that 'the lawsuit for the tort or the breach of contract is nothing more than an indirect attempt to appeal with is an internal academic decision when the proper procedure is judicial review.'"

[34]   Matters like scheduling and the competence of instructors are matters within the preserve of a university. Challenges to such decisions can be made by way of judicial review. While academic matters can be the subject of civil court proceedings for damages, the scope of civil courts in university matters is narrow, depending on the pleading. Any cause of action in contract must involve the very basis upon which the student agreed to attend a university. Any cause of action in tort must involve an intentional tort. Short of these exceptions, a pleading may be struck as disclosing no reasonable cause of action. Against this backdrop, the Plaintiff's Claim will be reviewed.

ANALYSIS

TUITION REFUND POLICY

[35]   On the basis of a wrong document being submitted, it would have been open to me to not even deal with this argument. I nevertheless would not have dismissed the action based on the tuition refund policy alone.

[36]   The affidavit in support of the motion is by Jordan Snel, Legal Advisor, Research and Copyright for the Defendant. The tuition refund policy is discussed at paras 16-20 of his affidavit.

[37]   It is suggested the policy was available for the Plaintiff to view on the university's website prior to accepting an offer of admission. That may be so but insufficient materials were supplied in the motion materials for me to decide that point.

[38]   It is not clear if the policy for foreign students is the same for all students, for instance, a student from Grimsby, Ontario. It is not clear if different rules apply for different programs. This is a motion to strike an action so the materials should have been more fulsome relative the tuition refund policy. The attack on the Plaintiff's Claim on this basis fails for the same reasons as in *Thode* outlined at para 29 above.

[39]   The limited tuition refund policy for someone in the Plaintiff's position would have been limited to illness precluding her from not only completing the program but also remaining in Canada. At first blush this is rather draconian. I am reminded of the case of *Tilden Rent-A-Car Co. v Clendenning*, (1978), 1978 CanLII 1446 (ON CA), 18 O.R. (2d) 601 where the signer to an unusual and onerous provision in a written contract was not bound by it. I reiterate there is not even any material before me to suggest there was a written offer and acceptance but the Defendant nevertheless seeks to rely on an onerous provision. If the enforceability of the tuition refund policy were the only issue on the motion, I would have dismissed the motion.

THE UNDERLYING CONCERN

[40]   It is evident the Plaintiff found Rose to be substandard in a number of ways. Four classes were cancelled over the first two months of the program. There was a lack of preparedness on one occasion. There was a lack of professional courtesy in advising the students with respect to a couple of the cancellations. As the expression goes, "where there's smoke, there's fire." It would appear there is some substance to the Plaintiff's concerns, the university circling the wagons to protect Rose. That observation, however, just outlines the nature of the complaints of the Plaintiff.

FIGURE 4.2 Continued

[41] Not satisfied with how her concerns were being addressed, the Plaintiff ultimately decided to deal with the issues by leaving the university and seeking a refund of all tuition and rent expenses, having been at the university but two months.

[42] Whether one considers the Plaintiff's decision brave or brazen, it ultimately has to be addressed against the backdrop of the legal principles set out earlier. Mr Shi submitted the Plaintiff left under duress. There is no such allegation in the Plaintiff's Claim.

WERE THE UNDERLYING ISSUES ACADEMIC IN NATURE?

[43] The Plaintiff's decision to leave after two months was ill-advised, even rash. Her rationale to do so was the PMPCP was short [a one year program] and her evident quality considerations.

[44] The timing and rescheduling of classes was part of the broad discretion of a university to implement curricula: *Gauthier* at para 47 and *Jaffer* at para 27. Per the affidavit of Mr Snel at para 25, there was time allotted within the academic calendar for makeup classes. The Plaintiff alleged some students were not available for the makeup classes. There was no suggestion the Plaintiff was not available for the makeup classes. Classes do get cancelled for good and bad reasons. I have to wonder if I would even be writing these reasons had the university been more forthcoming.

[45] While there appear to have been some valid concerns expressed by the Plaintiff about Rose's teaching skills, matters pertaining to allegations about an incompetent instructor are also part and parcel of the academic matters: *Gauthier* at paras 47 and 49.

[46] Timing of classes and instructor competence are academic disputes. Such matters are normally within the exclusive preserve of the university: *King* at para 10, *Murray* at paras 11 and 14 and *Turner* at para 37.

[47] Where it is sought to overturn the decision of a university on an academic dispute, the remedy is judicial review: *Gauthier* at 46, *Thode* at 29 and *Mortazavi* at para 33. The Plaintiff has not sought judicial review but a remedy through the civil courts.

DOES THE PLAINTIFF'S CLAIM STATE ONE OR MORE CAUSES OF ACTION?

[48] *Gauthier* outlines the narrow circumstances in which a core academic matter can be addressed in the civil courts, be it in contract or tort. This necessitates a further review of the Plaintiff's Claim.

CONTRACT

[49] There is nothing in the body—nor the 14 tabs—of the Plaintiff's Claim alleging the university "failed to fulfil an express or tacit obligation to which this institution had committed by accepting the student's registration": *Gauthier* at para 48. The Plaintiff did not agree to enrol in the PMPCP only if there were no cancelled classes and if she was satisfied with the quality of the instruction. It is very much an open question if any university would accept an application on that basis. The pleading does not show the Plaintiff has complied within the narrow range to ground a breach of contract action.

[50]   The responding motion record does not advance the Plaintiff's position. The occasional reference to "contract" does not deal with any underlying bargain amongst the parties.

TORT

[51]   The Plaintiff's Claim if anything is weaker on advancing any tort claim. I accept that the university owed the Plaintiff a duty of care but the pleading is devoid of any suggestion of an intentional tort to take away the broad discretion universities generally enjoy in dealing with the likes of complaints of incompetent instructors: *Gauthier* at 49. The sort of detail outlined in *Murray* at para 8 is simply lacking. As discussed above at paras 24-25 above re *Lobo*, properly pleaded, such a claim in tort could be advanced but only if there was an intentional tort.

[52]   Nothing in the Plaintiff's Claim nor submissions advanced would suggest there is a cause of action in either contract or tort.

NO LEAVE TO AMEND SOUGHT

[53]   Neither in the responding affidavit nor in submissions did Mr Shi seek leave to amend the pleading. I asked him about same in the course of the motion and no leave to amend was sought. Based on decisions like *Murray* and the appeal in *Mortazavi*, any such request would likely have been refused.

CONCLUSIONS UNDER R 12.02 (1)

[54]   With respect to clause (c), I would not have found the Plaintiff's Claim to be any of "inflammatory, a waste of time, a nuisance or an abuse of the court's process." The Plaintiff had some issues with the structure and teaching adequacy of the PMPCP. The shortcomings of how to deal with same were threefold: 1) deciding to leave the program 2) not seeking judicial review if she [felt] that the issues were that important and 3) proceeding in the civil courts without pleading appropriate causes of action in contract and/or tort. I do not view these shortcomings as the type of claims contemplated by clause (c).

[55]   Having gone the civil court route, the Plaintiff had to plead causes of action in contract and/or tort to take the matter outside of its normal resolution within the realm of academic matters. That has not been done and, frankly, could not have been done. There was nothing to suggest at day's end the matter was anything more than a dispute about class scheduling and instructor competence, matters that normally fall within academic matters. The further route sought was a civil action when it ought to have been judicial review. On that basis, I find there is no reasonable cause of action pleaded in the Plaintiff's Claim. I would strike the pleading on that basis and dismiss the action for failing to fall within the narrow exceptions outlined in *Gauthier*.

[56]   This matter was otherwise scheduled for trial on July 15, 2015. It should accordingly be removed from the trial list.

COSTS

[57]   This matter was not addressed by the parties. I have some sympathy to the Plaintiff's perceived dilemma. She ultimately was the authoress of her own misfortune in seeking to end her relationship with the university but it was her negative experience with the Canadian education system which was the initial problem. Even if the decision to leave amounted to an overreaction, it would be my inclination to award no costs of the motion nor the action.

[58]   If either side seeks a contrary disposition of costs, I would expect to be emailed, the other side copied, on or before June 16, 2015. The action is otherwise dismissed without costs.

[59]   Both parties through their representatives and the Court are being provided with an email version of this endorsement today.

June 9, 2015
"Marshall Deputy Judge"

FIGURE 4.3   Sample Case Brief

Title of Proceeding/Case Citation: *Liang v Brock University*, 2015 CanLII 31300 (ON SCSM)

Judge: Deputy Judge Marshall (Ontario Small Claims Court)

Facts: The plaintiff, Xiying Liang (the "plaintiff") was an international student who enrolled in the Professional Masters Preparation Certificate Program at Brock University (the "defendant"). The plaintiff was unhappy with the quality of her course instruction and the defendant's approach to dealing with her complaints. As a result, the plaintiff left the program and sought a tuition refund and other compensation; however, the defendant refused to compensate her. After the plaintiff commenced an action, the defendant brought a motion to dismiss the action.

Legal Issues: (1) Is program dissatisfaction a proper basis for a cause of action in either contract or tort law. (2) Do the plaintiff's pleadings or submissions support a cause of action in contract or tort law.

Decision: (1) No. Program dissatisfaction is not a proper basis for a cause of action in contract or tort law except in very narrow circumstances. (2) No. Neither the plaintiff's pleadings nor her submissions support a cause of action in either contract or tort law. The court dismissed the plaintiff's action.

Ratio: Courts will defer to universities regarding internal academic disputes, except in narrow circumstances in which the plaintiff's pleadings clearly identify material facts that support a cause of action in contract or tort law. Instructor incompetence and class rescheduling, on their own, will not generally be enough to base a cause of action in contract or tort. These kinds of disputes should not be the subject of civil court proceedings for damages except in very narrow circumstances in which the plaintiff's pleadings allege that the university failed to fulfill an express obligation that it committed to or the pleadings identify an intentional tort.

Reasoning:

Issue 1: Is program dissatisfaction a proper basis for a cause of action in either contract or tort law.

A student's dissatisfaction with an educational program is an academic issue and should be dealt with by the academic institution in most cases or by way of judicial review. However, the Court of Appeal for Ontario in *Gauthier v Saint-Germain* 2010 ONCA 309 (CanLII) held that courts can provide a remedy in some cases if the plaintiff can support a cause of action in contract or tort law.

In order to support a cause of action in contract, the plaintiff must show that the post-secondary institution expressly promised to fulfill an obligation to the student when the institution registered the student and that the institution subsequently failed to deliver that obligation.

Universities owe a duty of care to their students. However, in order to establish a cause of action based on negligence, the plaintiff must allege facts that establish this duty of care and that show the institution's conduct constitutes an intentional tort.

Issue 2: Do the plaintiff's pleadings or submissions support a cause of action in contract or tort law.

An action for breach of contract needs to establish that the academic institution did not honour an obligation it entered into with the student when accepting the student's registration. In this case, there was no such obligation. The plaintiff's enrollment at Brock University was not dependent on her satisfaction with the quality of the instructor. Nor did she agree to enroll only if there were no cancelled classes. The plaintiff's pleadings do not allege that the defendant accepted the plaintiff into its program on these terms.

The plaintiff's pleadings do not support a cause of action in tort. While the defendant owed the plaintiff a duty of care, the plaintiff failed to plead that the defendant owed her a duty of care. She also failed to plead facts that suggest an intentional tort on the part of the defendant.

Exercise 4.7

Writing a Case Brief

Read the Court of Appeal for Ontario decision *Fernandes v Peel Educational & Tutorial Services Limited (Mississauga Private School)*, 2016 ONCA 468 (CanLII) available at <https://www.canlii.org>. Draft a case brief summarizing the decision in the format discussed in this chapter.

Exercise 4.8

Locate one of the reported decisions listed below online at <https://www.canlii.org>. Read the decision and draft a case brief in the format discussed in this chapter.

1. *Hersch Harry Kopyto v Law Society of Upper Canada*, 2011 ONLSHP 0071
2. *HMQ (MOE) v Castonguay Blasting Ltd.*, 2011 ONSC 767

Summary

The ability to summarize and paraphrase is an effective communication tool for paralegals. When summarizing, a paralegal puts other people's words, substantially reduced, into his or her own words while retaining the meaning of the original. When paraphrasing, a paralegal demonstrates his or her understanding of a speaker's or writer's meaning. In most newspaper or popular magazine articles, authors reveal a particular point of view, or bias, on a topic. Facts supporting this bias are used to persuade the reader of the author's point of view. Paralegals should be able to identify bias in various forms of communication.

The ability to write a case brief is an important skill. It involves understanding a court's application of the law to a particular set of facts and summarizing it concisely using one's own words. It does not involve expressing a personal opinion about the decision. Following the case brief format suggested in Figure 4.1 will help paralegals summarize all relevant parts of a court decision in an organized manner.

Legal Argument

5

LEARNING OUTCOMES

After reading this chapter, you should be able to

- Describe the IRAC method of legal analysis.

- Understand the structure of a legal argument.

- Develop effective legal arguments.

Introduction

Developing a legal argument takes practice. A legal argument is a conclusion based on a coherent set of reasons intended to persuade someone to accept the conclusion as true. Making strong legal arguments is the essence of practising law. When representing clients before courts and tribunals, paralegals need to develop effective legal arguments to convince a judge or adjudicator why he or she should decide the case in favour of the paralegal's client. Paralegals must also develop strong legal arguments to persuade an opposing party of a certain position.

There are many ways to develop and organize an effective legal argument. This chapter introduces one way to do so. It also suggests tips for effectively organizing and presenting your legal arguments.

Structure of a Legal Argument

An important part of developing a legal argument is giving it an appropriate structure. There are different frameworks for structuring a legal argument, but all of them include most of the same elements. This chapter focuses on the IRAC framework.

The acronym IRAC represents the elements or stages of developing a legal argument: Issue, Rule, Application, and Conclusion.

As a paralegal, you will develop legal arguments based on a set of facts. A client will come to you to resolve a legal issue or problem, or a lawyer or paralegal in your firm may ask you to develop legal arguments in support of a particular legal position for the firm's client. You may present your legal arguments in a memorandum of law. Chapter 7 deals with writing memoranda.

FIGURE 5.1   IRAC

I ———▶ Issue
R ———▶ Rule
A ———▶ Application
C ———▶ Conclusion

The first step in developing a legal argument is to understand the facts. The next step is to research and understand the applicable law. Once you know the facts and the relevant law, you can start developing your legal arguments using the IRAC method. For example, assume you represent a plaintiff in a small claims court matter who is asking the court to order the defendant to pay her $5,000.00 in punitive damages. In addition to being found liable for the plaintiff's injuries, the defendant was also charged and convicted of a criminal offence in a separate proceeding for the same misconduct. Courts do not award punitive damages to every successful plaintiff. You will need to develop legal arguments to support your legal conclusion that the court should award punitive damages to your client. To do so, you would first analyze the facts of the case, then research the law on punitive damages to determine what the law requires for a punitive damages award. Often, statute and/or case law establishes a legal test for determining this.

Consider the fact scenario in Figure 5.2. The sections below refer to it to illustrate each stage in the IRAC method.

> **FIGURE 5.2   *Consumer Protection Act, 2002* Scenario**
>
> Sam signed a five-month gym membership agreement (a personal development services contract) with BigTown Fitness yesterday for a total of $180.00. Sam paid $60.00 up front and received a copy of the agreement that day. Today, Sam changed his mind. He called BigTown Fitness to cancel the membership and request a refund. He told the manger that he was exercising his rights under the *Consumer Protection Act, 2002*, SO 2002, c 30, Sch A (the "Act") to cancel his membership within the 10-day cooling off period provided for in the Act. BigTown Fitness refused to cancel the agreement.

Issue

The first step in the IRAC method is to identify the relevant issue(s) raised by a fact situation. This is a statement of the legal issue. The statement can be broad or narrow, depending on the situation. For example, using the small claims court example above, the issue might be

> Whether the plaintiff is entitled to an award of punitive damages.

or

> Whether the court should award punitive damages in this case when the defendant has already been punished criminally in a separate proceeding for the same misconduct.

The first issue statement is broad. The second issue statement is narrower, with a particular focus on whether the law allows for an award of punitive damages in a case where the defendant has already been punished in a criminal proceeding.

Using the fact scenario in Figure 5.2 above, the issues may be identified as follows:

1. Whether the cooling-off period in section 25(1) of the *Consumer Protection Act, 2002*[1] applies in this case.
2. If so, whether the cancellation notice is valid.

Rule

Identifying and explaining the relevant legal principles, laws, and legal tests—the rule(s)—is the next step in the IRAC method. Rules are found in statutes, regulations, and precedents (e.g., case law). As mentioned above, you should research the relevant law before developing your legal arguments so that you can easily break down the legal rule(s) into component parts.

When trying to identify the relevant rule(s), ask yourself: What does the law require to be proven in order for the rule to apply? In addition, you should identify whether there are any exceptions to the rule.

---

1   SO 2002, c 30, Schedule A.

Using the fact scenario in Figure 5.2 above, the relevant law is:

Consumer Protection Act, 2002, SO 2002, c 30, Sch A

• • •

29 (1)   Sections 30 to 36 apply in respect of personal development services or proposed personal development services for which,

(a)   payment in advance is required; and

(b)   the consumer's total potential payment obligation, excluding cost of borrowing, exceeds a prescribed amount.

• • •

Cancellation: cooling-off period

35 (1)   A consumer may, without any reason, cancel a personal development services agreement at any time within 10 days after the later of receiving the written copy of the agreement and the day all the services are available.

Source: *Consumer Protection Act, 2002*, SO 2002, c 30, Sch A, online: <http://canlii.ca/t/52x80>

Consumer Protection Act, 2002, O Reg 17/05

• • •

Prescribed amount

27.   The prescribed amount for the purpose of clause 29 (1) (b) of the Act is $50.

Source: *Consumer Protection Act, 2002*, SO 2002, c 30, Sch A, O Reg 17/05, online: <http://canlii.ca/t/52vg9>

Based on these provisions in the *Consumer Protection Act, 2002*, the relevant rule might be summarized as follows:

Section 35(1) of the *Consumer Protection Act, 2002*, SO 2002, c 30, Sch A (the "Act"), gives consumers a 10-day cooling off period during which they may cancel a personal development services agreement. However, this section applies only to contracts that meet the requirements listed in section 29(1) of the Act, which are:

1. The consumer made payment in advance; and
2. The consumer's payment obligation exceeds $50.00.

Application

This step requires applying the relevant legal rules identified in the previous step to the particular facts of the case or problem. This stage is the crux of the legal argument; therefore, it is important to not simply recite the facts of the case or the relevant law. The common mistake of copying verbatim the relevant provision in a statute or multiple paragraphs from a case is unacceptable and is not an application of the law to the facts; instead, the application must merge facts and law together. This involves showing how the facts of the case specifically meet or do not meet the requirements of the law (i.e., the rule).

Consider the fact situation in Figure 5.2. Knowing what the law requires in order for Sam to legally cancel his gym membership and receive a refund, identify the facts that meet those requirements as follows:

TABLE 5.1   Legal Requirements and Supporting Facts from the *Consumer Protection Act, 2002,* Scenario

Legal Requirement	Facts
The consumer made payment in advance (s 29(a)).	Sam paid $60.00 to the gym up front.
The consumer's payment obligation exceeds $50.00 (s 29(a) of the Act and O Reg 17/05, s 27).	The total cost for the gym membership under the terms of the agreement is $180.00.
A consumer may, without any reason, cancel a personal development services agreement at any time within 10 days after the later of receiving the written copy of the agreement and the day all the services are available (s 35(1)).	Sam called the gym to cancel the agreement the day after he signed the agreement and received a copy.

When applying the law to a set of facts, ask yourself: What particular facts support or do not support a legal requirement as set out in legislation or case law?

In the scenario in Figure 5.2, the cooling-off period applies in Sam's case because Sam paid $60.00 in advance when he signed the agreement and because the total payment obligation under the agreement exceeds $50.00. The cancellation is valid because Sam notified the gym of the cancellation within the required 10 days.

Conclusion

This step requires identifying the outcome resulting from the application of the law to the facts—the result of the argument.

Using the *Consumer Protection Act, 2002* fact scenario in Figure 5.2, the conclusion is that the cooling-off period applies to Sam's case and that the cancellation of the agreement is valid. This is the answer to the issue identified in the issue section. The reasons supporting this conclusion are the legal arguments, developed in the application step above.

Figure 5.3 provides another example of an IRAC analysis for a case involving a claim under the *Human Rights Code.*[2] Consider how the relevant facts are identified to support the requirements of the legal rule.

---

2   RSO 1990, c H.19

FIGURE 5.3   Sample IRAC Analysis

On November 1, 2016, Justine interviewed with a highly respected fashion house, VTM, for the position of Head Designer. Justine was one of only two people being interviewed for the position. She was also the most qualified. During the interview, the interviewer noted that the position required long hours and a lot of travel. The interviewer asked Justine what her plans were for having a family, and Justine responded that she was due to give birth in five months. The next day, the interviewer contacted Justine to advise her that she was not chosen for the position because she could not possibly fulfill the requirements of the position with a baby at home. Three weeks later, Justine was badly injured in a car accident. She spent the next 11 months recovering through intensive physiotherapy. On December 1, 2017, Justine consulted with you, a licensed paralegal, about a potential discrimination claim against VTM under the *Human Rights Code* (the "Code"). On December 22, 2017, you filed an application with the Human Rights Tribunal of Ontario on Justine's behalf alleging that VTM discriminated against her on the basis of sex. She is seeking $5,000 in compensation for injury to her dignity under section 45.2 of the Code. VTM's lawyer has scheduled a hearing for January 3, 2018, where VTM will argue that the Tribunal should dismiss Justine's application because it was not made within the one-year period required by the Code. As Justine's legal representative, what legal arguments might you make to convince the Tribunal to deny VTM's request to dismiss Justine's application?

Issue: Whether Justine's application should be dismissed on the basis that it was filed after the one-year period required by the Code.

Rule: The Code requires an applicant seeking an order from the Tribunal for compensation under section 45.2 of the Code to file his or her application within one year after the incident to which the application relates. Note, however, that the legislation provides an exception: the Tribunal may accept late applications if it is satisfied that the delay was incurred in good faith and that no substantial prejudice will result to any person affected by the delay.

The relevant law is as follows:

Human Rights Code, RSO 1990, c H.19

• • •

Application by person

34. (1) If a person believes that any of his or her rights under Part I have been infringed, the person may apply to the Tribunal for an order under section 45.2,

    (a)   within one year after the incident to which the application relates; or

    (b)   if there was a series of incidents, within one year after the last incident in the series.

Late applications

(2) A person may apply under subsection (1) after the expiry of the time limit under that subsection if the Tribunal is satisfied that the delay was incurred in good faith and no substantial prejudice will result to any person affected by the delay.

Source: *Human Rights Code*, RSO 1990, c H.19, online: <http://canlii.ca/t/52v2w>

In order for the tribunal to accept Justine's late application, Justine must show that

1. the delay was incurred in good faith; and

2. no substantial prejudice will result to any person affected by the delay.

Application: What are the facts of Justine's case that meet and/or do not meet the requirements of the rule?

Legal Requirements	Facts
34. (1) If a person believes that any of his or her rights under Part I have been infringed, the person may apply to the Tribunal for an order under section 45.2, (a) within one year after the incident to which the application relates;	Justine filed her application more than one year after the interview took place. The interview took place on November 1, 2016. She did not file her application until December 22, 2017.
The delay was incurred in good faith (s 34(2)).	Justine suffered serious injuries in a car accident three weeks after the interview. She spent at least 11 months recovering from her injuries. She was not in a position during this time to consider or pursue an application given her injuries. However, once she recovered, she sought legal advice and within a few weeks filed her application. This demonstrates good faith.
No substantial prejudice will result to any person affected by the delay (s 32(2)).	There is no evidence that VTM would be prejudiced by the delay.

In applying the rule to the facts, you could argue that Justine meets the rule under section 34(2) of the Code. The delay was incurred in good faith because, owing to her injuries, Justine was not in a position to obtain legal advice and pursue the claim for at least 11 months after the interview. Once she recovered, she acted quickly with respect to her claim by obtaining legal advice and filing an application with the Tribunal.

Conclusion: The Tribunal should not dismiss Justine's case and should allow her application to proceed.

Tips for Developing an Effective Legal Argument

As a practising paralegal, you must not only develop legal arguments but also present them as effectively and persuasively as possible. The following are some tips to consider when presenting your legal arguments:

1. *Deal with one issue at a time.* If there is more than one legal issue in a case, separate them and deal with each one separately. This will keep your arguments clear, logical, and organized for the reader. The *Consumer Protection Act, 2002* scenario in Figure 5.2 and the subsequent IRAC analysis is an example of how to deal with two issues separately.

2. *Put your strongest argument first.* Leading with your strongest argument takes advantage of the fact that readers' attention is usually highest at the beginning of a document. It may also influence how the reader thinks about your subsequent arguments.

3. *Address counter-arguments.* In a legal dispute, the opposing party will make counter-arguments and will point out the weaknesses in your legal argument(s). You should predict these and address them, because it is better to recognize any counter-arguments or weaknesses in your legal argument(s) and explain them away on your own terms before the other party brings them up.

   Consider the fact scenario in Figure 5.2 and the subsequent analysis. A counter-argument in that scenario might be that the cancellation notice is not valid because Sam gave notice over the phone and not in writing. To address this counter-argument, you could simply acknowledge that BigTown Fitness might take issue with the fact that Sam gave notice orally, then point out that the *Consumer Protection Act, 2002* does not require notice to be given in writing. As long as the evidence shows that notice was given, either orally or in writing, it will satisfy the notice requirement.

4. *Consider using headings and sub-headings when dealing with multiple legal arguments.* Good organization is important for effective legal writing, as discussed in Chapter 3. When you have many legal arguments to make, consider using headings and sub-headings to organize them logically for the reader. This allows the reader to quickly see what your next argument is and frames the paragraphs that follow, so that the reader is not confused as to whether you are still making your first argument or have moved on to the second. Using headings and sub-headings can also make your arguments flow better, which can help to persuade the reader.

5. *Use point-first writing.* As discussed in Chapter 1, point-first writing is one of an effective legal writer's most important skills, since it improves both clarity and persuasiveness. When developing legal arguments, consider beginning a paragraph by stating your conclusion, then stating the reasons supporting that conclusion. Lawyers and paralegals often make the mistake of starting a paragraph by explaining the relevant legal principle, rule, or law before stating the argument and conclusion. While this is not necessarily wrong, stating your conclusion and legal argument first, then explaining the relevant law, improves clarity and persuasiveness and is considered a more effective approach.

Exercise 5.1

Law Society Act

Jessie Bullock applied for a Class P1 licence to the Law Society of Ontario in 2018. His application disclosed that in 2009 he admitted to plagiarizing a paper written by someone else while he was a student in his first year of a Bachelor of Arts degree. He took another student's essay and submitted it as his own. Following the incident, Jessie attended nine counselling sessions that year to deal with the incident. He also wrote a letter to the student from whom he took the essay, apologizing for his behaviour. He subsequently attended law school, beginning in 2013, and graduated in June 2016. Jessie articled at a small firm in Toronto from 2016 through 2017. Over the past two years, Jessie has been heavily involved in the community: he volunteers with Meals on Wheels and coaches a local soccer team.

In investigating Jessie's plagiarism incident, the Law Society found out that he was involved in a second plagiarism offence, which he did not disclose in his application to the Law Society. The second incident occurred during the same year as the first, but in a different course. When confronted by the Law Society with the additional offence of plagiarism, Jessie admitted to it immediately. He wrote a letter to the Law Society admitting guilt and remorse. He also helped the Law Society to obtain information relating to the second offence. Section 27(2) of the *Law Society Act* requires that an applicant for a licence be of good character. A good character hearing is scheduled at the Law Society Tribunal on December 1, 2018. Jessie submitted a reference letter from one of his undergraduate professors attesting to his good character. The professor also stated that he noticed a change in Jessie's academic habits after attending counselling sessions during his first year at university. According to the professor, Jessie reached out to various professors and learning centre services for assistance with academic assignments. Jessie also submitted a reference letter from his articling principal, who speaks highly about his legal work as well as his involvement in fundraising efforts for the United Way. According to the articling principal, Jessie also spends his extra time mentoring young law students.

Using these facts and the relevant law below, develop legal arguments that support the conclusion that Jessie is of good character. Be sure to identify and address any counter-arguments or weaknesses in your legal arguments.

Law Society Act, RSO 1990, c L.8

• • •

LICENSING

• • •

Good character requirement

27(2) It is a requirement for the issuance of every licence under this Act that the applicant be of good character

---

Source: *Law Society Act*, RSO 1990, c L.8, online: <http://canlii.ca/t/527j8>

In *Armstrong v Law Society of Upper Canada,* 2009 ONLSHP 0029, the hearing panel described and considered five components that inform a good character analysis:

(a)   the nature and duration of the misconduct;

(b)   whether the applicant is remorseful;

(c)   what rehabilitative efforts, if any, have been taken and the success of such efforts;

(d)   the applicant's conduct since the misconduct; and

(e)   the passage of time since the misconduct.

Source: *Armstrong v Law Society of Upper Canada,* 2009 ONLSHP 0029, online: <http://canlii .ca/t/2fpn2>.

Exercise 5.2

Consumer Protection Act, 2002

Kim Vuong lives in Barrie, Ontario with her five teenage children. On September 1, 2017, Jeremy Bland knocked at Kim's door offering to sell her a mini microwave for $200.00. Jeremy is the owner and operator of AppliancetoGo, a company that sells small kitchen appliances. Surprisingly, Kim did not have a microwave in her kitchen, but she was in need of one. Her children regularly complained about how long it took them to warm up their meals on the stove. Kim decided that she needed a microwave for her family, so she signed a purchase agreement and wrote a cheque to Jeremy for $200.00. Three days later, Kim changed her mind. She contacted Jeremy to arrange to return the microwave and receive a refund. She knew that she was entitled to cancel the purchase agreement under the cooling-off provision in *Consumer Protection Act, 2002* ("CPA"). Jeremy refused, saying that the CPA did not apply to this type of purchase. Using these facts and the relevant legislative provisions of the CPA below, develop legal arguments in support of the conclusion that the Act applies to Kim's situation, specifically the purchase of the microwave.

Consumer Protection Act, 2002, SO 2002, c 30, Sch A

Interpretation

1   In this Act,

"consumer" means an individual acting for personal, family or household purposes and does not include a person who is acting for business purposes;

"consumer agreement" means an agreement between a supplier and a consumer in which the supplier agrees to supply goods or services for payment.

Note: On a day to be named by proclamation of the Lieutenant Governor, section 1 of the Act is amended by striking out the definition of "consumer agreement" and substituting the following:

"consumer agreement" means an agreement between a supplier and a consumer in which,

(a)   the supplier agrees to supply goods or services for payment, or

(b) the supplier agrees to provide rewards points to the consumer, on the supplier's own behalf or on behalf of another supplier, when the consumer purchases goods or services or otherwise acts in a manner specified in the agreement;

"consumer transaction" means any act or instance of conducting business or other dealings with a consumer, including a consumer agreement;

"supplier" means a person who is in the business of selling, leasing or trading in goods or services or is otherwise in the business of supplying goods or services, and includes an agent of the supplier and a person who holds themself out to be a supplier or an agent of the supplier;

• • •

Application

2   (1)   Subject to this section, this Act applies in respect of all consumer transactions if the consumer or the person engaging in the transaction with the consumer is located in Ontario when the transaction takes place.

Exceptions

(2)   This Act does not apply in respect of,

    (a)   consumer transactions regulated under the *Securities Act*;

    (b)   financial services related to investment products or income securities;

    (c)   financial products or services regulated under the *Insurance Act*, the *Credit Unions and Caisses Populaires Act, 1994*, the *Loan and Trust Corporations Act* or the *Mortgage Brokerages, Lenders and Administrators Act, 2006*;

    (d)   consumer transactions regulated under the *Commodity Futures Act*;

    (e)   prescribed professional services that are regulated under a statute of Ontario;

    (f)   consumer transactions for the purchase, sale or lease of real property, except transactions with respect to time share agreements as defined in section 20; and

    (g)   consumer transactions regulated under the *Residential Tenancies Act, 2006*.

Source: *Consumer Protection Act, 2002*, SO 2002, c 30, Sch A, online: <http://canlii.ca/t/52x80>

Consumer Protection Act, 2002, O Reg 17/05

Professional services regulated by statute

1.   A professional service provided by a person governed by, or subject to, any of the following Acts is exempt from the application of the Consumer Protection Act, 2002:

    1.   The *Architects Act*.

    2.   The *Certified General Accountants Act, 2010*.

    3.   The *Chartered Accountants Act, 2010*.

    4.   The *Drugless Practitioners Act*.

5. The *Law Society Act.*
6. The *Ontario College of Teachers Act, 1996.*
7. The *Professional Engineers Act.*
8. The *Professional Foresters Act, 2000.*
9. The *Professional Geoscientists Act, 2000.*
10. The *Public Accounting Act, 2004.*
11. The *Regulated Health Professions Act, 1991* and any Act named in Schedule 1 to the *Regulated Health Professions Act, 1991.*
12. The *Social Work and Social Service Work Act, 1998.*
13. The *Society of Management Accountants of Ontario Act, 1941.*
14. The *Surveyors Act.*
15. The *Veterinarians Act.*

Source: *Consumer Protection Act, 2002*, SO 2002, c 30, Sch A, O Reg 17/05, online: <http://canlii.ca/t/52vg9>.

Summary

Good legal writers develop legal arguments that are clear, concise, and organized. In order to do so, they should follow a structure when developing them. This chapter suggests using the IRAC method. You will see this method used in Chapter 7 in the context of writing a memorandum of law.

This chapter also suggests various tips for presenting legal arguments in the most persuasive way possible, including dealing with one issue at a time and always identifying and addressing counter-arguments and weaknesses in your own arguments. Consider these tips when developing legal arguments in the context of writing letters and memoranda in subsequent chapters.

Writing Letters

6

LEARNING OUTCOMES

After reading this chapter, you should be able to

- Describe different types of letters.
- Understand the proper layout and format of a letter.
- Write effective letters.
- Edit letters for clarity and conciseness.

Introduction

A paralegal will spend a great deal of his or her time writing letters to people outside his or her practice. In the legal environment, possibly even more than in other businesses, everything that takes place must be carefully recorded in writing so that all facts and information are available for future reference.

A paralegal will write letters to clients, opposing legal representatives, and other third parties, and will write different kinds of letters such as

- retainer letters
- non-engagement letters
- reporting letters
- opinion letters
- demand letters
- administrative or informative letters

All of these letters have different purposes. For example, you might use these kinds of letters to

- send information to a client;
- confirm your advice to a client or your understanding of facts;
- describe work done on a client's file or instructions given by a client;
- exchange information with lawyers and paralegals in other firms;
- provide a proposal to an opposing party;
- request that an opposing party comply with the law or terms of an agreement;
- notify another lawyer, paralegal, or opposing party of your involvement in the matter;
- correspond with government departments and other bodies from whom you must obtain information.

The first step in writing a letter is to identify its audience and its purpose. While the content will differ for each type of letter, the format and structure should always remain the same. This chapter examines the standard format and structure of a letter, as well as strategies for writing different kinds of letters.

In professional business letters, spelling, typing, and grammar errors are unacceptable. As you complete the in-chapter exercises, refer to the chapters on grammar and style.

Format

The basic business letter format appears in outline form in Figure 6.1. There are three different kinds of formats: the modified block style (shown in Figure 6.2), the semi-block style (Figure 6.3), and the full block style (Figure 6.4), which is the most common. Note that when using full block style, all paragraphs start at the left margin, with a double line space between them. The date, complimentary close, and signature line also start at the left margin. No paragraphs or lines are indented.

There are also two different styles of punctuation: mixed punctuation (Figures 6.2 and 6.3) and open punctuation (Figure 6.4). Mixed punctuation requires a colon after the salutation and a comma after the complimentary close. Open punctuation uses no punctuation after the salutation and the complimentary close.

FIGURE 6.1   Basic Business Letter Format

LETTERHEAD

Date

Method of delivery

Inside address (receiver's name and address)

Salutation

SUBJECT LINE

Body of letter

Complimentary close

Reference initials

Enclosures and attachments

Copies

FIGURE 6.2   Modified Block Style with Mixed Punctuation

SMITH, BROWN AND MARTINO LLP
4700 YONGE STREET, SUITE 500
TORONTO, ON M3X 2L9
TEL. 416-222-2222
FAX 416-222-2221

November 1, 2017

BY REGULAR MAIL

Mr. William Wilton
22 Penny Road
Toronto, Ontario M1R 2L2

Dear Mr. Wilton:

RE: Wilton v Lois—Small Claims Court Matter
File No. 17-1512

I write to advise you of your scheduled trial date.

Please note your trial is scheduled for **December 6, 2017, at 10:00 a.m.** at the
Ontario Small Claims Court, 47 Sheppard Avenue East, Toronto, Ontario M2N 5N1.
I enclose a map to the courthouse. Please arrive at the courthouse by 9:30 a.m.

I look forward to seeing you at the courthouse. In the meantime, if you have any
questions or concerns please contact me directly at 416-222-2222 ext. 233.

Yours truly,

SMITH, BROWN AND MARTINO LLP

Robert Martino
Robert Martino
Licensed Paralegal

RM/tm

Encl.

cc: Viktor Smith

Note: The date, complimentary close, and signature lines are centred horizontally.

FIGURE 6.3   **Semi-block Style with Mixed Punctuation**

SMITH, BROWN AND MARTINO LLP
4700 YONGE STREET, SUITE 500
TORONTO, ON M3X 2L9
TEL. 416-222-2222
FAX 416-222-2221

November 1, 2017

BY REGULAR MAIL

Mr. William Wilton
22 Penny Road
Toronto, Ontario M1R 2L2

Dear Mr. Wilton:

RE: **Wilton v Lois—Small Claims Court Matter**
              File No. 17-1512

I write following our meeting on October 25, 2017.

As you know, it is our policy to bill our clients once a month in order to keep them informed about their fees and disbursements. I enclose our recent invoice for the period of October 1, 2017, to October 31, 2017, showing a balance owing of $543.29. Kindly remit payment at your earliest convenience.

As always, if you have any questions regarding your account please contact my assistant Lianne Rogers at 416-222-2222 ext. 221.

Yours truly,

SMITH, BROWN AND MARTINO LLP

Robert Martino
Robert Martino

RM/lr

Encl. – Invoice No. 1031

Note: Indent first line of each paragraph. The date, complimentary close, and signature lines are centred horizontally.

FIGURE 6.4 **Full Block Style with Open Punctuation**

SMITH, BROWN AND MARTINO LLP
4700 YONGE STREET, SUITE 500
TORONTO, ON M3X 2L9
TEL. 416-222-2222
FAX 416-222-2221

November 1, 2017

BY REGULAR MAIL

Mr. William Wilton
22 Penny Road
Toronto, Ontario M1R 2L2

Dear Mr. Wilton

RE: **Wilton v Lois—Small Claims Court Matter**
            File No. 17-1512

I write following our meeting on October 25, 2017.

As you know, it is our policy to bill our clients once a month in order to keep them informed about their fees and disbursements. I enclose our recent invoice for the period of October 1, 2017, to October 31, 2017, showing a balance owing of $543.29. Kindly remit payment at your earliest convenience.

As always, if you have any questions regarding your account please contact my assistant Lianne Rogers at 416-222-2222 ext. 221.

Yours truly

SMITH, BROWN AND MARTINO LLP

Robert Martino
Robert Martino
Licensed Paralegal

RM/lr

Encl. – Invoice No. 1031

Layout and Style

When you are writing letters, be aware that certain stylistic conventions govern the format of the date, the inside address, the attention line, the salutation, the subject line, and the complimentary close. Generally speaking, avoid abbreviations such as *St.* for *Street*, not only in your headings but also in other parts of your letter (with the exception of titles such as *Dr.* for *Doctor* in your salutation). Abbreviations indicate a certain carelessness on your part, or a desire to get through the letter quickly.

Unless otherwise instructed, letters should be written in 12-point font with at least 1-inch margins. Use sans serif fonts such as Arial. You must take care to ensure that the fonts you use are compliant with the accessibility standards set by the *Accessibility for Ontarians with Disabilities Act, 2005.*[1] Arial is an accessible font type.

The following sections discuss the individual parts of a letter.

Date

The chronological order of everything that happens in a legal matter is important, so it is vital that your letters be dated. The date line is typically the first line you type after the letterhead. In Canada, the usual form is month followed by day, then a comma, then the year in full:

> January 15, 2018

Method of Delivery Notation

This notation appears under the date and indicates the method by which you are sending the letter. Start the line with *BY* or *VIA* and bold it. You may send a letter by regular mail, email, courier, or fax. For example:

> **BY FAX (416-222-2222)**
> **BY EMAIL (ksimpson@simpsonlaw.ca)**

If sending a letter by fax or email, it is good practice to include the recipient's fax number or email address in brackets, as shown above.

You may also send a letter by personal service. In this case, your delivery notation might be

> **BY PERSONAL SERVICE**

Special Notation

A special notation appears below the delivery notation and before the inside address. The words are bolded and typed in block capital letters. Some common special notations are

> **PRIVATE & CONFIDENTIAL**
> **WITHOUT PREJUDICE**
> **WITH PREJUDICE**

---

1   SO 2005, c 11

The phrase *without prejudice* means that the letter and its contents cannot be used in evidence at any future time without permission of the forwarding paralegal and the client. A paralegal may use this notation when he or she wants to put forward a position that has the potential to prejudice his or client's position at law or under a contract—for example, when sending a written offer to settle a case.

The phrase *with prejudice* indicates to recipients that the contents are admissible against them.

Inside Address, Attention Line, and Salutation

A typical inside address presents address information—personal or organization name, street address, city, jurisdiction, and postal code—on separate lines.

For example:

> Smith, Brown and Martino LLP
> 4700 Yonge Street, Suite 500
> Toronto, Ontario M3X 2L9

Note that there are two spaces between the province and the postal code.
The inside address uses very little punctuation, with the following exceptions:

- Use periods in abbreviated salutations such as "Mr." and "Mrs."
- If a firm name uses commas, the inside address uses them as well.
- A comma follows the street name if a suite number appears on the same line. Do not use a comma if the suite number appears on its own line.
- A comma follows the city name, separating it from the jurisdiction name.

The form of the inside address depends on whether you are addressing the letter to a business entity, such as a company or firm, or to an individual. This choice also governs the attention line and the salutation. As a rule of thumb, the first line of the inside address should "match" the salutation.

If you are addressing the letter to a company, you still need to give someone's name so that the mailing department will know where to deliver the letter. In that case, you need an *attention line*. This goes beneath the inside address, separated by one line space. It is important to note that, because you are addressing the company, the salutation should reflect this fact and should not mention the person's name.

You can "salute" the company as follows:

> The Provincial Bank
> 123 Main Street
> Royston, Ontario R8H 2Y7
>
> Attention: Robert Brown
>
> Dear Sirs/Mesdames:

If your letter is addressed to Mr. Brown, you do not need an attention line and you should "salute" Mr. Brown as follows:

Mr. Robert Brown, Vice President
The Provincial Bank
123 Main Street
Royston, Ontario R8H 2Y7

Dear Mr. Brown:

In this example, the recipient of the letter, Robert Brown, has the business title of *vice president*. It is customary to show such a title in the inside address. You can place the title on the same line as the name, separated by a comma as shown, or on its own line, below the name, without a comma.

You can use the recipient's given name or a number of courtesy titles (Ms., Miss, Mrs., Mr., or Dr.) in the salutation. Much will depend on how the person wishes to be addressed. When writing to someone for the first time, always use a courtesy title and the last name. For example, if you receive a letter signed "Mrs. Edna Jones," send a reply to "Mrs. Edna Jones" with the salutation "Dear Mrs. Jones." Otherwise, however, *Ms.* is the standard courtesy title for women. If the person has a gender-neutral name, such as Jean or Terry, contact the organization and find out which courtesy title should be used. See Figure 6.5 for information on correct titles and forms of address.

FIGURE 6.5   Titles and Forms of Address

People with a professional title or academic degree(s) often append the title or degree abbreviation(s) to their name. The title or abbreviation appears on the same line as the person's name, and is separated from the name by a comma. For a person with an advanced academic degree, such as a PhD (doctor of philosophy) or JD (doctor of jurisprudence), the usual courtesy title (Mr., Ms., Miss, Mrs.) is omitted from the inside address. The courtesy title "Esq" (for "Esquire") is sometimes used by male lawyers, and appears after the name and before the title or degree. The form of the salutation depends on the degree or title. Some common titles and degrees and their use in the inside address and salutation are shown below.

Degree/title	Inside address form	Salutation
JD (doctor of jurisprudence)	Paula Szacki, JD	Dear Ms. Szacki
MD (doctor of medicine)	James Sinclair, MD	Dear Dr. Sinclair
PhD (doctor of philosophy)	Mary Barrington, PhD	Dear Dr. Barrington
Esq (esquire)	Alistair Willins, Esq	Dear Mr. Willins
QC (Queen's counsel)	Alistair Willins, QC	Dear Mr. Willins
	Alistair Willins, Esq, QC	Dear Mr. Willins

FIGURE 6.5   Continued

There are also prescribed forms of addressing and saluting government officials and judges. Some of these are shown below.

Title/position	Inside address form	Salutation
Governor general	Her Excellency the Right Honourable Julie Payette	Excellency
Prime minister	The Right Honourable Justin Trudeau	Dear Mr. Prime Minister *or* Dear Prime Minister
Lieutenant governor	Her Honour, the Honourable Elizabeth Dowdeswell	Your Honour
Provincial premier	The Honourable Kathleen Wynne	Dear Premier *or* Dear Madame Premier
Mayor	His Worship Mayor John Tory	Dear Mayor Tory
Supreme Court chief justice	The Right Honourable Beverley McLachlin, PC, Chief Justice of Canada	Dear Madam Justice McLachlin
Supreme Court justice	The Honourable Mr Justice John C. Major	Dear Mr. Justice Major
Federal Court chief justice	The Honourable John D. Richard, Chief Justice	Dear Mr. Justice Richard
Federal Court justice	The Honourable Madam Justice Karen Sharlow	Dear Madam Justice Sharlow
Provincial high court justice	The Honourable Mr. Justice Doe	Dear Mr. Justice Doe
Provincial or county court judge	Judge Roe	Dear Judge Roe

Subject Line

The subject line prepares your reader's mind for the information in your letter, so it is important to make it as clear and useful as possible. In legal writing, the line usually begins with *RE:* (short for *regarding*), which is why it is sometimes called the "Re Line."

The subject line should be bolded or underlined (not both). It should include the matter name and file number. Some firms have a standard format for subject lines, which, of course, you will follow if you work for a firm.

Here are some possibilities:

> **RE:**   **Bartholomew v Nicodemus**
> **File No. 17-2121**

Note: a litigation matter between Bartholomew and Nicodemus.

> **RE:**   **Bartholomew ats Nicodemus**
> **File No. 17-2121**

Note: Bartholomew "at the suit of" Nicodemus; Nicodemus is suing Bartholomew.

> **RE:**   **Bartholomew v Nicodemus, Our File No. 17-2121**
> **Your File No. SC2121**

Note: when writing to another law firm, you might also include their file number for their convenience.

When citing the names of the parties in a subject line, always put your client's name first. For example, in a letter from another firm with the subject line

> **RE:**   **Bartholomew v Nicodemus**

Bartholomew is the other firm's client, who is suing your client, Nicodemus. When you write back, you should change the subject line to

> **RE:**   **Nicodemus ats Bartholomew**

Complimentary Close

Commonly used complimentary closes include *Yours truly* and *Sincerely yours*. Do not capitalize the first letter of the second word. Other acceptable forms include *Sincerely*, *Regards*, and *Yours very truly*. Never use *From*, *Cheers*, or *Thanks* to close a formal business letter.

For companies, it is generally enough to leave four to six line spaces after the complimentary close, followed by the sender's name and, if you wish, the sender's title. The sender will then sign inside the space.

Law firms almost always sign letters with the firm name before the signature space and the writer's name. The rationale for this is that the author writes the letter on behalf of the firm itself, not on his or her own behalf. When a paralegal works as a sole practitioner, his or her name and title should follow the complimentary close. When sending a letter, licensed paralegals should always identify themselves as such.

Here are two examples of different complimentary close formats you might use:

Yours truly,   Yours very truly,

SMITH, BROWN AND MARTINO   Samantha Lau
LLP   Licensed Paralegal

Robert Martino
Licensed Paralegal

Reference Initials

Reference initials indicate that someone other than the author typed the letter. The initials of the author appear in capitals, followed by the typist's initials in lowercase letters. The two sets of initials are separated with a slash or a colon.

If you are simply typing a letter on behalf of another person, do not sign your name as the sender. Rather, indicate that you are the typist by using typist initials, as follows:

> Yours sincerely,
>
> SMITH, BROWN AND MARTINO LLP
>
> Marilyn Benson, Licensed Paralegal
> MB/ab

Copies

When you send copies of your letter to people other than the recipient, you should add a line that begins *cc:, CC:, or c.c.:*, two lines below the writer's name. The abbreviation stands for "carbon copy" and is a vestige of the days when copies were made using a typewriter and carbon paper. Some firms have replaced the abbreviation with the words *Copy to.*

Regardless of how the copy line begins, leave two spaces after the colon and add the name of the person receiving a copy of the letter. If more than one person is receiving a copy, list them one below the other.

Sometimes you will see *bcc:*, which means "blind carbon copy." This notation appears only on copies of the letter, not on the original. You use *bcc:* when you do not want the primary recipient of the letter to know who received copies.

Enclosures and Attachments

Very often you will send the recipient copies of items to which you refer in your letter. These items can be either *enclosures*, which are separate from the letter, or *attachments*, which are stapled. To indicate that you are sending something with a letter, add a final line to the letter stating either *Enc.* or *Encl.* This line goes two lines below the copy line or, if there are no copies, two lines below the writer's name.

Enclosures are often named in the enclosure line, and it is particularly useful to name them when there are several. List the names of the documents you are enclosing, one below the other. This helps you ensure that you have enclosed all the necessary items, and it is also useful to the reader in identifying the documents.

As you have seen from some of the examples, there are some variations in letter format and style. Many firms provide staff with a detailed manual that outlines how letters are to be formatted, sometimes going so far as to specify which fonts to use and exactly where to place each element of the letter. Other firms may not formalize their policies in a manual but will still prescribe certain conventions. In all cases, if you work for a firm, follow its conventions. If you practise on your own, make sure you remain consistent with the letter formatting and style you use.

Structure and Content

The structure and content of a letter's body will depend on what kind of letter you are writing. However, it is helpful to consider a general structure of a letter's body that you can follow regardless of the type of letter.

It is helpful to think of a letter as having three parts:

1. Introductory paragraph.
2. Middle paragraphs.
3. Closing paragraph.

Introductory Paragraph

The first paragraph in a letter should always explain why you are writing, in order to situate the letter for the recipient. Here are several examples:

> I write in response to your letter dated December 15, 2017.
>
> I write following our meeting on November 3, 2017, regarding your careless driving charge.
>
> I write to propose dates for a hearing in the above noted matter.
>
> I write to report to you following my appearance at the Ontario Small Claims Court today.
>
> I write following our meeting on November 22, 2017, regarding your small claims court matter.

When writing to a recipient for the first time, always introduce yourself. Here is an example of how *not* to introduce yourself in the first paragraph:

> RE: **Bartholomew v Nicodemus**
>   **File No. 17-2121**
> My name is Sam Burton. I'm a paralegal. I am writing to you on behalf of my client, Mr. Bartholomew.

Never write, "My name is [name]," because the recipient can see your name in the signature part of the letter. Here is the proper way to introduce yourself:

> RE: **Bartholomew v Nicodemus**
>   **File No. 17-2121**
> I represent [*or* I am assisting] Mr. Bartholomew in the above noted matter. I write with respect to your client's offer to settle.

Many times you will write a letter to respond to a client's email or an opposing advocate's letter. When doing so, always identify the date of the letter you are responding to. For example:

> RE: **Bartholomew v Nicodemus**
>   **File No. 17-2121**
> I am responding to your letter dated October 15, 2017, regarding your disclosure request.

Middle Paragraphs

The content of a letter's middle paragraphs will depend on the type of letter you are writing. Regardless of its content, however, a letter should present information in an accurate, concise, organized, and complete manner by using separate paragraphs. A paragraph consists of several sentences and contains one main idea. There is no rule for how long a paragraph must be; some main ideas will require a longer paragraph, and others a shorter one. Using both short and long paragraphs can also help break up the information for the reader.

You may need to write various types of paragraphs: narration (telling a story), description (describing something with an appeal to the senses), exposition (explaining how something is done), comparison/contrast (pointing out similarities or differences between two or more subjects), and cause and effect (describing the effect of one thing on another).

If you are writing a letter with a lot of content, such as an opinion letter or a reporting letter, consider using headings and sub-headings to help organize the information for the reader. This not only helps the reader follow the message but also provides ease of reference for future discussions or correspondence. This is especially important if you are presenting a lot of information to a client who does not have legal training. Chapter 3 discusses headings as a way to organize information for a reader.

When presenting a lot of information, you should also consider how to make the important information stand out to the reader. Bold text, bullets, and numbered lists can help identify important information; for example, bold important dates and deadlines. Never use all capital letters to make information stand out, as this signals to the reader that you are yelling.

Consider the use of bold in the following paragraph to highlight a deadline:

> Please note that the deadline to issue your claim with the Ontario Small Claims Court is **August 28, 2017**. **You must issue it by this date; otherwise, you will lose your right to do so.**

This example uses capital letters for the same purpose:

> Please note that the deadline to issue your claim with the Ontario Small Claims Court is AUGUST 28, 2017. YOU MUST ISSUE IT BY THIS DATE; OTHERWISE, YOU WILL LOSE YOUR RIGHT TO DO SO.

The use of all capital letters signals an angry tone, which is unprofessional.

Closing Paragraph

End your letter with a goodwill closing paragraph, providing necessary details, requesting additional information, or requesting action. If your letter asks someone to do something, your closing paragraph can include the date by which it should be done and the consequences of its not being done, as in this closing paragraph in a letter from a paralegal to a client who missed an appointment:

> Please contact me at 416-221-2121 to reschedule your appointment. If I do not hear from you by December 12, 2017, I will assume you are not interested in retaining me for your small claims court matter and I will close my file.
>
> Yours truly,

A simple administrative or informative letter to a client may simply indicate that the client can contact you with any questions or concerns (see Figures 6.2 and 6.3).

Writing Strategies

This section reviews different types of letters and offers strategies for writing content in letters from a paralegal to clients, opposing parties or advocates, and other third parties. Please note that this section does not cover all possible types of letters but focuses on a select few.

Letters to Clients

Letters to clients are probably a paralegal's most important correspondence, because they document progress on a client's file. Documenting information, advice, and instructions will prevent future misunderstandings with clients, which is an important part of practice management.

Letters to clients must always be courteous and professional. Even when your client is not cooperative, never communicate in a threatening, aggressive, or unpleasant way. Recall a paralegal's ethical obligations under the *Paralegal Rules of Conduct* to communicate in a professional, civil, and respectful tone, as discussed in Chapter 3.

Retainer Letter

A retainer letter confirms the terms of a client's engagement with a paralegal. When a client **retains** a paralegal to assist him or her with a legal matter, the paralegal should send a retainer letter to the client or have the client sign a retainer agreement.

The content of a retainer letter or agreement will differ depending on the client and the type of legal matter. It may cover things such as scope of the paralegal's services to the client (e.g., type of legal services the client will receive), fees and disbursements (how much the paralegal will charge the client), and withdrawal of representation (when the paralegal may withdraw from representing the client).

The terms set out in the retainer letter should be clear and concise. Consider using headings and sub-headings to organize the information for the client, and bold to highlight important information such as hourly rate.

Consult the Law Society of Ontario's website at <http://www.lsuc.on.ca/with.aspx?id=2147490137> for a sample retainer letter.

Non-engagement Letter

A non-engagement letter is the opposite of a retainer letter: it provides notice to a **prospective client** that a paralegal is *not* representing him or her.

A paralegal should write a non-engagement letter to any prospective client he or she has had contact with but is not representing, because some prospective clients may believe that the paralegal represents him or her despite not having actually retained the paralegal. A non-engagement letter makes it clear to the prospective client that the paralegal is not taking any steps on his or her behalf and is not responsible for his or her matter.

A non-engagement letter should include references to time limits or limitation periods, if relevant. In some cases, a prospective client may have limited time to file a claim before it expires. A non-engagement letter should clearly outline any approaching deadlines and the consequences of not acting before those deadlines.

Consult the Law Society of Ontario's website at <http://www.lsuc.on.ca/with.aspx?id=2147490137> for a sample non-engagement letter.

Reporting Letter

A reporting letter describes a paralegal's work on a file and any results achieved for the client. It is usually sent to a client to update him or her about the case. A paralegal may send several reporting letters to a client over the course of that client's matter.

A reporting letter also confirms the client's instructions to the paralegal. If a file results in a claim against the paralegal, reporting letters will help determine what did and did not happen.

Once a paralegal completes a case, he or she should always send **a final reporting letter** to the client that

- confirms the retainer and the scope of representation (i.e., what the paralegal was asked to do)
- outlines the steps taken on the client's behalf to resolve the matter, according to the client's instructions
- confirms that the client's matter is complete
- confirms any remaining obligations the client needs to complete (e.g., future deadlines, limitation dates, payments to a third party)
- confirms that the client's original documents have been returned (or that the client should arrange to pick up the documents)
- confirms that the final account has been paid (or attach invoice)
- thanks the client for allowing the paralegal to assist him or her.

A sample reporting letter appears in Figure 6.6.

FIGURE 6.6 Sample Reporting Letter

SMITH, BROWN AND MARTINO LLP
4700 YONGE STREET, SUITE 500
TORONTO, ON M3X 2L9
TEL. 416-222-2222
FAX 416-222-2221

November 1, 2017
BY REGULAR MAIL

Mr. Landon Lui
221 Lincoln Road
Toronto, Ontario M1R 2L2

Dear Mr. Lui:

RE: **Lui v Brown—221 Lincoln Road, Suite 201, Toronto, Ontario**
File No. 17-1255

I write to report to you following our attendance at the Landlord and Tenant Board (the "Board") on October 12, 2017.

You will recall that you retained me to file an application on your behalf to terminate the tenancy between you and your tenant, Sam Brown, for non-payment of rent.

As you will recall, the Board made a number of orders in your favour. In particular, the Board ordered as follows:

1. The tenant must pay you $2,750.00 by November 15, 2017. This amount represents the amount of rent owing up to November 15, 2017;

2. The tenancy between you and the tenant is terminated as of November 15, 2017. The tenant must vacate the rental unit on or before November 15, 2017; and

3. If the tenant does not vacate the unit on or before November 15, 2017, then starting November 16, 2017, you may file the Board's order with the Court Enforcement Office so that the sheriff can enforce the order.

In accordance with the Board's order, the tenant must pay you $2,750.00 by November 15, 2017. He must also move out of the property on or before November 15, 2017.

If the tenant still occupies the unit as of November 16, 2017, you may request that the sheriff physically remove the tenant from the property. To do so, you must file the Board's order with the Court Enforcement Office. Please note that you cannot change the locks or physically remove the tenant yourself. Only the sheriff can enforce the eviction order.

As your matter is now complete, I enclose my final invoice for your kind attention. You will note that there is a total balance owing of $1,567.90. Kindly send a cheque payable to Smith, Brown and Martino LLP by November 21, 2017. I confirm that I have returned all of your original documents to you.

Thank you for allowing me to assist you. Please do not hesitate to contact me if I can assist again in the future.

Yours truly,

SMITH, BROWN AND MARTINO LLP

Robert Martino

Robert Martino, Licensed Paralegal

RM/tm

Encl. – Invoice No. 17-2121

Exercise 6.1

Draft a Reporting Letter

Using the details below, write a final reporting letter to your client, Frances Hamlin, in full block mixed punctuation format. Include an appropriate matter name and file number. Send the letter today by courier.

- You filed an application on Frances' behalf with the Human Rights Tribunal of Ontario, alleging discrimination in employment on the basis of creed under section 5 of the Ontario *Human Rights Code*, RSO 1990, c H.19 (the "Code").

- Frances lives at 45 Ontario Drive, Toronto, Ontario M2P 1B1. Her email address is fhamlin@gmail.com.

- Frances claimed that the respondent, VP Enterprises, excluded her from various employee meetings and eventually fired her because she practises ethical veganism. She testified at the hearing about five incidents in which she claimed that she suffered discrimination in the workplace because she is an ethical vegan.

- VP Enterprises filed a response to Frances' application.

- The parties appeared before the Tribunal for a hearing one month ago.

- You argued that ethical veganism fits within the definition of creed under the Code.

- You called Frances and her former colleague, Vanessa Santos, as witnesses to testify as to the incidents of discrimination that occurred in the workplace.

- Frances also testified about the emotional and financial impact of the discrimination.

- You received the Tribunal's decision seven days ago. The Tribunal found that the five incidents constituted repeated and wilful discrimination against Frances on the basis of creed, and ordered VP Enterprises to pay Frances $10,000 as compensation for her loss of dignity resulting from the repeated infringement of her right under section 5 of the Code.

- You received a $10,000 certified cheque from VP Enterprises' lawyer yesterday, payable to Frances. You are enclosing it with the letter.

- You have also returned all original documents to Frances.

- Frances has already paid your final invoice in the amount of $2,455.00.

Exercise 6.2

Rewrite a Reporting Letter

Below is an example of a poorly drafted reporting letter from a paralegal to his client. Rewrite the body of the letter in full block mixed punctuation format, using effective style and correct grammar. Follow the basic format and layout described above.

Hey Sam Smith!

I'm writing to you to update you on your case. I've contacted the paralegal for the defendant to get dates for a settlement conference. We've agreed on December 12, 2018 as the date for the settlement conference at the Ontario Small Claims Court. Do you know what a settlement conference is? It's when the parties get together with their representatives before a small claims court judge to discuss the issues in dispute. It's meant to encourage settlement and avoid going to trial. It's meant to resolve or narrow the issues in the action, expedite the disposition of the action, assist the parties in trial preparation. Pursuant to the Rules of the Small Claims Court, a settlement conference must be held in every defended action. A settlement conference is mandatory for you. If you do not attend the settlement conference, the court may impose certain sanctions on you such as ordering you to pay the plaintiff's costs. IT'S IMPORTANT THAT YOU ATTEND. PLEASE diarize this date. The Rules also require you to disclose to the plaintiff the following documents at least 14 days before the date of the settlement conference:

- A copy of any document to be relied on at the trial
- A list of proposed witnesses and of other persons with knowledge of the matters in dispute in the action

I will have to provide these documents to the plaintiff's rep by November 27, 2018 the latest. Please provide any documents that you think might be relevant to the proceeding and the names of any individuals who may have knowledge of the matters in your proceeding to me by **September 15, 2018.**

I will now start preparing for the settlement conference. I look forward to receiving from you the documents and information requested. In the meantime, please contact me if you have any questions or concerns.

From,

Thomas B.

Opinion Letter

An opinion letter is a letter from a paralegal to a client that offers a legal opinion on the client's matter and confirms legal advice given to a client. The letter also describes the facts and the law that the paralegal relied on to form his or her opinion. A sample opinion letter appears in Figure 6.7.

There are several elements in an opinion letter:

1. *The introductory paragraph*: Indicate why you are writing (to provide an opinion on a particular legal matter, to answer the client's questions, to recommend a course of action, etc.).

2. *Conclusion*: State your conclusion or recommended course of action. Always state that your conclusion is based on the facts as you understand them. When explaining your conclusion to your client, go over essential elements your client will need to prove, possible defences, problems, alternatives, and anything else the client needs to know to understand your legal conclusion.

3. *Facts*: Outline the facts on which you relied on in reaching your conclusion. Ask the client to read the facts carefully and advise you if there are any errors or any facts missing. This is important because missing or misstated facts can change your conclusion.

4. *Applicable law*: Explain the relevant law to the client clearly and concisely. Refer to the style tips in Chapters 1 and 3, which will help you explain the law in plain English.

5. *Closing*: Outline what needs to happen next. You might need documents from your client or instructions from your client on how to proceed. For example, if you recommended that your client file a claim in the Ontario Small Claims Court for breach of contract, advise your client that you will need to review the relevant documents and prepare a draft plaintiff's claim.

FIGURE 6.7   **Sample Opinion Letter**

SMITH, BROWN AND MARTINO LLP
4700 YONGE STREET, SUITE 500
TORONTO, ON M3X 2L9
TEL. 416-222-2222
FAX 416-222-2221

December 10, 2017

BY EMAIL (vsimms@gmail.com)

Ms. Victoria Simms
205 – 32 Yonge Street
Toronto, Ontario M1R 2L2

Dear Ms. Simms:

RE: **Simms v 24 Fitness—Gym Membership**
          File No. 17-1414

It was a pleasure meeting with you on December 8, 2017, regarding your 24 Fitness gym membership. I write to outline our discussion and to confirm my advice to you regarding your membership renewal.

As you will recall, you advised that you entered into a one-year membership contract ending December 31, 2017, with 24 Fitness (the "Club") and that you did not want to renew it.

Based on the facts as I understand them, I advised you to send a letter to the Club's manager notifying him that you do not wish to renew your membership. As mentioned, if you fail to do this before **December 31, 2017**, the Club may renew your contract and bill you. However, the law requires the Club to send you a renewal notice at least 30 days before the end of your contract. If it does not, any renewal or billing under a new agreement would likely be invalid.

I have based my advice to you on the following facts. Kindly advise me immediately if any facts are incorrect or any facts are missing:

- You signed a one-year gym membership contract with the Club ending on December 31, 2017.
- The agreement includes an automatic renewal provision, meaning that the terms of your membership will automatically renew for another year on the same terms as the agreement you signed. You were clear that you did not want to commit to another contract.
- You have not received any notice from the Club about the upcoming renewal of your contract.

The *Consumer Protection Act, 2002*, SO 2002, c 30, Sch A (the "Act"), requires that the Club follow certain rules before it can enforce its contract renewal clause. One of these rules is that it must send you a renewal notice at least 30 days before the contract expires. The Club must also give you a copy of the contract noting any changes to the original contract.

I understand from you that you did not receive a renewal notice from the Club about the upcoming renewal of your contract. Based on this fact, I advise that the Club is in breach of the requirements of the Act. Therefore, as explained above, any membership renewal beyond December 31, 2017, would be invalid and you would be entitled to demand that the Club return any money paid after the end of your original one-year contract.

In order to avoid any problems going forward, I recommend that you send a letter to the Club advising that you do not wish to renew your membership. You should do this before December 31, 2017.

I would be happy to write the letter to the Club on your behalf. Please contact me by December 20, 2017, if you would like me to assist in this regard.

As always, I invite you to contact me with any questions or concerns.

Yours truly,

SMITH, BROWN AND MARTINO LLP

Robert Martino

Robert Martino

Licensed Paralegal

Exercise 6.3

Draft an Opinion Letter

You are a paralegal who has just finished a meeting with your client Liam Kettle. Using your meeting notes below, write an opinion letter to Liam confirming the advice you gave him during your meeting today. The letter should be in full block mixed punctuation format. Include an appropriate matter name and file number. You will send the letter today by regular mail.

- Met with Liam Kettle today regarding his gym membership with Lagon Fitness.
- Liam lives at 12 Fairlawn Avenue, Suite 200, Toronto, Ontario M2L 3R3.
- Yesterday, Liam signed up for a one-year gym membership with Lagon Fitness. The cost for the year is $1,200. He is billed on a per-month basis.
- His membership started yesterday. He also received a copy of the agreement yesterday after he signed it.
- Today, he changed his mind about joining the gym. He tried to cancel by calling the gym, but the manager said he could not cancel the contract because he had already signed it.
- Section 35(1) of the *Consumer Protection Act, 2002*, SO 2002, c 30, Sch A, provides a 10-day cooling off period for consumers, such as Liam. It states, "A consumer may, without any reason, cancel a personal development services agreement at any time within 10 days after the later of receiving the written copy of the agreement and the day all the services are available."
- The gym membership agreement in this case is a personal development services agreement.
- During the meeting, Liam asked me if he could cancel his gym membership and, if so, what he should do to cancel it.
- I advised him about the 10-day cooling off period under the Act.

Exercise 6.4

Rewrite an Opinion Letter

Below is an example of a poorly drafted opinion letter from a paralegal to her client. Rewrite the body of the letter in full block mixed punctuation format, using effective style and correct grammar. Refer to Chapters 1 to 3 for guidelines on grammar and style.

Dear Karen Greene,

Throughout our meeting yesterday, you were freaking out about your dance studio membership. You said that two days ago you signed an agreement for a two-year membership at X Dance Studios for the amount of $2,000.00 per year. You told me that you realized you can't afford it and are freaked out by the thought that you will be locked in for 2 years!!!! Don't worry Karen! I've checked into the law. Section 31(1) of the *Consumer Protection Act, 2002*, SO 2002, c 30, Sch A provides as follows:

31 (1) No personal development services agreement may be made for a term longer than one year after the day that all the services are made available to the consumer.

Under the law, your dance studio membership contract is considered a personal development services agreement and therefore the studio is prohibited by law from having you enter into an agreement that is longer than one year. It's outrageous that they would allow that. Also, the CPA has a 10-day cooling off period during which you can completely and fully cancel the entire contract without giving a reason. All you have to do is advise the studio within ten days after receiving a signed copy of the agreement that you are cancelling it. It's as simple as that.

Hope that helps.

Always:

Lester Buttle

Encl.

Administrative or Informative Letters

Paralegals write administrative or informative letters to their clients for a number of reasons, such as confirming a hearing or settlement conference date; requesting that a client provide documents by a specific date; or providing an invoice. An example of an administrative letter to a client appears in Figures 6.2 and 6.3.

Paralegals often send simple requests or information to clients via email rather than a formal letter. Examples of these kinds of communications appear in Chapter 8, which covers email communications.

Exercise 6.5

Rewrite an Administrative Letter to a Client

Below is an example of a poorly drafted letter from a paralegal to her client regarding a missed appointment. Rewrite the body of the letter in full block mixed punctuation format, using effective style and correct grammar. Refer to Chapters 1 to 3 for guidelines on grammar and style.

To Mindy Bryce,

I refer to our meeting scheduled for today at 10:00 a.m. for which you did not attend. I specifically took time out of my busy scheduled to meet with you to discuss preparing a plaintiff's claim. The limitation period is coming up fast and it CANNOT be extended! You MUST file your claim in the Ontario small claims court by May 26, 2018! If you do not, all will be lost!

Mindy, I have many files that need my attention. I lost two hours today that could have been spent working on another file. Our firm's policy is that you must cancel any appointment by giving at least 24 hours notice. If you don't want my help anymore just tell me. If you want to call me to see if I can squeeze you in next week, please do so. I can't do anything to help without you telling me what you want me to do.

From,

Marco

Exercise 6.6

Draft an Administrative Letter to a Client

You are a paralegal representing Lee Han in a provincial offences matter. Lee was charged with careless driving under section 130 of the *Highway Traffic Act*, RSO 1990, c H.8. You recently obtained disclosure from the prosecutor and are now preparing for Lee's trial in a few months. It is your policy to bill your clients once a month. Write a letter to Lee enclosing your interim account for services rendered over the last 30 days. All accounts are payable within 14 days. The letter format should be full block mixed punctuation. Include an appropriate matter name and file number. You will send the letter by email today. Make up any information regarding Lee's address and email.

Letters to Opposing Parties or Opposing Legal Representatives

This section gives an overview of letters to opposing parties and opposing legal representatives, focusing specifically on two types of letters: demand letters and administrative or informative letters.

As discussed in Chapter 3, an important element of effective legal writing is using appropriate tone. When writing letters to opposing parties or opposing legal representatives, you must ensure that the tone of your letter is always professional, civil, and respectful. Never write in an abusive or offensive manner. You must also avoid ill-considered criticism of another licensee's competence, conduct, or advice. Remember that you can disagree with an opposing party or legal representative while still remaining pleasant and professional.

Demand Letter

A demand letter acts as a formal notice to an individual demanding that he or she fulfill an alleged legal obligation by a certain date. A paralegal may send a demand letter on behalf of a client to demand that the recipient of the letter refund money owed or carry out a contractual obligation. The letter will give the recipient a deadline to carry out the requested action or respond to the letter. The letter will usually advise what may happen if the recipient does not do as requested or respond by the deadline, such as starting legal proceedings or consulting with the paralegal's client.

A demand letter has four elements:

1. Describe the facts leading up to the demand.

2. Describe what your client wants the recipient of the letter to do (e.g., refund money paid, fix the damage to property, pay rent arrears).

3. Explain why your client is entitled to receive what you are asking the recipient for. Identify and explain the law that gives your client the right to make such a demand.

4. Indicate a specific date by which the recipient must do what you are demanding (or by which he or she must respond to your letter). You should give the recipient a reasonable amount of time to respond to your request.

If you are writing a demand letter to an unrepresented party, clearly indicate that you represent your client and not the recipient. You should also suggest that the recipient obtain legal advice or representation.

FIGURE 6.8   Sample Demand Letter

SMITH, BROWN AND MARTINO LLP
4700 YONGE STREET, SUITE 500
TORONTO, ON M3X 2L9
TEL. 416-222-2222
FAX 416-222-2221

December 10, 2017
BY FAX (416-312-2121)

Fun Fitness
331 Keegan Avenue West, Suite 101
Toronto, Ontario M5M 3T1

Attention: Ken Hawthorne

Dear Sirs/Mesdames:

RE: Sim v Fun Fitness—Gym Membership
**   File No. 17-1414**

I represent Ms. Victoria Sim in the above noted matter.

I understand that Ms. Sim signed a one-year gym membership with Fun Fitness on December 2, 2017, and was billed $53.21 on December 2, 2017, for the first month. I also understand that Ms. Sim cancelled the contract by sending an email to your assistant manager, Jordan Eves, on December 3, 2017. I enclose a copy of the email for your reference.

According to the *Consumer Protection Act, 2002* (the "Act"), Ms. Sim is entitled to cancel the contract and receive a refund of $53.21. She notified Fun Fitness of the cancellation within the 10-day cooling-off period in accordance with the Act. However, she has yet to receive her refund.

Please cancel Ms. Sim's contract immediately and refund her $53.21 by sending a cheque to my office. If I do not hear from you by December 20, 2017, I will consult with my client regarding next steps.

Yours truly,

SMITH, BROWN AND MARTINO LLP

Robert Martino
Robert Martino
Licensed Paralegal

Encl. – Copy of email

cc. Fun Fitness Head Office, Legal Department

Exercise 6.7

Draft a Demand Letter

You are a licensed paralegal representing Jeffrey Barry, a landlord, in a residential tenancies matter. Mr. Barry has asked you for assistance in collecting rent arrears from his tenant, Wilfred Buttle, who rents 121 Orchard View Lane, Unit 605, Toronto, Ontario M8P 2L2. Using the details below, write a demand letter to Wilfred Buttle on your client's behalf. The format should be full block mixed punctuation. Include an appropriate matter name and file number. You will send the letter by courier. Use today's date.

- Six months ago, Wilfred Buttle signed a one-year lease to rent Jeffrey's condominium for $1,750.00 per month plus utilities. The lease requires Wilfred to pay rent on the first of every month.

- As of today, Wilfred has not paid rent for the past three months. Wilfred owes Jeffrey $5,250.00 in rent.

- Jeffrey wants Wilfred to pay the rent arrears; otherwise, he wants to terminate the tenancy and evict Wilfred.

- The *Residential Tenancies Act, 2006*, SO 2006, c 17, allows a landlord to terminate a tenancy before the end of the lease term if a tenant fails to pay rent owing under a tenancy agreement. In other words, Jeffrey does not have to wait until the end of the one-year lease term to terminate the tenancy.

- The first step in terminating a tenancy for non-payment of rent is to serve the tenant with a Notice to Terminate a Tenancy for Non-payment of Rent.

- Jeffrey instructs you to write a demand letter to Wilfred demanding that he pay the rent arrears. If he does not pay within a reasonable time, Jeffrey wants to start proceedings to terminate the tenancy and evict Wilfred.

- You will send the letter to Wilfred today.

Administrative or Informative Letters

A paralegal may write numerous kinds of administrative or informative letters to an opposing party or legal representative. This section reviews a few of these.

For example, a letter to an opposing party or legal representative might

- request available dates for a hearing, mediation, or case conference;
- request disclosure;
- provide disclosure; or
- serve legal documents.

FIGURE 6.9 **Sample Administrative Letter to Opposing Legal Representative**

SMITH, BROWN AND MARTINO LLP
4700 YONGE STREET, SUITE 500
TORONTO, ON M3X 2L9
TEL. 416-222-2222
FAX 416-222-2221

December 10, 2017
BY COURIER

Brett Robertson
Robertson Paralegal Services
31 Sheppard Avenue West, Suite 200
Toronto, Ontario M2H 3H3

Dear Mr. Robertson:

RE: **Ronaldi v Kanson**
File No. 17-14233

I represent Mr. Ken Ronaldi in the above noted matter. I understand you represent Ms. Kanson.

Please find enclosed Mr. Ronaldi's Plaintiff's Claim, which is hereby served upon you in accordance with the *Rules of the Small Claims Court*.

Yours truly,

SMITH, BROWN AND MARTINO LLP

Robert Martino
Robert Martino
Licensed Paralegal

Encl. – Plaintiff's Claim

Exercise 6.8

Draft a Letter to an Opposing Legal Representative

You are a licensed paralegal acting for John Ingalls in a small claims court matter. The plaintiff, William Button, is suing your client for negligence. A lawyer, Sasha Leonard, represents the plaintiff. You spoke to Ms. Leonard today to confirm that both parties and their legal representatives will have a four-way meeting at Ms. Leonard's office in seven days from today at 10:00 a.m. The purpose of the meeting is to canvass the issues and see if a settlement is possible. Write a full block mixed punctuation letter to Ms. Leonard confirming the meeting and setting out the date, time, and place for the meeting. Include an appropriate matter name and file number. Ms. Leonard's address is 400 Sheppard Avenue East, Suite 500, Toronto, Ontario M8L 2J2. Her fax number is 416-911-9233. Send the letter by fax today. Create your own letterhead.

Exercise 6.9

Rewrite a Letter to Opposing Counsel

Below is an example of a poorly drafted letter from a paralegal to an opposing advocate, which uses an inappropriate tone. Rewrite the body of the letter in a full block mixed punctuation format, using effective style, correct grammar, and acceptable tone. Refer to Chapters 1 to 3 for guidelines on grammar, style, and tone.

Dear Sir:

I refer to my letters dated November 3, 15, and 30, 2017. I have now requested from you on 3 different occasions copies of your client's medical records from Dr. Caleb Hanson. What is your problem? I can only assume that you and your client have something to hide. As you probably do not know, the Rules of the Small Claims Court require the parties exchange all documents that are relevant to the issues in the proceeding. My client has abided by this rule—I sent you his disclosure on October 27, 2017; yours hasn't. I don't know what kind of poor advice you are giving your client, but your client must disclose! He must disclose by December 20, 2017! If he doesn't, I'm telling the judge and your client will pay!

Sam Brown

Licensed Paralegal

Letters to Other Third Parties

In addition to opposing parties or their legal representative, a paralegal may write letters to other third parties for a variety of reasons. Most commonly, a paralegal will write to a client's doctor to obtain medical documents and reports that may be relevant to a case. A paralegal may also write to a client's previous lawyer or paralegal to obtain a copy of the client's file.

When requesting documents from third parties on behalf of your client, you will need to provide an Authorization and Direction signed by your client. An Authorization and Direction authorizes a named individual to release certain documents and information about the authorizing person to another person. It must clearly identify what documents and information can be released and to whom. A sample template appears in Figure 6.10.

FIGURE 6.10   Sample Authorization and Direction

AUTHORIZATION & DIRECTION

TO: Dr. Allison Meeks
54 Front Street, Suite 400, Toronto, Ontario M2L 3H3

FROM: Victoria Smith

RE: Medical Documentation

DATE: January 15, 2018

I, Victoria Smith, authorize and direct you, Dr. Allison Meeks, to release any and all documents, including medical records, medical reports, correspondence, notes, and all other information written or otherwise recorded, contained in my medical file, to my paralegal, Robert Martino, Smith, Brown and Martino LLP, 4700 Yonge Street, Suite 500, Toronto, Ontario M3X 2L9, or any representative of Smith, Brown and Martino LLP.

AND this authorization and direction shall be your good and sufficient authority for so doing.

DATED at Toronto, the 15th day of January, 2018.

_____   _____
Witness   Victoria Smith

Exercise 6.10

Rewrite a Letter

Rewrite the following letter, correcting all grammar, form, spelling, and punctuation errors. Remove any unnecessary words and phrases, and correct awkward sentence construction. Arrange the material in appropriate paragraphs.

November 1, 2017

Dr. Norman Wattingford, Doctor of Chiropractic,
2100 Robinson Boulevard,
Suite 207,
Abbotsford, Ontario L6J 4M2

Dear Doctor Wattingford

Big Bad Machinery Company v Langham

We are acting as solicitors for mrs Dorothy Langham who is also a chiropractic patient of yours. It is our understanding from our discussions with dorothy that she suffered a accident on the factory floor of Big Bad Machinery Co where she works on December 14 2016. As a result of said acident (on which a large piece of heavy metal machinery accidently broak of it's hinges and fell at ms Langhams' feet landing on her big toe of her right foot leading to great pain) Ms. Langham has been suffering excrutiating pain since the accident. Because of the above reasons she has not worked since the date of the accident. It is my understand that you are the doctor who has treated Mrs Langham for her injuries and you agree she is not in a condition to return to her place of work in case she further injures her toe. Furthermore she is seeing a psychiatrist because of pain and sufering which she has caused her to be afraid of the big machinery so how can she now earn her living with it? Can you please send me all your reports exploring Dorothys' history with this trouble so that as her solicitors I can act on her behalf in dealing with her employer the Big Bad Machinery Company and trying to get her some form of compensation form them. I have enclosed an authorization and direction from Ms Langham authorizing you to release these documents to us. Please kindly contact me with this information at your earliest possible convenience.

Best,

WILSON Smith & JONES

Billy Smith

Summary

Writing letters is an important part of a paralegal's practice. When writing a letter, a paralegal should ensure that the letter follows an acceptable format and layout. The body of every letter generally has three parts, as discussed above. Remembering this structure will help a paralegal write letters that are clear, concise, and persuasive.

A paralegal will write letters to clients, opposing parties and legal representatives, and other third parties. This chapter reviewed different kinds of letters such as retainer letters, non-engagement letters, reporting letters, opinion letters, administrative or informative letters, and demand letters. It also discussed writing strategies for composing these types of letters.

Practise your letter-writing skills by completing the in-chapter exercises. When doing so, use the grammar and style skills you learned in the previous chapters to ensure letters are error free.

Writing Memoranda

LEARNING OUTCOMES

After reading this chapter, you should be able to

- Describe the different types of memoranda.

- Understand the purpose, form, and layout of memoranda.

- Write an information or instruction memorandum.

- Write a memorandum of law.

- Understand the basic rules of legal citation.

Introduction

A memorandum ("memo") is often used for internal communication within a law firm or other organization. Paralegals use memos for different purposes; the most common types are

- information or instruction memos,
- problem-solving memos,
- opinion or proposal memos (note that the opinion memo is not the same as an opinion letter, which is a formal document sent by a firm to a client), and
- memorandum of law.

This chapter examines the standard format of memos, the different types of memos, and basic legal citation rules.

Format

Memos can be either formal or informal, depending on their intended use. Whatever the situation, there are certain guidelines to follow. A memo always has a header and a body. Figure 7.1 shows a basic memo format.

FIGURE 7.1   Memo Format

MEMORANDUM

TO:	Recipient
FROM:	Sender/Author
DATE:	Date the author sends the memo to the recipient
SUBJECT:	Matter Name
	File Number

[Body—Singled spaced]

Copy to:

Author's initials and typist's initials (only if author's initials are different from typist's initials)

Recipient

A memo always names a recipient. A paralegal may write a memo to another employee to update him or her about a client or general office matter, creating a written record of developments either on a client file or in the office.

A paralegal may also write a memo to file to record developments on a client file, such as a meeting with the client during which a paralegal gave advice. In a firm, several paralegals and/or lawyers might be working on the same file; to determine the progress on a file, a paralegal could simply consult any memos to file. The recipient in this case would simply be "File," as shown in Figure 7.2.

A paralegal may also address a memo to a third party. For example, many paralegals and lawyers rely on **process servers** to file legal documents such as pleadings, affidavits, and other legal forms with various courts and tribunals. In such cases, a memo will provide the information the process server needs to file the documents. An example of a memo to a process server appears in Figure 7.3.

If there is more than one recipient, add an additional recipient line under the first recipient line, as indicated in Figure 7.4. Regardless of how many recipients there are, write their names clearly. Include the names of all individuals who are being directly addressed by the contents of the memo. Name the individuals who are only receiving a copy for their information in the "Copy to" line at the bottom of the memo.

Sender/Author

The sender or author of the memorandum indicates his or her name in the "From" line. If asked to type the memo on behalf of someone else, such as a senior lawyer, the paralegal does not put his or her name as the sender. Instead, the paralegal's initials are included at the bottom of the memo as the typist of the memo. Refer to Chapter 6 for further information on typist initials.

Date

The "Date" line gives the date when the author sends the memo to the recipient, using the proper format of month, day, and year (e.g., September 12, 2017). To ensure clarity, numerals should not be used for dates (e.g., 12/09/2017).

Subject Line

The "Subject" line should not be a complete sentence. If the memo relates to a particular client file, the subject line should always include the matter name and file number. For example:

>Subject: Singh v Anderson
>File No. 17-1212

>Subject: Lee ats Newman—Small Claims Court Matter
>File No. 17-1213

If the memo relates to a general office matter rather than a client file, provide a short description of what the memo is about. Make it as brief and to the point as possible. For example, the subject line of a memo announcing changes to the photocopying policy at a place of employment might be look like this:

>Subject: Changes to Photocopying Policy

Body

As discussed above, a memo can have many different purposes. Regardless of the purpose, the body of the memo always provides information to the reader. Limit your memo to one topic. If you have two topics to discuss, send two memos.

The body of the memo should use a font size of at least 12 points and should be single spaced. If there is a lot of information to communicate, use paragraphs throughout the body, separated by line spaces. Each paragraph begins at the left margin (i.e., do not indent the first line).

Remember that the contents of the memo's body should be polite, courteous, and professional. The information should also be accurate, complete, and free from confusing or irrelevant details. Use the skills learned in previous chapters to increase the readability of memos.

Closing

Unlike a letter, a memo does not use a complimentary close (e.g., "Yours truly," "Sincerely,"). A memo should close with the author's initials and the typist's initials, if different from the author's. The closing should also include the names of anyone who will receive a copy of the memo but is not the recipients.

Types of Memoranda and Writing Strategies

Memos fall into categories according to their purpose: informative or instruction memo, problem-solving memo, opinion or proposal memo, and memo of law.

While there are no hard-and-fast rules for writing memos (except for the format discussed above), the following guidelines will help you write memos that fall into these categories.

Information or Instruction Memo

An information or instruction memo is used, for instance, to notify others in the firm of developments on a client file, such as a meeting with a client. For example, you may write a memo to a senior paralegal to inform him or her about a telephone conference, meeting, or other developments on a client file. You might also write this type of memo "to file" as a written record of developments on the file. Figure 7.2 shows a sample of this kind of memo.

In addition, you may write an information or instruction memo when instructing a process server to file documents with the court (see Figure 7.3 for an example). Here are some things to remember when writing information or instruction memos:

1. *Main message:* State the main reason for writing. For example, you might be reporting your recent telephone conference with a client who instructed you to commence legal proceedings.

2. *Details:* State the information or instructions in as much detail as necessary. For example, in a memo about a meeting with a client, indicate when it occurred,

what you discussed, any advice you gave the client, and any instructions the client gave you. Some memos may need an additional paragraph or two to convey all the information or instructions.

3. *Action required or proposed:* If you need instructions on how to proceed, ask for them; if you are going to take action yourself, inform the reader what action you will take. For example, if a client has instructed you to commence a small claims court proceeding, indicate that you will now prepare a draft Plaintiff's Claim for the client's review. If no action is required, simply tell the reader that this memo is for information only.

FIGURE 7.2   Information Memo to File

MEMORANDUM

TO: File
FROM: Fatima Brown
DATE: October 1, 2017
SUBJECT: Smith v LaFontagne—Small Claims Court Matter
              File No. 17-1233

I spoke to our client, Rex Smith, today regarding his small claims court matter.

We discussed the process for commencing a breach of contract claim against Ms. LaFontagne. I explained to Mr. Smith that we would prepare a Plaintiff's Claim on his behalf and that Ms. LaFontagne would likely serve and file a Defence. I further explained that the Small Claims Court Rules require parties to attend a Settlement Conference prior to attending trial. We also discussed possible costs involved in starting a proceeding.

Mr. Smith instructed me to prepare a Plaintiff's Claim. I asked Mr. Smith to provide the following documents by October 10, 2017:

1) The contract;
2) Any receipts for payment; and
3) Any photographs of the unfinished kitchen.

Mr. Smith agreed to provide these documents by October 10, 2017.

Once I receive these documents, I will prepare a draft Plaintiff's Claim for Mr. Smith's review.

FB

FIGURE 7.3   Information Memo to Process Server

MEMORANDUM

TO:	Antoine Baker
FROM:	Fatima Brown
DATE:	December 15, 2017
SUBJECT:	Smith v LaFontagne—Small Claims Court Matter
	File No. 17-1233

Kindly attend at the Ontario Superior Court of Justice—Small Claims Court at 47 Sheppard Avenue East, Toronto, Ontario M2N 5N1 to issue the Plaintiff's Claim in the above noted matter.

Enclosed are the following items:

1) Plaintiff's Claim (Form 7A) (3 copies); and
2) Cheque payable to the Minister of Finance for $95.00.

Please contact Fatima Brown at 416-222-2222 ext. 23 with any questions.

FB/tj

Exercise 7.1

Draft a Memo to File

Using the details below, prepare a memo to file summarizing your meeting with your client, Eileen Hanson. The matter name is *Hanson v Braun*. The file number is 17-1555. Use today's date.

- Met with Eileen Hanson today regarding her rental property and issues with her tenant.
- Eileen Hanson owns a rental property at 45 Ingles Crescent, Toronto, Ontario. Her tenant, Victoria Smith, signed a one-year lease five months ago. Victoria pays $3,200.00 per month in rent.
- Victoria has not paid rent for the past three months. Eileen called Victoria approximately five times over the past three months to request that Victoria pay. Eileen left voicemail messages on all five occasions, but Victoria has not responded.
- Eileen wants to evict Victoria. Wants to know if she has to wait until the end of the one-year lease term before she can evict Victoria. Wants to know if she can change the locks on the house.
- Explained to client that she cannot change locks. Needs order from Landlord and Tenant Board. Once there is an order, only sheriff can physically evict a tenant.
- Explained to client process for evicting tenant on basis of non-payment of rent. Must serve tenant with Form N4: Notice to End Your Tenancy Early for Non-Payment of Rent.

- Explained failure to pay rent is a ground on which property owner can terminate tenancy before end of the term.
- Explained tenant will have 14 days after receiving the Notice to pay the rent arrears. If tenant does not pay, can start an Application at the Landlord and Tenant Board.
- Client wants us to prepare Form N4 and serve on tenant.
- Client asked to provide copy of lease agreement and contact info for tenant within 14 days. Client agreed to provide by this date.
- Will need to prepare Form N4 and letter to tenant advising we represent Eileen.

Exercise 7.2

Draft a Memo to a Process Server

You are a paralegal representing Richard Fulbright in a small claims court matter. Monica Green is suing Richard Fulbright for breach of contract. You recently served Ms. Green with your client's Defence. You now need to file the required documents with the Small Claims Court. Using these facts and the facts below, prepare a memo to the process server, Alexis Sutton, instructing him to file documents with the Small Claims Court. Use today's date.

- File number is 17-1232
- Court address is 45 Sheppard Avenue East, Toronto, Ontario M2N 5N1
- Documents to be filed are Defence (Form 9A), Affidavit of Service, and cheque payable to the Minister of Finance for $50.00 dollars
- Alexis can contact you at 416-212-2122

Problem-Solving Memo

A sample problem-solving memo appears in Figure 7.4. Keep the following elements in mind when writing this kind of memo:

1. *Statement of the problem:* You want the reader to care about the problem before you provide a solution, so state it from his or her perspective or from the perspective of the firm. For example, suppose that you want to host a paralegal student for the rest of the summer to help with client files. Point out that the vacation backlog has already resulted in missed deadlines, late submission of expense reports, and other consequences of importance to the reader.

2. *Analysis:* Go into some detail about where and why the problems arise. In this case, provide financial numbers to illustrate the cost and anything else the reader should know.

3. *Proposed solution:* Describe your solution and explain how it would work. Again, provide cost figures for comparison, so that the reader can clearly see the financial benefit.

4. *Proposed action:* Request permission to go ahead, stating exactly what you propose to do.

FIGURE 7.4   Problem-Solving Memo

MEMORANDUM

TO:	Amanda Jean, Managing Partner
FROM:	Heather Armstrong
DATE:	July 15, 2017
SUBJECT:	Proposed hosting of a paralegal student

An increase in new files has recently led to a number of inefficiencies in managing the firm's files. First, a number of new files remain unopened in our computer system, which means a paralegal is unable to start working on them. Second, this backlog of unopened files almost caused us to miss one deadline. Third, we are behind on billings.

There are two reasons for these problems:

1) Mary is on maternity leave until September 20, 2017, and we did not hire a replacement assistant. This leaves Lianne as the firm's only legal assistant; and

2) Our new online billing system is complicated and the learning curve has been steep.

I recommend we host a paralegal student to assist us with our files. I contacted Sarah Lynn, the Program Coordinator of the paralegal field placement program at Simpson College, to discuss its field placement program. She recommended a student for our firm who would complete 120 hours over a four-week period in matters within the paralegal scope of practice.

I believe that hosting a student for field placement will help us catch up on files to ensure our usual level of efficiency while providing a paralegal student with some practical experience.

Kindly advise whether we can move forward with hosting a paralegal student.

Copy to: Lianne Jones

HA

Opinion or Proposal Memo

Figure 7.5 shows a sample opinion or proposal memo. When writing this type of memo, try to include the following elements:

1. *Statement of opinion:* Suppose you want to recommend a course of action your firm should take on a file. Begin with a clear statement such as "I recommend …" or "In order to … I would suggest …" or "Based on my research, I recommend …"

2. *Reason for suggestion:* State the potential positive outcome if your recommendation is accepted.

3. *Examples:* Provide examples to illustrate the reasons underlying your opinion.

4. *Benefits of change:* Do not exaggerate, but use positive language and facts to portray your opinion in a good light.

5. *Possible disadvantages:* Presumably, since you are making this recommendation, you have thought through the pros and cons and still believe in your idea. Now you must mention any possible drawbacks, but do so in such a way that they appear outweighed by the benefits.

6. *Action requested:* Request action, such as a meeting to discuss your ideas further or to schedule a telephone conference with a client to obtain instructions.

FIGURE 7.5   **Opinion Memo**

MEMORANDUM

TO: Viktor Lee
FROM: Cassie Singh
DATE: September 1, 2018
SUBJECT: Buttle v The Law Society of Ontario
              File No. 17-2222

I believe Ms. Buttle is likely to show that she meets the test for good character under the *Law Society Act*, RSO 1990, c L.8 (the "Act"). If successful in proving she meets this test, Ms. Buttle will receive her P1 license to practise law as a paralegal in Ontario. If the Law Society Hearing Panel finds she does not meet the test for good character, section 49.32(1) of the Act allows Ms. Buttle to appeal the decision to the Appeal Division.

A determination of good character requires the consideration of five factors:[1] (1) the nature and duration of the misconduct; (2) whether the applicant is remorseful; (3) what rehabilitative efforts, if any, have been undertaken, and the success of such efforts; (4) the applicant's conduct since the misconduct; and (5) the passage of time since the misconduct.

The following are the reasons underlying my opinion:

The Nature and Duration of the Misconduct

The event giving rise to the complaint occurred over a short time period of one week. While Ms. Buttle's actions were aggressive, it was an isolated incident.

---

1   *Ryan Jesse Manilla v Law Society of Upper Canada*, 2010 ONLSHP 92.

FIGURE 7.5   Continued

The Applicant's Remorse

Ms. Buttle showed remorse for her behaviour immediately after the incident. She expressed remorse in a number of ways. First, she wrote an apology letter to her neighbour three days after the incident occurred. Second, she admitted in her Application for a P1 Licence that her conduct was inappropriate.

The Applicant's Rehabilitation

Ms. Buttle spent a significant amount of time rehabilitating herself. For example, she enrolled in anger management classes immediately after the incident.

The Applicant's Conduct

Ms. Buttle took a leave of absence from her part-time job as a cashier following the incident in order to attend anger management classes.

The Passage of Time

While the incident occurred only two years ago, the decision in *Smith v The Law Society of Upper Canada*, 2010 ONLSHP 111, notes that two years is still a significant amount of time. Further, an analysis of the four remaining factors in the context of Ms. Buttle's case supports a finding of good character.

Conclusion:

While all five factors are relevant, I recommend highlighting the isolated nature of Ms. Buttle's actions and her rehabilitation efforts since the incident occurred.

CS

Planning Your Memo

Advance planning will make the task of writing a memo much easier and faster. Decide which type of memo you need, write down the relevant elements listed above, and make notes of what to include in each. Having the message clear in your own mind will help you make it clear on paper for your reader.

Language, Grammar, and Style

Use the material covered in Chapters 1–3 when writing a memo. Even the best-planned and best-formatted memo will be ineffective if it is grammatically incorrect or full of stylistic problems.

When necessary, follow the tips in Chapter 5 to develop legal arguments.

Memorandum of Law

The most specialized form of memo written by a paralegal is the memorandum of law ("memo of law"). This is essentially a memo that reports the results of legal research.

For example, to decide on a course of action in a case, a paralegal may need to examine previous case law for similar parameters and circumstances. A memo of law presents the results of this research, along with an application of the law to a particular set of facts. As a paralegal, you may do this for yourself or for a senior paralegal; in either case, you must know how to format and write a memo of law correctly.

A memo of law can follow different formats. This book focuses on the following format:

1. *Question* (optional): State the question you have been asked to research.

2. *Facts:* State the facts on which you have relied in researching the question. If you have made assumptions, say that they are assumptions. Emphasize essential facts and delete any irrelevant facts.

3. *Issue(s):* Clearly state the issue or issues of law that you examined. Here you must define the legal issues that emerge from the facts you are dealing with.

4. *Brief answer(s):* Briefly state the answer(s) to the issue(s) stated above.

5. *Analysis:* Analyze the statutes or regulations and the available case law in light of the facts. In doing so, set out the law governing the case law you have found. If you refer to statutes, you must state the provisions of the law exactly as they appear in the statutes, with full citations set out in the **prescribed** manner (see below). Identify legal arguments for both sides of the issue(s).

6. *Conclusion:* State what you have concluded after applying the law to the facts of the current situation.

Writing a Memorandum of Law

Writing a memo of law is a complex process, and it is important that the end result be an accurate description of your research and the conclusions you have reached. You should not rush it. You may write several drafts, or at least do several rounds of heavy editing, before the final version is ready. It is worth the time and effort to produce an effective memo of law.

The following steps will guide you through the process:

1. *Analyze the fact situation.*

2. *Research the law.* Once you have done this, you will be able to look at the facts and decide which ones are relevant to the principles of law involved.

3. *Prepare a draft memo of law.* At this point, you should try to see the problem as a whole, and this is necessary in preparing your memo. A draft memo of law gives you a chance to try out different ideas about what you think is going on from a legal point of view and to settle on the true issues, the important facts, and the relevant law. You may have to revise your draft once or twice before you are satisfied that you have approached the problem from the correct angle.

4. *Edit to produce a final memo of law.* You should spend a significant amount of time editing your draft memo. Refer to Appendix A for a sample editing checklist. Remember that a memo of law is not a 5,000-word term paper; keep it short and to the point.

Figure 7.6 shows an instruction memo from a senior paralegal to an associate requesting that the associate prepare a memo of law based on the facts provided. The instructing paralegal wants to know whether a court is likely to find that police conduct violated a client's rights under the *Canadian Charter of Rights and Freedoms* and whether a court is likely to exclude from trial the evidence obtained as a result of the *Charter* violation. Figure 7.7 shows the resulting memo of law prepared by the associate paralegal.

FIGURE 7.6   Instruction Memo

MEMORANDUM

TO: Vincent Lau
FROM: Patricia Keeting
DATE: November 1, 2017
SUBJECT: R v Kessel
             File No. 17-1299

Our client, Henry Kessel, is charged with knowingly permitting a place to be used for the purposes of a common gaming and betting house contrary to section 201(2)(b) of the *Criminal Code*, RSC 1985, c C-46 ("*Criminal Code*").

The facts are as follows:

Henry is the owner of a detached house in a residential neighbourhood at 233 Mountain Street, Toronto, Ontario. While Henry is the owner of the property, he lives in the basement and rents out the main floor to his tenant, Brian Sutton. Brian and Harry share a common kitchen on the main floor of the house. Brian is charged with keeping a common gaming and betting house contrary to section 202(1) of the *Criminal Code*. He has his own counsel. Brian operated a casino on the main floor of the house for which patrons paid an entrance fee to gain access to the casino facilities. As part of the enterprise, Brian installed four slot machines and two blackjack tables in the house. The slot machines and blackjack tables were located at the back of the first floor of the house.

Several months after Brian started his casino operation, the Toronto Police Service ("TPS") received an anonymous tip regarding the existence of the operation. Acting on this tip, the TPS asked the local utility supplier to install a digital recording ammeter ("DRA") on the power line that delivers electricity to the house. The power line was located on public property outside the property line. The utility company complied with the request, even though the TPS did not obtain a search warrant.

A DRA records electricity use in the home and discloses patterns of electricity use. After 14 days, the DRA revealed above-average electricity use in the home, consistent with a gaming operation. With this information and the anonymous tip, the TPS applied for and obtained a warrant to search Henry's house. When the TPS arrived at the house with the search warrant, they seized evidence that confirmed a gaming and betting operation.

Our client says that he did not know about Brian's gaming and betting operation and had nothing to do with it. He says that he only ever went upstairs to the main floor to use the kitchen, which is nowhere near the rooms Brian used for his operation. While Henry regularly heard large numbers of people coming and going to the house, he says he thought Brian was just a "big partier" with many friends. Yet Henry now stands charged under the *Criminal Code* for knowingly permitting a place to be used for the purposes of a common gaming and betting house.

The TPS search warrant appears problematic. The TPS obtained their search warrant based on the information provided by the DRA. The DRA's installation on the property's power line may have violated Henry's right to be secure from unreasonable search and seizure under the Charter. If it did, the search warrant may be invalid and therefore Henry may apply under section 24(2) of the Charter to exclude from trial the evidence seized from the house.

Please prepare a memorandum of law on whether the court is likely to find a Charter violation based on these facts and whether the court is likely to exclude the evidence obtained during the search of the house.

PK

FIGURE 7.7 **Memo of Law**

MEMORANDUM

TO: Patricia Keeting
FROM: Vincent Lau
DATE: November 15, 2017
SUBJECT: R v Kessel
                  File No. 17-1299

FACTS

Henry Kessel is charged with knowingly permitting a place to be used for the purposes of a common gaming and betting house contrary to section 201(2)(b) of

FIGURE 7.7 **Continued**

the *Criminal Code*, RSC 1985, c C-46. Henry owns property in Toronto in which he lived in the basement and rented the main floor to his tenant, Brian Sutton. Brian operated a casino on the main floor of the house, which included slot machines and blackjack tables. After several months of the casino's operation, the Toronto Police Service ("TPS") received an anonymous tip regarding its existence. Acting on this tip, the TPS asked the local utility supplier to install a digital recording ammeter ("DRA") on the power line that delivers electricity to the house in order to measure electrical consumption patterns in the house. The power line was located on public property outside the property line. The utility company complied with the request, even though the TPS did not obtain a search warrant. The information generated from the DRA revealed above-average electricity use in the house, consistent with a gaming operation. With this information and the anonymous tip, the TPS applied for and obtained a warrant to search Henry's house. In searching the house, the TPS seized evidence that confirmed a gaming and betting operation. The TPS subsequently arrested and charged Henry.

ISSUES

(1) Did the installation of a DRA on the power line delivering power to Henry's house without prior judicial authorization constitute a violation of Henry's right to be secure from unreasonable search and seizure under section 8 of the *Canadian Charter of Rights and Freedoms*, Part I of the *Constitution Act, 1982*, being Schedule B to the *Canada Act 1982* (UK), 1982, c 11 (the "Charter").

(2) If so, was the search warrant valid.

(3) If Henry's section 8 right was violated, should the evidence obtained in breach of his right be excluded from trial under section 24(2) of the Charter.

BRIEF ANSWERS

(1) No.

(2) No.

(3) No.

ANALYSIS

Did Henry Have a Reasonable Expectation of Privacy in the Information Obtained by the DRA.

According to the test laid out in *R v Edwards*, [1996] 1 SCR 128 ("*Edwards*"), in order to establish that his section 8 right was violated, Henry must demonstrate that he had a reasonable expectation of privacy in the information obtained by the DRA and that the DRA installation was an unreasonable intrusion on that privacy interest. In *Hunter et al v Southam Inc*, [1984] 2 SCR 145, the Court established that the guarantee of security from unreasonable search and seizure only protects a reasonable expectation of privacy, and therefore police conduct interfering with a reasonable expectation of privacy without prior judicial authorization constitutes an unreasonable search within the meaning of section 8 of the Charter.

According to *Edwards*, the existence of a reasonable expectation of privacy is determined by considering the subject matter obtained by the technology, the existence of a subjective expectation of privacy in the subject matter, and whether the reasonable expectation of privacy is objectively reasonable. In Henry's case, the DRA measures the amount of electrical consumption within the house. Binnie J in *R v Tessling*, [2004] 3 SCR 432 ("*Tessling*"), held that privacy interests protected by section 8 include personal, territorial, and informational privacy. Henry clearly has a reasonable expectation of privacy in the subject matter obtained by the DRA, as it relates to activities within his home. Henry also has a subjective expectation of privacy in the subject matter because the police were interested in obtaining the information for what it might reveal about the activities in his house. According to *Tessling*, a person cannot have a reasonable expectation of privacy in information he voluntarily exposes or abandons to the public. The Crown could argue that because Henry took no steps to conceal the information, he had no subjective expectation of privacy in it; however, Henry had no reasonable reason to conceal his use of electricity, as he himself was using it for purposes unrelated to the casino operation. It would also have been impossible for Henry to conceal his use of electricity.

In determining whether Henry's reasonable expectation of privacy is objectionably reasonable, the conclusion must be based on what the technology discloses. In *R v Wong*, [1990] 3 SCR 36 at para 48, the Court held that "the nature of the place in which the surveillance occurs will always be an important factor to consider …. It is not, however, determinative." In Henry's case, the Crown could argue that the DRA was not placed on Henry's property and that it only measures information that exists outside the home and is therefore capable of being in public view. However, because the information is unobservable without the use of the device, it is not in public view. In addition, contrary to the facts in *R v Plant*, [1993] 3 SCR 28 ("*Plant*"), it cannot be said in Henry's case that the information was in the possession of third parties prior to its detection by the DRA device.

Henry's privacy interest is informational. Therefore, the Court will analyze the nature and quality of the information obtained by the DRA in determining whether there was an intrusion on Henry's privacy interest. In considering the police intrusion into the privacy interest and the nature of the details exposed by the technology at issue, a number of lower courts have held that the installation of a DRA device is not intrusive because the nature and manner of the collection of electronic information involves no physical restraint or interference with the accused person or his house. However, this proposition presupposes that the privacy interest is territorial in nature rather than informational. In *Tessling*, Binnie J held that when informational privacy is at issue, intrusion must be determined by focusing on the nature and quality of the information obtained by the technology.

Section 8 of the Charter protects a biographical core of personal information. The majority in *Plant* held that electrical consumption does not reveal a biographical core of personal information, specifically intimate details of the lifestyle and personal choices of the individual, as it cannot identify the exact source or nature of the activity using the electricity. In *Tessling*, the Court held that the device did not reveal intimate personal details of the occupant's lifestyle because it could not identify the source or nature of the activity generating the information. Based on this reasoning, the Crown could argue that the amount of electrical consumption within the house does not reveal any intimate details relating to Henry's personal

FIGURE 7.7 **Continued**

activities because it cannot establish the exact source of the electrical consumption. While the DRA can detect the amount of electricity used within the house, it cannot distinguish between the various activities the electricity is used for. The amount of electrical consumption does not sufficiently support the inference that a gambling or betting operation is taking place within the home, because there are many legal activities that could produce such data. Further, the Supreme Court of Canada found in *R v Gomboc*, [2010] 3 SCR 211, that the DRA used by police in that case did not disclose intimate details of the lifestyle and personal choices of the individual that form part of the biographical core of data protected by the Charter.

Based on the facts in Henry's case, it would be difficult to argue that the DRA reveals a biographical core of personal information. It does not reveal information about a specific activity that an individual engages in within the house. As a result, it cannot indicate any type of personal choice Henry made to engage in a certain activity, such as the use of a computer, television, etc.

Therefore, based on the consideration of the totality of circumstances, it is unlikely that Henry has a reasonable expectation of privacy in the information obtained by the DRA. This device, in its present information-generating capabilities, does not intrude on Henry's reasonable expectation of privacy because it is not able to detect any specific activity occurring within the home.

Was the Search Warrant Valid.

According to *R v Wiley*, [1993] 3 SCR 263, police may not rely on facts obtained by *Charter* breach to obtain a search warrant. However, because the installation of the DRA will likely not be found to have violated Henry's section 8 right, the search of Henry's house will likely be found reasonable.

However, if the Court finds that it did violate Henry's section 8 right, the search of Henry's house will be reasonable only if the anonymous tip provides sufficient reasonable and probable grounds that there was an illegal gaming and/or betting operation within the house.

Can Henry Apply to Exclude the Evidence Obtained from the House at Trial.

As it is not likely that the Court will find a section 8 Charter violation, Henry cannot apply to exclude from trial the evidence obtained in breach of a Charter right under section 24(2) of the Charter.

CONCLUSION

It is likely that Henry will not be able to show that the installation of a DRA constituted a violation of section 8 of the Charter, given the technological nature of the device. Consequently, the search of Henry's house is not likely to be found unreasonable, given that the information obtained from the DRA and the anonymous tip provide sufficient reasonable and probable grounds for the issuance of the search warrant. Therefore, Henry is unable to apply to exclude the evidence obtained during the search under section 24(2) of the Charter.

VL

Legal Citation

An essential part of the formatting of a memo of law is what is known as *legal citation*. All aspects of the case law or legislation are cited in the memo in a prescribed manner. You must become familiar with the rules of legal citation. See Figure 7.7 for a sample memo of law with proper legal citations.

Case Citations[1]

A correct legal citation of a case consists of several parts, as illustrated in the following examples, explained below:

1	2	3	4	5	6	7
Malette v Shulman	(1990),	67	DLR	(4th)	321	(Ont CA)
Pettkus v Becker,	[1980]	2	SCR		834	

1. STYLE OF CAUSE OR GENERAL HEADING

The style of cause of the citation sets out the names of the parties (last names only). The names of *all* the parties to the action are not always included in the citation. In a reported case, the editors of the report series will have given the case a short style of cause as well as the complete one if it is long. The names of the parties are separated by a lowercase *v* (short for the Latin *versus*, meaning "against"), and the entire style of cause is italicized.

2. YEAR

The year in which the case is decided or reported—that is, published in a report series—follows the style of cause and is enclosed in either round or square brackets.

Some report series number their volumes sequentially no matter what the year, and it is not essential to know the year in which the case was reported in order to find it in the report series. In that case, the year is placed in round brackets—( )—and is followed by a comma.

Other report series start a new set of volume numbers each calendar year, and it is essential to know the year in order to find the case in the report series. In this case, the year appears in square brackets—[ ]—and is preceded by a comma. For example, in each calendar year, the first volume of the *Supreme Court Reports* is volume 1. To find a case located in volume 1, you must know the year in which the case was reported to find the appropriate volume 1.

3. LAW REPORT VOLUME NUMBER

This number tells you the volume number of the report series in which your case can be found. Some law report volumes are identified simply by volume number (as in the first

---

1   Note that the *Canadian Guide to Uniform Legal Citation*, 7th ed. (Toronto: Carswell, 2010), removed periods from citations and that this citation practice continues in the 8th edition (Toronto: Carswell, 2014). While this chapter follows this practice, note that the removal of periods in citations has not been universally accepted. Some courts, organizations, and employers continue to use periods in their citations. You should follow the preference of your employer or the practice guidelines of particular courts, if any.

example above), while others are also identified by the year of publication. More than one volume may be published in one year, as illustrated in the second example above. If the report series starts a new sequence of volume numbers each year, then you must make sure you look for the volume number for the correct year. In the example of *Pettkus v Becker*, you are looking for volume 2 of the year 1980.

4. NAME OF THE LAW REPORT SERIES

This part of the citation tells you the name of the law report series in which the case is reported, generally in abbreviated form. In the example of *Malette v Shulman*, "DLR" stands for *Dominion Law Reports*; in the example of *Pettkus v Becker*, "SCR" stands for *Supreme Court Reports*. (For these and other categories of abbreviations used in legal citation, refer to a resource such as the appendices to the *Canadian Guide to Uniform Legal Citation*, 8th ed.)

5. LAW REPORT SERIES NUMBER

Many reports do not continue past a certain number of volumes. When the report reaches, for example, volume 75 or volume 100, that series ends and a new one begins. Subsequent editions are identified by "2d," "3d," "4th," and so on (*not* "2nd," "3rd"). If a series or edition number is provided in a citation, be sure that you have the right series as well as the right volume number of the report. In the *Malette v Shulman* citation, the case can be found in the 67th volume of the 4th series of the DLR.

6. PAGE NUMBER

This number tells you the page number on which the case begins in the report volume. In a correct citation, no abbreviation such as "p.," "pp.," or "pg." is used before the page number.

7. JURISDICTION AND COURT

The abbreviation for jurisdiction and the level of court is given in round brackets following the page number of the case. This information is omitted if the jurisdiction and/or court level is obvious from the name of the reporter series.

If the citation refers to a report series that includes cases for one province only, such as the *Ontario Reports* or the *British Columbia Reports*, only the level of court is needed. For example, the citation of a Court of Appeal case published in the *Ontario Reports* will end with "(CA)"; however, the citation for the same case in the *Dominion Law Reports* (which publishes cases from across Canada) will end in "(Ont CA)."

If the citation refers to a report series for one court only, the level of court is not included in the citation. For example, the *Supreme Court Reports* reports only Supreme Court of Canada decisions. Therefore, a citation for that report series will omit both the jurisdiction and the level of court, as illustrated in the example of *Pettkus v Becker*.

Sometimes the name of the judge who decided the case is included in the citation. If the citation does not include the court, the judge's name appears in round brackets at the end of the citation. If the court is included, the name follows the court, separated by a long (em) dash: for example, "(Ont CA—Robins J)." The "J" stands for *judge* or *justice*; it is not the initial of the judge's first name. "JJ" stands for *justices* and "JJA" stands for *justices of appeal*. "CJ" stands for *chief justice*. A judge's own initial is used only if it is necessary to distinguish between two judges with the same last name—for example, "R.E. Holland J" and "J. Holland J."

Parallel Citations

If a case is reported in more than one report series, "parallel" citations are given. A parallel citation provides other places to find the same case. The citation for any official report series is given first. For example:

> *R v Carosella*, [1997] 1 SCR 80, 142 DLR (4th) 595, 112 CCC (3d) 289.

This citation means that the case can be found in the *Supreme Court Reports*, the *Dominion Law Reports*, and *Canadian Criminal Cases*. Parallel citations are separated by commas.

When parallel citations are given, the reader can choose any one of the report series to find the text of the case. However, if a case has been reported in an official report series, you should read and copy the case from that report series, if it is available to you.

Statute Citations

A correct legal citation of a statute consists of several parts, as illustrated in the following examples, explained below:

1	2	3	4
Courts of Justice Act,	RSO 1990,	c C.43,	s 22(1)
Residential Tenancies Act, 2006,	SO 2006,	c 17,	s 95(1)

1. NAME OF THE STATUTE

The citation begins with the short title of the statute, italicized, followed by a comma. Note that short titles of some statutes also include the year, as shown above in the citation for the *Residential Tenancies Act, 2006*. In this case, the year must also be italicized because it forms part of the short title of the statute.

2. VOLUME TITLE ABBREVIATION AND YEAR

The name of the statute is followed by the abbreviated name of the statute series in which it appears and the year of publication. A comma follows the year of publication. Note that no comma separates the abbreviated volume title and the year, as shown above.

3. CHAPTER NUMBER

Part 3 of the statute citation identifies the chapter number assigned to the statute in the volume. Abbreviate *chapter* as "c" and add a space before the chapter number, as shown above. Note that style of the chapter number depends on the particular statute volume. Some statute volumes include a letter, as shown in the *Courts of Justice Act* citation above.

4. SECTION NUMBER

If you refer to a particular section of a statute in your memo of law, the statute citation must include the section number. Abbreviate *section* as "s" and *subsection* as "ss," and add a space before the number. If your reference is to a subsection of a section, put the subsection in brackets after the section number, as shown above.

Exercise 7.3

Draft a Memo of Law

Write a memo of law addressed to the managing partner of your firm, Alexis DuPont, based on the following facts. The matter name is *Simpson v Brantford*. The file number is 17-1301. Use November 30, 2017, as the date.

The firm's client, Marie Simpson, retained the firm to assist her with a possible breach of contract matter. Marie hired David to install a new front and back deck on her house for $8,500.00. They entered into a written agreement on March 1, 2017, in which David agreed to complete the work by May 19, 2017, which was the start of the Victoria Day weekend. Marie paid David a $2,000.00 deposit. Marie had hired David in the past to complete various small jobs on her house, and she had been pleased with his work. David did not complete the work by May 19, 2017. It was not until September 8, 2017 that David finished the work, and once it was done, it was not to Marie's liking. Marie complained to David about the quality of the decks and the delay in completing the work. Marie became frustrated and stopped the work. In October 2017, Marie hired a contractor from Innis Renovations to complete the work. Innis Renovations completed the work for $5,333.29, which Marie paid. Marie wants to start a Small Claims Court proceeding against David for breach of contract. She wants David to pay her $5,333.29 to cover the cost of having Innis Renovations complete the work as well as $7,000.00 in aggravated or punitive damages.

Prepare a memo of law on whether Marie's case is likely to merit an award of punitive damages.

Summary

Paralegals must be able to write different types of memoranda. Whether writing an information or instruction memo, a problem-solving memo, an opinion or proposal memo, or a memo of law, it is important to follow the appropriate format. The suggestions in this chapter on format and writing style will assist paralegals in developing their memo writing skills.

An important part of writing memos of law is proper legal citation. This chapter reviewed the basic rules for case and statute citations. Paralegals should follow the rules of legal citation when composing a memo of law.

Email and Social Media Communication

8

LEARNING OUTCOMES

After reading this chapter, you should be able to

- Understand the different types of email messages.

- Write effective email messages.

- Edit emails for clarity and conciseness.

- Understand social media as a form of communication in the legal profession.

- Describe various guidelines for appropriate social media communication.

Introduction

Online communication plays a significant role in legal practice today. *Online communication* refers to communication between individuals or organizations via the Internet, including email and social networking sites such as Twitter, Facebook, and LinkedIn.

Paralegals should take care when writing emails and other types of online communication. This chapter explores the different types of emails a paralegal might send as well as strategies for writing effective email messages. It also suggests some guidelines to consider when using social media to communicate for marketing, professional, or personal purposes. While this chapter does not provide an exhaustive list of guidelines to consider, the guidelines discussed are helpful when thinking about appropriate online communication.

Email

Because email is simply a vehicle for transmitting messages, it requires fewer formatting or composition guidelines than letters and memoranda. Remember, you can write a letter or a memorandum and send it by email. You should approach the writing of email messages with the same care and focus as if you were putting the content on paper.

Writing Effective Email Messages

The general guidelines that follow will help you write effective email messages. While these guidelines do not necessarily deal specifically with writing, they do deal with communication.

Subject Line

Always use an effective subject line. People are overwhelmed with huge volumes of email, and your subject line can influence your reader either to open your email or to delete it without reading it.

In your subject line, avoid words that will trigger an email provider's or organization's "spam filters," such as *free*, *dollar*, *girls*, *bargain*, *profit*, *additional income*, *billing address*, *avoid bankruptcy*, and *your income*. Such lists are growing all the time, so you might use words that are perfectly legitimate and relevant to your message, such as *billing address*, only to have your message caught in the recipient's spam filter and never delivered. For up-to-date lists, search online for "words that trigger spam filters."

Emails to clients should include the words "Personal and Confidential" in the subject line. Also consider including your firm name in the subject line so that a client can more easily find and recognize the email. For example:

> Subject: Amanda Lane, Licensed Paralegal – Personal and Confidential
> Subject: Kenwood Paralegal Services – Personal and Confidential

Emails to opposing advocates should include the file's matter name. For example, assume you represent the plaintiff, Kent Teale, who is suing the defendant, Michael Swoon, in a small claims court matter. You compose an email to the defendant's paralegal to follow up on a disclosure request. Your subject line might be:

> Subject: Teale v Swoon – Small Claims Court Matter

You may also consider including the opposing paralegal's file number, as follows:

> Subject: Teale v Swoon – Your File No. 17-2232

Salutation

If, in a printed letter, you would normally use a salutation with a courtesy title, such as *Dear Mr.* or *Dear Ms.*, use the same salutation in your email message.

While email messages are less formal than letters, they should not be inappropriately informal. Always address the recipient by the appropriate courtesy title and last name, and continue to do so until the recipient requests that you communicate on a first-name basis. Use "Dear," "Hello," or "Hi" in your salutation; never use "Hey" or "To."

Here is an example of an improper salutation in an email to a client:

> Subject: Amanda Lane, Licensed Paralegal – Personal and Confidential
> Hey Sam!

In this case, the salutation should be revised as follows:

> Subject: Amanda Lane, Licensed Paralegal – Personal and Confidential
> Dear Mr. Jones,

or

> Subject: Amanda Lane, Licensed Paralegal – Personal and Confidential
> Hello Mr. Jones,

Many people do not mind being called by their first name, but some relationship building is needed before you start addressing people by their first name in emails.

Body of Email

Write the body of your email as you would in a written letter. Maintain an acceptable level of formality. Do not use slang or other informal language. It is acceptable to use contractions in email messages, however. Refer to Chapter 3 for tips on avoiding informal language, expressions, and slang.

Use upper and lower case as you would on paper. As mentioned in Chapter 6, using all capital letters for emphasis creates the impression that you are shouting; in an email message, text in "all caps" is also likely to trigger spam filters. If you omit capital letters altogether, on the other hand, your work will be not only grammatically incorrect but difficult to read and inappropriately casual.

Divide your message into paragraphs, and keep paragraphs short. Large blocks of text on a computer screen are hard on the eyes and difficult to read, creating an automatic barrier to communication. Follow the guidelines in Chapter 6 on writing paragraphs. Each paragraph should contain one main idea. Leave an extra line space between paragraphs, just as you would on paper.

Never use smiley faces, emoji, or other "emoticons" in email messages. These have no place in professional business emails. Your words must speak for themselves.

Always consider the tone of your email message. Sometimes email messages can be written and sent very quickly, and as a result, you might not realize that your tone was inappropriate until after sending the email. If not carefully considered, an email message might appear insulting, aggressive, or disrespectful despite not being intended that way.

Avoid replying to an email message immediately, especially when you are not happy with the content of the message you received. Recall a paralegal's duty of civility under the *Paralegal Rules of Conduct*, as discussed in Chapter 3. Chapter 3 also includes tips on ensuring that your communication uses an appropriate tone.

Remember to proofread your email for grammar, spelling, and style before sending. An email is a business document, and must be just as error free in all respects as if it were on paper. Correct grammar and spelling and appropriate style are necessary. Always type in full sentences and never in point form. Never use method of delivery as an excuse for careless work.

Close

The same types of complimentary closes discussed in Chapter 6 in the context of writing letters should also be used in professional email communications. For example, use "Sincerely," "Yours truly," or "Regards" to end your email. Never use "From" or "Cheers."

Include your contact information at the end of the message, together with your name. Following your name, identify yourself as a licensed paralegal. The easiest way to do this is with email signatures, available in all major email programs.

Never use "PS" at the end of your email message. The abbreviation "PS" stands for *postscript* and was traditionally used to include additional or updated information after the writer concluded a handwritten letter. If you need to include additional or updated information to an email message you have drafted, simply add it at an appropriate place in the text.

Distribution Lists

Use distribution lists wisely. A list of people in your firm, for example, can be useful when the message is for everyone, but sending copies of all your messages to everyone on the list is unnecessary and annoying.

Other Email Fields

Email programs offer three recipient fields: "To," "BCC," and "CC." It is important to use these fields properly. In the To field, always use the email address of the person you are sending the email to. Use the BCC field when emailing a group of contacts who do not know each other. When you copy other people using BCC, the actual recipient will not see these names.

Use the CC field when copying other people on an email who are involved in the matter. Usually, these people will know each other and have one another's contact information already. For example, a paralegal might send an email to a client to schedule a meeting and include his or her assistant in the CC field so that the assistant receives a copy of the email and can update the firm's calendar.

Keep in mind that when writing emails to clients, you should never copy any other person on that email (either CC or BCC line) unless it is another person in your firm who is involved in the matter. This is because paralegals owe a duty of confidentiality to their clients under the *Paralegal Rules of Conduct*. Subject to certain exceptions, "a paralegal must, at all times, hold in strict confidence all information concerning the business and affairs of a client and shall not disclose any information."[1] Copying another person on an email to a client or to another person involved in a client's matter may breach this rule. Be careful when using BCC and CC.

---

1   Law Society of Ontario, *Paralegal Rules of Conduct* (1 October 2014; amendments current to 28 September 2017), Rule 3.03, online: <https://www.lsuc.on.ca/paralegal-conduct-rules>.

Types of Email Messages

Like letters, email messages come in many types. However, emails are usually much shorter than letters. Email is best used to send short messages—for example, to

- request documents from a client or opposing party,
- request a meeting,
- reply to a request for documents,
- reply to a request for a meeting,
- inform a client of a hearing date and location,
- deliver an interim account or final account,
- follow up on a previous email or letter, or
- provide a client with draft documents for review.

Figures 8.1, 8.2, and 8.3 show examples of some of these types of emails. Use these examples to practise your email writing skills by completing the in-chapter exercises below. When doing so, refer to Chapters 2 and 3 on grammar and style.

FIGURE 8.1   Sample Email Request to Client

> To: Vanessa Greenwood
>
> Date: August 27, 2017
>
> From: Lee Vu
>
> Subject: Lee Vu, Licensed Paralegal – Personal and Confidential
>
> ---
>
> Hello Ms. Greenwood,
>
> As discussed during our meeting yesterday, I am attaching your draft plaintiff's claim for your review.
>
> Kindly review the claim and advise me whether you would like any changes or clarifications.
>
> I look forward to hearing from you.
>
> Sincerely,
>
> Lee Vu
>
> ....
>
> Lee Vu, Licensed Paralegal
> 121 Bedford Avenue, Suite 101
> Toronto, ON M2P 3L9
> Tel: 416-978-5454
> Fax: 416-978-2222
> Email: lee@leevuparalegal.ca

FIGURE 8.2 **Sample Email to Client**

To: Saher Singh

Date: September 10, 2017

From: April Stone

Subject: Stone Paralegal Services – Personal and Confidential

---

Dear Ms. Singh,

I am attaching my invoice for services rendered between September 1, 2017 and September 30, 2017.

You will note that we applied the monies held in trust on your behalf to your account, leaving a balance owing of $1,233.54.

Kindly send a cheque payable to Stone Paralegal Services within the next 15 days.

Thank you for allowing us to assist you with your small claims court matter.

As always, please contact me if you have any questions or concerns.

Regards,

April

....

April Stone, Licensed Paralegal
Stone Paralegal Services
1500 Markham Road, Suite 202
Toronto, ON M3P 4L4
Tel: 416-777-0909
Fax: 416-777-8888
Email: april@stoneparalegalservices.ca

FIGURE 8.3   Sample Reply Email to Opposing Advocate

To: Kenneth Jones

Date: August 27, 2017

From: Jennifer Smith

Subject: Leone ats Buttle – Your File No. 16-3434

Dear Mr. Jones,

I am responding to your email dated August 26, 2017.

Please note that I will be meeting with my client on August 31, 2017 to sign the documents, and will courier them to your office shortly thereafter.

Thank you for your patience.

Regards,

Jennifer

....

Jennifer Smith
Licensed Paralegal
25 Burnaby Street
Toronto, ON M6M 2V2
Tel: 647-233-5959
Fax: 647-233-5000
Email: jennifer@smithparalegal.ca

Exercise 8.1

Write an Email to a Client

Using the details below, write an email to your client, Frances Hamlin, to request a meeting with her to discuss her upcoming hearing at the Human Rights Tribunal of Ontario ("HRTO"). Include an appropriate subject line and email signature. Make up any details regarding your contact information that are not included below.

- You are a licensed paralegal working for Littlewood Paralegal Services.
- Your address is 191 Wood Lane, Suite 450, Toronto, ON M2P 3L3.
- You would like to schedule a meeting with Ms. Hamlin to discuss her upcoming hearing.
- Frances applied to the HRTO alleging that she was discriminated against by her employer, LCK Consulting Services.
- Suggest a number of dates for the meeting.
- Ask her to bring copies of the emails from her employer.

Exercise 8.2

Write an Email to an Opposing Advocate

You are a licensed paralegal acting for a tenant, Mr. Viktor Jones, in a residential tenancies matter. A lawyer, Francesca Little, acts for the landlord who filed an application with the Landlord and Tenant Board ("LTB") to evict Mr. Jones. Write an email to Ms. Little requesting that she provide you with her and her client's available dates to schedule a hearing before the LTB. Include an appropriate subject line and email signature. Make up any details regarding your contact information that are not included below.

- The landlord's name is Jennifer Harrison.
- The address of the property is 1200 Restampton Road, Unit 1500, Toronto, ON M2R 3L3.
- Suggest available dates.
- Ask her to respond as soon as possible so that you can schedule the hearing with the LTB.
- Your address is 59 Littlewood Street, Toronto, ON M2X 3M3.

Exercise 8.3

Write an Email to an Opposing Advocate

You are a licensed paralegal acting for the plaintiff, Mr. Wilfred Sampson, in a small claims court matter. A paralegal, Kaitlyn Barry, represents the defendant, Karen Brown. You had a telephone conference scheduled with Ms. Barry two days ago at 4:30 p.m. to discuss the case. However, Ms. Barry was not available to speak at that time and the call was rescheduled to this afternoon at 2:00 p.m. Ms. Barry emailed you to confirm the call and advised that she would call you today at 2:00 p.m. However, when you did not receive a call at 2:00 p.m. you called her office and Ms. Barry's law clerk advised you that she was not in the office today. You need to speak to Ms. Barry because your client wants to finalize the outstanding issues before the end of the month. Using these facts, write an email to Ms. Barry. Include an appropriate subject line and email signature.

Exercise 8.4

Rewrite an Email to a Client

Below is an example of a poorly drafted email from a paralegal to her client regarding a scheduled settlement conference. Rewrite the email using effective style, correct grammar, and appropriate tone. Refer to Chapters 1–3 for guidance on grammar and style.

To: Brendan Watson   Date: November 15, 2017
From: Alexander LeBlanc
Subject: Hey!

Hey Brendan,

I'd thought I'd send you a quick note to let you know that you're settlement conference is scheduled for January 15, 2018 at 10 am at the Toronto Small Claims Court. Please be on time. You are required to be there. Last time I represented you for your speeding ticket you were late for the hearing and the judge was by all means not very impressed. We don't want that to happen again. The defendant and his lawyer will be there of course because they are required to be, but I'll handle them!

See you then!

Alex

P.S. DON'T FORGET TO BE ON TIME!

Exercise 8.5

Rewrite an Email to an Opposing Advocate

Below is an example of a poorly drafted email from a paralegal to the paralegal representing the opposing party in a small claims court matter. Rewrite the email using effective style, correct grammar, and appropriate tone. Make up any information needed to complete the exercise. Refer to Chapters 1–3 for guidance on grammar and style.

To: Lianne Jacobs   Date: November 20, 2017
From: Alexander LeBlanc
Subject: Last Email!

Lianne,

This is my LAST email to you. I've sent you my client's disclosure brief over 2 WEEKS AGO! Where is your client's brief? I have not received it. I have sent you email after email (Oct 25, Nov 1, Nov 13 and today) asking for it! When am I going to hear from you? Please don't make me have to bring a motion before the court compelling you to produce. The trial date is fast approproaching and I require your client's disclosure to prepare properly for the trial as per common sense and basic principles of law.

I await your immediate response or else I will have no choice.

Alex

Social Media

Social media is a communication tool that many lawyers and paralegals use as part of their practice. The general term *social media* refers to websites that allow users to connect with other users. Many websites also allow users to create and share content. Some examples are Twitter, Facebook, and LinkedIn.

Using social media can enhance business and professional development. For example, many lawyers and paralegals use social media to market their legal practice, educate the public about the law, and build relationships with other legal professionals.

Paralegals should use social media carefully. A paralegal's social media presence can affect his or her reputation. In addition, inappropriate use of social media may be considered professional misconduct under the *Paralegal Rules of Conduct* (the "Rules"), even though social media are not specifically mentioned in the Rules.

The following are some things to consider when using social media to communicate as a licensed paralegal:

- *Does your communication constitute marketing?* In presenting and promoting your practice, you must comply with the Rules regarding the marketing of legal services. For example, Rule 8.03(2) prohibits a paralegal from marketing legal services in a misleading, confusing, or deceptive manner. The marketing must also be demonstrably true, accurate, and verifiable. Ensure that your social media communications follow the Rules.

- *Are you inadvertently creating a paralegal–client relationship?* Be careful when communicating with third parties using social media, especially when engaging in conversations that involve answering legal questions. Social media users might assume that you represent them because of your conversation. Avoid giving any legal advice through social media platforms.

- *Does your communication disclose confidential information?* The Rules require paralegals to hold in strict confidence all information concerning the business and affairs of a client acquired in the course of their professional relationship. A simple communication about winning a client's case on social media may breach this duty, especially if a client has not consented to the disclosure.

- *Does your communication comment about particular judges or members of a tribunal?* Rule 6.01(2) of the Rules requires paralegals to "take care not to weaken or destroy public confidence in legal institutions or authorities by making irresponsible allegations or comments particularly when commenting on judges or members of a tribunal."[2] Paralegals have a broad obligation to encourage respect for the administration of justice. Do not make negative comments or allegations about judges on social media. In fact, avoid making any kind of comments about judges, adjudicators, opposing counsel, or colleagues. Otherwise, you risk breaching the Rules.

---

2 *Ibid*, Rule 6.01(2).

- *Have you considered the implications of your online communication before posting?* It is easy to react quickly and rashly to an online comment that we feel strongly about. Do yourself a favour and think long and hard about the implications of your response. Your response may be available online for a long time. A disrespectful online comment can negatively impact your personal reputation for many years.

- *Have you proofread your communication several times over?* Proper grammar, spelling, and tone are important when communicating through social media. The slightest spelling or grammar mistake may cause people to question your competence and professionalism. Always proofread your online communications before posting.

- *Does your communication bring discredit upon the paralegal profession?* If you use social media in your personal life (not as part of your firm marketing, etc.), consider the fact that your tweets (Twitter posts) or Facebook posts could create problems for you with the Law Society of Ontario (the "Law Society"). Rule 9.01(12) permits the Law Society to discipline a paralegal for "conduct unbecoming a paralegal," defined as "conduct in a paralegal's personal or private capacity that tends to bring discredit upon the paralegal profession."[3]

Summary

Email communication plays a significant role in legal practice. Lawyers and paralegals rely heavily on email to communicate quickly and effectively with clients, opposing advocates, and other third parties. When writing emails, a paralegal should ensure that each message includes an acceptable subject line, salutation, and closing. The message's body should also be clear, concise, and free of errors.

Social media can enhance a paralegal's career. Paralegals and lawyers use social media to share information, market their practice, and communicate with other legal professionals. If not used properly, however, social media communication can negatively affect a paralegal's reputation. Paralegals should learn how to communicate using social media in an ethical manner. This involves asking the questions discussed in this chapter and being familiar with a paralegal's professional obligations under the *Paralegal Rules of Conduct*.

---

3 *Ibid,* Rule 9.01(12).

Legal Forms

9

LEARNING OUTCOMES

After reading this chapter, you should be able to

- Understand the authorized areas of practice for paralegals.

- Understand the different kinds of legal forms.

- Complete legal forms using correct grammar and spelling and appropriate style.

- Proofread legal forms to identify and correct grammatical and stylistic problems.

Introduction

There are literally hundreds of forms involved in routine and non-routine legal transactions. This chapter covers a selection of those that paralegals are most likely to see and use in the course of their work. The scope of practice for licensed paralegals is limited. After a brief introduction to the areas in which paralegals can practice, this chapter will focus on a few selected forms in various areas of practice relevant to paralegals. In each case, a brief introductory narrative is followed by the forms.

Each of the forms in this chapter has a specific purpose; each one also has a number of general purposes, the most important being to transmit information inside and outside the paralegal practice. Completing these forms sometimes involves the use of skills learned earlier in this book, such as summarizing skills and developing effective legal arguments. Completing these forms also requires the excellent spelling and grammar skills, clarity, and accuracy that are trademarks of the legal profession. These forms are models of the forms that you will encounter in practice. Some forms have been completed to suggest proper formats, content, and context appropriate to each situation. Others have not been completed and are simply provided to show the layout and fields in the form. There are several in-chapter exercises that require completing various forms based on fact scenarios provided. When completing the exercises, remember the skills learned in previous chapters.

Paralegal Scope of Practice

Paralegals are regulated by the Law Society of Ontario ("LSO"). This means that paralegals must meet education and licensing requirements set by the LSO in order to practise law as a paralegal. A paralegal's conduct while licensed is also regulated by the LSO through various by-laws and rules including the *Paralegal Rules of Conduct*.[1]

The scope of practice for licensed paralegals is limited by the LSO. By-Law 4 of the LSO[2] allows paralegals to represent someone only before specific courts and tribunals:

1. Small Claims Court.
2. Ontario Court of Justice for proceedings under the *Provincial Offences Act*.[3]
3. Ontario Court of Justice for summary offences under the *Criminal Code*.[4]
4. Administrative Tribunals such as the Landlord and Tenant Board, the Human Rights Tribunal of Ontario, the Social Benefits Tribunal, and the Licence Appeal Tribunal.

---

1   Law Society of Ontario, *Paralegal Rules of Conduct* (1 October 2014; amendments current to 28 September 2017), online: <https://www.lsuc.on.ca/paralegal-conduct-rules>.
2   Law Society of Ontario, *By-Laws* (amendments current to 23 February 2017), By-Law 4, online: <https://www.lsuc.on.ca/uploadedFiles/By-Law-4-Licensing-02-23-17.pdf>.
3   RSO 1990, c P.33.
4   RSC 1985, c C-46.

Licensed paralegals can also represent clients in a limited area of immigration and refugee law, such as representing clients in a hearing before the Immigration and Refugee Board.

Paralegals cannot represent clients in the areas of real estate law, corporate law, wills and estates, or family law. Only lawyers can provide legal services in these areas. This means that paralegals cannot appear in the Ontario Superior Court of Justice (other than the Small Claims Court), nor can they represent a client in a family law proceeding, including a case in the Ontario Court of Justice.

However, the Ministry of the Attorney General and the Law Society of Ontario are currently considering whether paralegals should be allowed to practise in some areas of family law. In 2017, the Honourable Annemarie E. Bonkalo submitted a report to the Ministry of the Attorney General and the LSO recommending that a special licence be created to allow paralegals to provide certain types of family legal services. The Attorney General and the LSO are currently considering the report's recommendations.

Legal Forms

As legal documents, forms must be filled in accurately and completely. Attention to detail is of paramount importance. If a name is misspelled, an address is incorrect, or a piece of vital information is left out, your client could suffer legal or monetary consequences. Such errors may also raise questions about your competence as a paralegal and affect your reputation as a legal professional.

You will note that the forms presented in this chapter generally require the following information:

- Who?
- What?
- Where?
- When?
- Why?
- How?

Stylistically, the content of the legal forms should always be

- clear;
- concise;
- complete;
- correct; and
- consistent.

Examine the forms presented over the next several pages, noting their purposes, contents, and the specific details that make each unique.

Administrative Tribunals

Paralegals can represent clients before administrative tribunals. **Administrative tribunals** are independent quasi-judicial bodies established by legislation to implement legislative policy. They are specialized bodies that settle disputes involving government rules and regulations. Although they render decisions, administrative tribunals are not part of the court system.

There are hundreds of administrative tribunals in Ontario. Some examples are

- The Landlord and Tenant Board.
- The Human Rights Tribunal of Ontario.
- The Social Benefits Tribunal.
- The Licence Appeal Tribunal.
- The Criminal Injuries Compensation Board.
- The Law Society Tribunal.
- The Workplace and Safety Insurance Board.
- The Ontario Municipal Board.
- The Assessment Review Board.
- The Consent and Capacity Board.

The pages that follow deal with only a selection of forms from the Landlord and Tenant Board, the Human Rights Tribunal of Ontario, and the Licence Appeal Tribunal.

The Landlord and Tenant Board

The *Residential Tenancies Act, 2006*, SO 2006, c 17, establishes the Landlord and Tenant Board (the "LTB"). The LTB's role is to resolve disputes between residential landlords and tenants.

FIGURE 9.1   Residential Landlord and Tenant Scenario

Victoria Thomas lives at 202 – 15 Bartlett Street, Toronto, ON M3P 2L9. She rents the unit from the property owner, Alicia Lorrie. Alicia lives in unit 100 in the same property. Victoria signed a one-year lease in April 2017 and agreed to pay $1,200.00 in rent per month. Her tenancy started on March 1, 2017. Victoria has not paid rent to Alicia for two months. She missed the October 1 and November 1, 2017 payments. Alicia called Victoria approximately five times over the past two months asking her to pay the outstanding rent, but Victoria has not responded. Alicia wants to evict Victoria for non-payment of rent. However, she does not know whether she has to wait until the end of the one-year lease to evict her. In November, Alicia hires a licensed paralegal, Kevin Simpson, to assist her. He tells her that she can terminate the tenancy before the end of the one-year term for non-payment of rent.

The relevant sections of the *Residential Tenancies Act, 2002*, are the following:

Non-payment of rent

59 (1) If a tenant fails to pay rent lawfully owing under a tenancy agreement, the landlord may give the tenant notice of termination of the tenancy effective not earlier than,

(a) the 7th day after the notice is given, in the case of a daily or weekly tenancy; and

(b) the 14th day after the notice is given, in all other cases.

Contents of notice

(2) The notice of termination shall set out the amount of rent due and shall specify that the tenant may avoid the termination of the tenancy by paying, on or before the termination date specified in the notice, the rent due as set out in the notice and any additional rent that has become due under the tenancy agreement as at the date of payment by the tenant.

Notice void if rent paid

(3) The notice of termination is void if, before the day the landlord applies to the Board for an order terminating the tenancy and evicting the tenant based on the notice, the tenant pays,

(a) the rent that is in arrears under the tenancy agreement; and

(b) the additional rent that would have been due under the tenancy agreement as at the date of payment by the tenant had notice of termination not been given.

Source: *Residential Tenancies Act, 2006*, SO 2006, c 1, online: <https://www.canlii.org/en/on/laws/stat/so-2006-c-17/latest/so-2006-c-17.html>.

Kevin prepared the Notice of Termination (Figure 9.2) and the Application (Figure 9.3). Alicia hand delivered the Notice of Termination to Victoria on November 16, 2017.

Forms

The pages that follow show some of the LTB forms relevant to the Residential Landlord and Tenant matter in Figure 9.1.

FIGURE 9.2   Form N4: Notice to End Your Tenancy Early for Non-payment of Rent

Notice to End your Tenancy
For Non-payment of Rent
N4

To: (Tenant's name) include all tenant names	From: (Landlord's name)
VICTORIA THOMAS	ALICIA LORRIE

Address of the Rental Unit:

202 -15 BARTLETT STREET
TORONTO, ON M3P 2L9

This is a legal notice that could lead to you being evicted from your home.

The following information is from your landlord

I am giving you this notice because I believe you owe me $ | | 2 , 4 0 0 . 0 0 | **in rent.**

See the table on the next page for an explanation of how I calculated this amount.

I can apply to the Board to have you evicted if you do not:

- **pay this amount by** 3 0 / 1 1 / 2 0 1 7 . This is called the termination date.
  dd/mm/yyyy

Or

- **move out by the termination date.**

If another rent payment becomes due on or before the date you make the above payment to your landlord, you must also pay this extra amount.

WHAT YOU NEED TO KNOW

The following information is provided by the Landlord and Tenant Board

The termination date

The date that the landlord gives you in this notice to pay or move out must be at least:
- 14 days after the landlord gives you the notice, if you rent by the month or year, or
- 7 days after the landlord gives you the notice, if you rent by the day or week.

What if you agree with the notice?

If you agree that you owe the amount that the landlord is claiming, you should pay this amount by the termination date in this notice. If you do so, the landlord cannot apply to the Board to evict you based on this notice.

If you do not pay the amount owing, you do not have to move out. However, the landlord can apply to the Board to evict you. If the landlord applies to the Board to evict you and the Board orders the eviction, you will likely have to pay the landlord's filing fee, in addition to what you owe.

What if you disagree with the notice?

You do not have to move out if you disagree with this notice. You could talk to your landlord. You may also want to get legal advice. If you cannot work things out, the landlord may apply to the Board for an order to evict you. The Board will schedule a hearing where you can explain why you disagree.

What if you move out?

If you move out by the termination date in this notice, your tenancy will end on the termination date. However, you may still owe money to your landlord. Your landlord will not be able to apply to the Board but they may still take you to Court for this money.

v. 30/11/2015   Page 1 of 2

How will you know if the landlord applies to the Board?	The earliest date that the landlord can apply to the Board is the day after the termination date in this notice. If the landlord does apply, the Board will schedule a hearing and send you a copy of the application and the *Notice of Hearing*.
What you can do if the landlord applies to the Board	• Talk to your landlord about working out a payment plan. • Go to the hearing where you can respond to the claims your landlord makes in the application; in most cases, before the hearing starts you can also talk to a Board mediator about mediating a payment plan. • Get legal advice immediately; you may be eligible for legal aid services.
How to get more information	For more information about this notice or about your rights, you can contact the Landlord and Tenant Board. You can reach the Board by phone at **416-645-8080** or **1-888-332-3234**. You can also visit the Board's website at sjto.ca/LTB.

The following information is from your landlord

This table is completed by the landlord to show how they calculated the total amount of rent claimed on page 1:

Rent Period From: (dd/mm/yyyy)	To: (dd/mm/yyyy)	Rent Charged $	Rent Paid $	Rent Owing $
01/10/2017	31/10/2017	1,200.00	0.00	1,200.00
01/11/2017	30/11/2017	1,200.00	0.00	1,200.00
/ /	/ /	.	.	.
			Total Rent Owing $	2,400.00

Signature   ○ Landlord   ● Representative

First Name
K E V I N

Last Name
S I M P S O N

Phone Number
(4 1 6) 2 9 2 - 2 5 5 5

Signature

Date (dd/mm/yyyy)

Representative Information (if applicable)

Name KEVIN SIMPSON, LICENSED PARALEGAL	LSUC # P12334	Company Name (if applicable) SIMPSON PARALEGAL	
Mailing Address 1200 STEELES AVENUE WEST, SUITE 500		Phone Number 416-292-2555	
Municipality (City, Town, etc.) TORONTO	Province ON	Postal Code M2N 3Y1	Fax Number 416-292-0000

FIGURE 9.3 **Form L1: Application to Evict a Tenant for Non-payment of Rent and to Collect Rent the Tenant Owes**

Social Justice Tribunals Ontario
Providing fair and accessible justice
Landlord and Tenant Board

Application to Evict a Tenant for Non-payment of Rent and to Collect Rent the Tenant Owes
FORM L1

PART 1: ADDRESS OF THE RENTAL UNIT COVERED BY THIS APPLICATION

Street Number: 1 5

Street Name: B A R T L E T T

Street Type (e.g. Street, Avenue, Road): S T R E E T

Direction (e.g. East):

Unit/Apt./Suite: 2 0 2

Municipality (City, Town, etc.): T O R O N T O

Prov.: O N

Postal Code: M 3 P 2 L 9

PART 2: TOTAL AMOUNT THE TENANT OWES

The following information is from your landlord

I am applying to the Landlord and Tenant Board for an order:
- to evict you because you owe rent, and
- to collect the money you owe me.

I believe that you owe me a total of $ 2 , 5 9 0 . 0 0 as of 0 1 / 1 2 / 2 0 1 7 .
dd/mm/yyyy

This amount includes the filing fee for this application. **You may also owe me any new rent that comes due after I file this application.** To see how I calculated this amount, go to page 5.

The following information is from the Landlord and Tenant Board

IF YOU AGREE with the amount the landlord claims you owe:

If you agree with the amount the landlord claims you owe, you can pay everything you owe or work out a payment plan. However, read the options before you decide. You may want to get legal advice first.

OPTION 1:
Pay everything you owe

If you pay all the rent you owe plus the landlord's filing fee before the Board issues an order about this application, the landlord will not be able to evict you for not paying the rent.

The amount you have to pay includes:

- the amount set out above that the landlord is claiming in this application, plus
- any new rent that has come due after the landlord filed this application.

You can pay these amounts to the landlord directly, or to the Board in trust. Be sure to get a receipt for any amounts you pay to the landlord.

Go to the hearing, where you can tell the Board what you've paid. If the landlord gave you receipts for amounts you paid, bring them to the hearing.

OPTION 2:
Work out a payment plan

If you cannot pay everything you owe right now, you can talk to your landlord to see if they are willing to work out a payment plan.

If you and the landlord agree to a payment plan, go to the hearing where you can explain the payment plan to the Board.

OFFICE USE ONLY

File Number:

v. 16/01/2017

Page 1 of 6

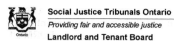

Social Justice Tribunals Ontario
Providing fair and accessible justice
Landlord and Tenant Board

**Application to Evict a Tenant for Non-payment of Rent
and to Collect Rent the Tenant Owes
FORM L1**

OPTION 2: **Work out a** **payment** **plan -** **continued**	The Board also has a *Payment Agreement* form that you and your landlord can fill out and file with the Board before the hearing. If you or your landlord files the *Payment Agreement* form with the Board before the hearing, the Board can issue a consent order without holding a hearing. The consent order will be based on the payment plan set out in the *Payment Agreement* form. If the Board issues the consent order, you will **not** have to go to the hearing. However, if the Board has not issued a consent order by the date of the hearing, go to the hearing.

IF YOU DO NOT AGREE with the amount the landlord claims you owe:

Talk to your landlord to see if both of you can agree on a different amount. You may want to get legal advice first.

If you and **your landlord** **agree on a** **different** **amount**	If you and your landlord can agree on the amount you owe, read the options above called **Pay everything you owe** and **Work out a payment plan**. You can follow one of these options, but use the different amount you and your landlord have agreed on. Go to the hearing unless the Board has issued a consent order based on a *Payment Agreement*.
If you and **your landlord** **do not agree** **on a different** **amount**	If you and your landlord cannot agree on the amount you owe, go to the hearing, and, at the hearing, explain why you disagree with the amount the landlord claims you owe. If the Board decides that you owe money, you can ask for more time to pay it.
Go to the **hearing**	As described in this form, there are different options for dealing with the claims your landlord made in this application depending on whether or not you agree with the amount the landlord claims you owe. However, whatever you choose to do, it is important to go to the hearing. The date, time and location of the hearing are shown on the Notice of Hearing that is attached to this application. (Exception: you do not have to attend the hearing if, before the hearing date, the Board issues a consent order based on a *Payment Agreement* form - however, if you and your landlord filled out the *Payment Agreement* form and you haven't received the consent order by the hearing date, go to the hearing.) At the hearing, the landlord will have to prove the claims they made in the application and the *Notice to End your Tenancy*. You will have an opportunity to respond to the landlord's application. For example, you can explain why you disagree with the amount the landlord claimed you owe, or explain why you think you should not be evicted. You can also ask the Board for more time to pay the money you owe. If you have paid everything you owe before the hearing, or if you and your landlord have worked out a payment plan, you can tell the Board at the hearing. You can also raise other issues such as maintenance problems or harassment. If you plan to raise other issues at the hearing, it is important that you bring evidence to support your case. If the Board accepts your evidence, the Board may order the landlord to pay you money. If you owe arrears of rent, this may reduce the amount you owe.
Mediation is **available**	If you would like to resolve this application by mediation instead of the formal hearing process, in most cases you can speak to a Board mediator on the day of your hearing.
After the **hearing**	The Board will make a decision and issue an order that will be sent to you by mail. The order will tell you what the Board decided, including what you have to pay. You should read the order to be sure it is correct and that you understand it.

For more information:

You can contact the Landlord and Tenant Board at **416-645-8080** or toll-free at **1-888-332-3234** or visit the Board's website at sjto.ca/LTB.

FIGURE 9.3 **Continued**

Social Justice Tribunals Ontario
Providing fair and accessible justice
Landlord and Tenant Board

Application to Evict a Tenant for Non-payment of Rent and to Collect Rent the Tenant Owes
FORM L1

THE LANDLORD'S APPLICATION

Read the instructions carefully before completing this form. Print or type in capital letters.

PART 3: GENERAL INFORMATION

Landlord's Name and Address

First Name (If there is more than 1 landlord, complete a *Schedule of Parties* form and file it with this application.)

ALICIA

Last Name

LORRIE

Company Name (if applicable)

Street Address

15 BARTLETT STREET

Unit/Apt./Suite: 100   Municipality (City, Town, etc.): TORONTO   Prov.: ON   Postal Code: M3P2L9

Day Phone Number: (647) 222-1514   Evening Phone Number: ( ) -   Fax Number: ( ) -

E-mail Address

ALORRIE@GMAIL.COM

Tenant Names and Address

Tenant 1: First Name (If there are more than 2 tenants, complete a *Schedule of Parties* form and file it with this application.)

VICTORIA

Tenant 1: Last Name

THOMAS

Tenant 2: First Name

Tenant 2: Last Name

Mailing Address (if it is different from the address of the rental unit)

15 BARTLETT STREET

Unit/Apt./Suite: 202   Municipality (City, Town, etc.): TORONTO   Prov.: ON   Postal Code: M3P2L9

Day Phone Number: (647) 988-2929   Evening Phone Number: ( ) -   Fax Number: ( ) -

E-mail Address

VTHOMAS@SIMPATICO.CA

Related Applications

If you or your tenant filed other applications that relate to this rental unit and those applications have not been resolved, list their file numbers below.

File Number 1

File Number 2

Page 3 of 6

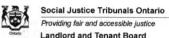

Social Justice Tribunals Ontario

Providing fair and accessible justice

Landlord and Tenant Board

Application to Evict a Tenant for Non-payment of Rent and to Collect Rent the Tenant Owes

FORM L1

PART 4: REASONS FOR YOUR APPLICATION

Shade the box completely next to each reason on which you based this application.

I am applying for an order to end the tenancy and evict the tenant and to collect:

☒ the rent the tenant owes me up to the date they move out of the rental unit, and

☐ an amount for charges related to NSF cheques the tenant gave me.

The tenant must be in possession of the rental unit when you file this application. Shade the circle completely to answer whether or not the tenant is still in possession of the rental unit on the date you file this application.

⦿ Yes   ◯ No   If you answer no, you cannot file this application

Shade the circle completely to show whether the tenant is required to pay rent by the:

⦿ month   ◯ week   ◯ other (specify) _____

The amount of rent currently on deposit: $ [ ][ ][ ][ ][ ] . [ ][ ]

The date the rent deposit was collected: [ ][ ] / [ ][ ] / [ ][ ][ ][ ]
dd/mm/yyyy

The last rental period for which the tenant was paid interest on the rent deposit: [ ][ ] / [ ][ ] / [ ][ ][ ][ ] **to** [ ][ ] / [ ][ ] / [ ][ ][ ][ ]
dd/mm/yyyy   dd/mm/yyyy

PART 5: DETAILS OF THE LANDLORD'S CLAIM

Section 1. Rent Owing

I have calculated the amount of rent the tenant owes me as follows:

Rent Period From: (dd/mm/yyyy)	To: (dd/mm/yyyy)	Rent Charged $	Rent Paid $	Rent Owing $
0 1 / 1 0 / 2 0 1 7	3 1 / 1 0 / 2 0 1 7	1 , 2 0 0 . 0 0	0 . 0 0	1 , 2 0 0 . 0 0
0 1 / 1 1 / 2 0 1 7	3 0 / 1 1 / 2 0 1 7	1 , 2 0 0 . 0 0	0 . 0 0	1 , 2 0 0 . 0 0
/ /	/ /	.	.	.

Total Rent Owing $ [ ] 2 , 4 0 0 . 0 0

Section 2. NSF Cheque Charges

Fill in the table below if you are applying to collect money from the tenant because you had bank or administration charges for NSF cheques the tenant gave you.

I have calculated the amount of NSF bank charges and my related administration charges the tenant owes me as follows:

Cheque Amount $	Date of Cheque dd/mm/yyyy	Date NSF Charge Incurred dd/mm/yyyy	Bank Charge for NSF Cheque $	Landlord's Administration Charge $	Total Charge $
.	/ /	/ /	.	.	.
.	/ /	/ /	.	.	.
.	/ /	/ /	.	.	.

Total NSF Related Charges Owing $ [ ][ ][ ][ ][ ] . [ ][ ]

Attach additional sheets if necessary.

Page 4 of 6

FIGURE 9.3 **Continued**

Social Justice Tribunals Ontario
Providing fair and accessible justice
Landlord and Tenant Board

Application to Evict a Tenant for Non-payment of Rent and to Collect Rent the Tenant Owes
FORM L1

PART 6: TOTAL AMOUNT OWING

Total rent owing:
(from Part 5, Section 1)

$ 2 , 4 0 0 . 0 0

Total NSF cheque related charges owing:
(from Part 5, Section 2)

$.

Application Fee:

$ 1 9 0 . 0 0

Total: $ 2 , 5 9 0 . 0 0

PART 7: SIGNATURE

Landlord/Representative's Signature

/ /
dd/mm/yyyy

Who has signed the application? Shade the circle completely next to your answer.

○ Landlord   ◉ Representative

Information About the Representative

First Name
K E V I N

Last Name
S I M P S O N

LSUC #   Company Name (if applicable)
P 1 2 3 4   S I M P S O N   P A R A L E G A L

Mailing Address
1 2 0 0   S T E E L E S   A V E   E A S T

Unit/Apt./Suite   Municipality (City, Town, etc.)   Prov.   Postal Code
5 0 0   T O R O N T O   O N   M 2 N 3 Y 1

Day Phone Number   Evening Phone Number   Fax Number
(4 1 6) 2 9 2 - 2 5 5 5   ( ) -   (4 1 6) 2 9 2 - 0 0 0 0

E-mail Address

Page 5 of 6

FIGURE 9.4   Certificate of Service

Social Justice Tribunals Ontario
Providing fair and accessible justice
Landlord and Tenant Board

Certificate of Service

File Number ☐☐☐☐☐☐☐☐☐☐

Address of Rental Unit:

Unit /Apt. /Suite: | Street Address:

Municipality (City, Town, etc): | Postal Code:

I, _____ , **certify that on** ☐☐ / ☐☐ / ☐☐☐☐ ,
dd/mm/yyyy

I gave a copy of the following document(s):
☐ Notice of Termination Form # _____
☐ Application Form # _____
☐ Notice of Hearing
☐ Motion to Set Aside an Ex Parte Order
☐ Request to Review an Order
☐ Other _____
(insert name of document)

to the following person(s):
○ the tenant   ○ the landlord   ○ other

_____
(insert the name of the person you gave the document to)
○ more than one tenant, who is a party to the same application, on the same date and in the same way.
   (If you shade this circle, attach a list of the names and addresses of the people you served.)

by the following method of service:
○ handing the document(s) to the person(s).
○ handing the document(s) to an authorized employee of the landlord.
○ handing the document(s) to an adult person in the tenant's rental unit.
○ leaving the document(s) in the mailbox, or place where mail is normally delivered.
○ placing the document(s) under the door of the rental unit or through a mail slot in the door.
○ sending the document(s) by courier to the person(s).
○ sending the document(s) by fax to fax number: _____
○ sending the document(s) by mail or Xpresspost to the last known address of the person(s), at:

○ a different method of service (provide details)

Notes:
1. The only document that can be properly served by posting it to the door of the rental unit is a notice of intent to enter a rental unit given under section 27 of the *Residential Tenancies Act, 2006*, unless a Member orders otherwise pursuant to the Landlord and Tenant Board's Rules of Practice.
2. It is an offence under the *Residential Tenancies Act, 2006* to file false or misleading information with the Landlord and Tenant Board.

Signature   ○ Landlord   ○ Tenant   ○ Representative   ○ Other
First Name

Last Name

Phone Number
(___) ___ - ___

v. 30/11/2015

Signature (the person who served the documents must sign the form) | Date (dd/mm/yyyy)

OFFICE USE ONLY:
Delivery Method: ○ In Person ○ Mail ○ Courier ○ Email ○ Efile ○ Fax   FL ☐☐

Under section 185 of the *Residential Tenancies Act, 2006*, the Landlord and Tenant Board has the right to collect the personal information requested on this form. We use the information to resolve your application. After you file the form, your information may also be available to the public. If you have questions about how the Board uses your personal information, contact one of our Customer Service Officers at **416-645-8080** or **1-888-332-3234 (toll free)**.

EXERCISE 9.1

Complete a Certificate of Service

Using the facts in Figure 9.1 and the completed forms in Figures 9.2 and 9.3, complete the Certificate of Service form in Figure 9.4 for the service of the Notice of Termination on Victoria.

The Human Rights Tribunal of Ontario

The Human Rights Tribunal of Ontario ("HRT") is established under the *Human Rights Code*, RSO 1990, c H.19 (the "Code") to resolve claims of discrimination and harassment brought under the Code.

FIGURE 9.5   Human Rights Scenario

Sharon Lingh is a 72-year-old woman who lives in Toronto. About two years ago, Sharon joined a social club in Toronto, the Pineridge Senior Association, as a member. Over the past year, Association Council members confronted her on two occasions about her beliefs in Raelism. The members did not know that she practised Raelism before she joined. Raelism is a movement whose members believe that life on Earth was scientifically created by extraterrestial beings. Sharon has practised Raelism for approximately three years. She considers it to be of great importance to her, and she credits it with improving her physical and emotional health. Six months ago, Sharon attended a breakfast organized by the Association. One of the Council members, Victor Hee, asked her how she kept herself in such good health. Sharon told him that she practised Raelism. An argument then took place about the merits of Raelism. According to Sharon, Victor yelled, "Only crazy people practise Raelism. We cannot let it infiltrate our society or else our kids will disappear!" Two weeks after this event, the Association's President, Liam Smith, called Sharon to advise her that Council had revoked her membership in the Association. When Sharon asked him why, he said, "Raelism is an evil sickness." These incidents and the ultimate decision to revoke her membership have had a serious emotional impact on Sharon. Before her membership was revoked, she had made more than 30 friends through the Association's activities. Now that she is no longer a member, none of these people speak to her anymore. She feels embarrassed and believes that this treatment and the Council's decision damaged her dignity and reputation in the community. She feels shame, which has resulted in a decrease in appetite and problems sleeping.

The HRT forms relevant to the Human Rights Scenario in Figure 9.5 above can be found online. Complete the following exercise using the appropriate online legal form.

EXERCISE 9.2

Prepare an Application to the Human Rights Tribunal of Ontario (Form 1)

You are a licensed paralegal representing clients in human rights matters. You work for VT Paralegal Services, 233 Birch Street, Toronto, ON M2L 3M3. Your licence number is P3232. Sharon comes to you for assistance. She feels the Pineridge Senior Association discriminated against her and she wants to file an application with the HRT for an order granting her $5,000.00 in damages for injury to her dignity. She also thinks Council members should be ordered to undergo cultural sensitivity training and that the Association should develop policies to prevent discrimination.

Using the facts in Figure 9.5 and the relevant law, prepare an application to the HRT on Sharon's behalf. The application form appears online. Make up any information that you require to complete the form but do not have.

In order to complete the form accurately, you will need to familiarize yourself with the *Human Rights Code*.[5] The website of the Ontario Human Rights Commission is also helpful.[6]

The Licence Appeal Tribunal

The Licence Appeal Tribunal ("LAT") is established under the *Licence Appeal Tribunal Act, 1999*, SO 1999, c 12, Sch G. It hears appeals and resolves disputes relating to a number of different matters including liquor licences, motor vehicle impoundment, and, most recently, accident benefits.

Forms

As of April 1, 2016, LAT adjudicates all new accident benefits disputes under the Statutory Accident Benefits Schedule.[7] These matters involve a dispute between an individual and an insurance company over accident benefits.

Several forms relating to applications to LAT under the Statutory Accident Benefits Schedule can be found online. Figure 9.6 shows one of those relevant forms—the Declaration of Representative.

---

5 *Human Rights Code*, RSO 1990, c H.19, online: <https://www.canlii.org/en/on/laws/stat/rso-1990 -c-h19/latest/rso-1990-c-h19.html>.

6 Ontario Human Rights Commission, online: <http://www.ohrc.on.ca/en>

7 O Reg 34/10.

FIGURE 9.6   Declaration of Representative

Ontario

Safety, Licensing Appeals and
Standards Tribunals Ontario
Licence Appeal Tribunal

Declaration of Representative

Automobile Accident Benefits Service

Mailing Address: 77 Wellesley St. W.,
Box 250, Toronto ON M7A 1N3

In-Person Service: 20 Dundas St. W.,
Suite 530, Toronto ON M5G 2C2

Tel.:   416-314-4260
         1-800-255-2214
TTY: 416-916-0548
         1-844-403-5906
Fax: 416-325-1060
         1-844-618-2566

Website: www.slasto.gov.on.ca/en/AABS

Important Information

- If you have a representative for a matter before the Tribunal, have them fill in this form clearly and completely and provide it to the Tribunal **and** all other parties immediately (available at www.slasto.gov.on.ca/en/AABS).

- Only persons licensed by the Law Society of Upper Canada (LSUC) **or** who fall within the exceptions or exemptions approved by the LSUC may represent a party before the Tribunal.

- For the current list of exemptions for unlicenced representatives, visit the LSUC website at www.lsuc.on.ca or contact them at 416 947-3300 or toll-free 1 800 668-7380.

Tribunal File No.

Representative Information

Last Name	First Name	Initial

Company Name

Address

Unit Number	Street Number	Street Name	PO Box

City/Town	Province	Postal Code
	▼	

Telephone Number	Fax Number

Declaration of Representative

I am representing:

Name of Party:

Last Name	First Name

OR

I am representing:

Name of Insurance Company

Before the Licence Appeal Tribunal in the matter of

Name of Applicant:

Last Name	First Name

and Name of Respondent:

Last Name	First Name

Acknowledgement

check one

☐ I acknowledge that I am licensed by the Law Society of Upper Canada (LSUC) to provide legal services.

My LSUC No. is

☐ I acknowledge I am an unlicensed representative covered by an exemption allowed by the LSUC.

The exemption I fall under is

Last Name	First Name

Signature

Signature of Representative	Date (yyyy/mm/dd)

The Licence Appeal Tribunal collects the personal information requested on this form under section 3 of the *Licence Appeal Tribunal Act, 1999*. This information will be used to determine appeals under this Act. After an appeal is filed, all information may become available to the public. Any questions about this collection may be directed to the Licence Appeal Tribunal at 416 314-4260 or toll-free at 1 800 255-2214.

Clear Form   Print Form

EXERCISE 9.3

Prepare a Declaration of Representative

You represent Marion DeSousa. Marion was injured in a car accident on September 1 of last year. Her insurer, Plate State Inc., denied her application for statutory accident benefits as provided for under the *Statutory Accident Benefits Schedule*, O Reg 34/10. Marion has retained you to file an appeal with the Licence Appeal Tribunal to resolve her dispute with Plate State Inc. You must deliver a Declaration of Representative form to the Tribunal and all other parties to notify them that you are representing Marion. Based on this information, prepare this form, found in Figure 9.6. You can make up any information that has not been provided.

Litigation (Small Claims Court)

The Small Claims Court is a branch of the Ontario Superior Court of Justice that hears civil claims for up to and including $25,000.00. Civil claims over $25,000.00 must be heard in the Ontario Superior Court of Justice. Recall that paralegals can appear in Small Claims Court but not in the Ontario Superior Court of Justice. Each of these courts has its own procedural rules. Civil proceedings in the Superior Court are governed by the *Rules of Civil Procedure*,[8] while civil proceedings in the Small Claims Court are governed by the *Rules of the Small Claims Court*.[9]

FIGURE 9.7 Small Claims Scenario

On August 25, 2017, plaintiff Danny Gill brought suit against defendants My Gas Bar and Gas Bar Limited. He claims that when he stopped on their property to buy gas, he slipped on black ice and fell, sustaining serious personal injuries. The plaintiff's paralegal, Linda Hawthorne, prepared the Plaintiff's Claim and served it on the defendants on August 27, 2017, in accordance with the *Rules of the Small Claims Court*. Linda hired a process server, Dan Smith (of the City of Toronto), to serve the defendants. On August 27, 2017, he left a copy of the Plaintiff's Claim with Neil Simmons, President of 99999 Ontario Inc. (My Gas Bar), at its head office. He also left a copy of the Plaintiff's Claim with Suzanne Foster, assistant, at Gas Bar Limited. On September 14, the plaintiff offered to settle the action out of court.

Forms

Figures 9.8 through 9.11 show the forms involved in the Small Claims Scenario described in Figure 9.7. The first three forms have been completed for you.

---

8   RRO 1990, Reg 194.
9   O Reg 258/98.

FIGURE 9.8   **Plaintiff's Claim**

ONTARIO
Superior Court of Justice

Plaintiff's Claim
Form 7A Ont. Reg. No.: 258/98

Ontario
Small Claims Court

Claim No.

Seal

47 Sheppard Avenue East
Toronto, ON M2N 5N1

Address

416-326-3554
Phone number

Plaintiff No. 1   ☒ Additional plaintiff(s) listed on attached Form 1A.   ☐ Under 18 years of age.

Last name, or name of company		
Gill		
First name	Second name	Also known as
Danny		
Address (street number, apt., unit)		
29 Princess Avenue		
City/Town	Province	Phone no.
Toronto	**ON**	
Postal code		Fax no.
M2P 3E3		
Representative		LSUC #
Linda Hawthorne		**P12221**
Address (street number, apt., unit)		
2100 Yonge Street, Suite 400		
City/Town	Province	Phone no.
Toronto	**ON**	**416-299-8000**
Postal code		Fax no.
M3L 4T5		**416-299-7000**

Defendant No. 1   ☒ Additional defendant(s) listed on attached Form 1A.   ☐ Under 18 years of age.

Last name, or name of company		
99999 Ontario Inc. carrying on business as My Gas Bar		
First name	Second name	Also known as
Address (street number, apt., unit)		
999 North Street		
City/Town	Province	Phone no.
Toronto	**ON**	**647-455-3000**
Postal code		Fax no.
M2P 5K5		
Representative		LSUC #
Address (street number, apt., unit)		
City/Town	Province	Phone no.
Postal code		Fax no.

Les formules des tribunaux sont affichées en anglais et en français sur le site www.ontariocourtforms.on.ca. Visitez ce site pour des renseignements sur des formats accessibles.

SCR 7.01-7A (November 1, 2016) CSD

Continued on next page

FIGURE 9.8 Continued

FORM 7A   PAGE 2   -------------------------------
                                                              Claim No.

REASONS FOR CLAIM AND DETAILS

Explain what happened, including where and when. Then explain how much money you are claiming or what goods you want returned.

If you are relying on any documents, you **MUST** attach copies to the claim. If evidence is lost or unavailable, you **MUST** explain why it is not attached.

What happened?
Where?
When?

1. The Plaintiff claims:

(a) Special damages in the amount of $8,000.00;

(b) General damages in the amount of $10,000.00;

(c) Pre-judgment interest pursuant to Section 128 of the Courts of Justice Act, RSO 1990, c C.43;

(d) The costs of this action, and HST on costs; and

(e) Such further and other relief as this Honourable Court deems just.

2. The Plaintiff waives any amounts over $25,000.00.

3. The Plaintiff resides in the City of Toronto.

4. The Defendant, 99999 Ontario Inc., carrying on business as My Gas Bar, is a corporation incorporated under the law of the Province of Ontario with its head office in the City of Toronto, in the Province of Ontario and at all material times was an occupier of a service station at 999 North Street, in Toronto (the service station).

5. The Defendant, Gas Bar Limited, is a corporation incorporated under the laws of the Province of Ontario with its head office at the City of Toronto, in the Province of Ontario, and was at all material times the owner and occupier of the service station.

6. On Saturday, March 14, 2016, the Plaintiff stopped at the service station to buy gasoline.

7. The Plaintiff parked his vehicle at the northern-most filling island and put gasoline into his vehicle.

8. After pumping gasoline, the Plaintiff walked backed to his vehicle around the northern side of the filling island, to go into the service station office to pay.

9. As the Plaintiff walked past the filling island, he suddenly slipped and fell on black ice, suffering serious personal injuries.

10. The Plaintiff states that the incident occurred as a result of the negligence, breach of contract and the breach of the Occupiers' Liability Act of the Defendants, and the servants, agents and employees of these Defendants, the particulars of which are as follows:

SCR 7.01-7A (November 1, 2016) CSD   **Continued on next page**

FORM 7A   PAGE 3

                                                               Claim No.

(a) They failed to see that the service station was reasonably safe for persons entering it;

(b) They failed to keep the service station free of ice and snow;

(c) They failed to sand or salt the area around the filling island at the service station;

(d) They failed to regularly inspect the area around the filling island to ensure that it was kept in a safe condition for people using the service station;

(e) They knew or should have known that ice was likely to form given the weather conditions that prevailed on the day of the incident;

(f) They failed to take reasonable care, or any care, to ensure that the Plaintiff, Danny Gill, would be reasonably safe while using the service station;

(g) They premitted or allowed ice to accumulate on the paved surface surrounding the filling island, thereby creating a danger and a trap to persons using the service station;

(h) They failed to take reasonable steps, or any steps, to implement a program or a procedure for the routine removal of ice from the service station;

(i) They employed incompetent servants, agents and employees;

(j) They failed to instruct properly, or at all, their servants, agents, or employees in the proper methods and procedures to be followed to prevent the accumulation of ice;

(k) They failed to supervise properly, or at all, the removal of ice;

(l) They caused or prevented the area where the Plaintiff was walking to become or to remain a danger and a trap to the Plaintiff;

(m) They had at the service station salt and sand available for use, but failed to apply it;

(n) They failed to take such care as in all the circumstances was reasonable to see that the Plaintiff was safe while on the premises.

11. As a result of this incident, the Plaintiff suffered serious, lasting and permanent personal injuries including a fracture of the right distal tibia into the ankle joint and tearing of the muscles, tendons, ligaments in the lower right extremity.

12. As a result of the incident, the Plaintiff also suffered headaches, dizziness, shock, anxiety, depression, emotional trauma, insomnia, weakness, diminished energy and stiffness, which continue to the present.

13. The Plaintiff sustained and will continue to sustain pain and suffering, loss of enjoymnet of life and loss of amenities.

14. The Plaintiff was unable to participate in recreational, social, household and athletic activities to the extent which he participated in such activities prior to the incident.

 For information on accessibility of court services for people with disability-related needs, contact:
Telephone: 416-326-2220 / 1-800-518-7901   TTY: 416-326-4012 / 1-877-425-0575

SCR 7.01-7A (November 1, 2016) CSD

FIGURE 9.8   Continued

FORM 7A   PAGE 4   _____
                                                         Claim No.

15. The Plaintiff's ability to walk on slopes and uneven ground is impaired because of the incident.

16. As a further result of the incident, the Plaintiff has undergone and will continue to undergo in the future, hospitalization, therapy, and rehabilitation. In addition, the Plaintiff has received and will continue to receive medication.

17. The Plaintiff has also incurred and will continue to incur expenses, including expenses for hospitalization, medication, therapy, rehabilitation, home care, the use of special equipment, medical treatment, and other forms of care, the full particulars of which are not within the Plaintiff's knowledge at this time.

18. The Plaintiff has sustained a loss of income.

19. The Plaintiff is unable to perform handyman chores and housekeeping tasks for himself to the extent he was able to do so before the accident and reuslting injuries, and he will require assistance in the future to complete such chores and tasks.

20. As a result of the negligence, breach of contract, and breach of the Occupiers' Liability Act of the Defendants, the Plaintiff has suffered other pecuniary damages up to the present and will continue to suffer pecuniary damages in the future, the full particulars of which are not known at this time.

21. The Plaintiff pleads and relies upon the Occupiers' Liability Act, RSO 1990, c O.2 as amended, and specifically, Section 3 thereof.

22. The Plaintiff pleads and relies upon the Negligence Act, RSO 1990, c N.1 as amended, and specifically, Section 1 thereof.

23. The Plaintiff proposes that this action be tried in the City of Toronto, in the Province of Ontario.

  For information on accessibility of court services for people with disability-related needs, contact:
Telephone: 416-326-2220 / 1-800-518-7901   TTY: 416-326-4012 / 1-877-425-0575

SCR 7.01-7A (November 1, 2016) CSD

How much? $ ....20,000.00.....................

(Principal amount claimed)

☒   **ADDITIONAL PAGES ARE ATTACHED BECAUSE MORE ROOM WAS NEEDED.**

The plaintiff also claims pre-judgment interest from March 14, 2017   under:

(Date)

(Check only   ☒ **the *Courts of Justice Act***
one box)
                     ☐ **an agreement at the rate of** _____ **% per year**

and post-judgment interest, and court costs.

Prepared on: **August 25,**   , 20 **17**   _____

(Signature of plaintiff or representative)

Issued on: _____ , 20 _____   _____

(Signature of clerk)

CAUTION TO DEFENDANT:	**IF YOU DO NOT FILE A DEFENCE** (Form 9A) and an Affidavit of Service (Form 8A) with the court within twenty (20) calendar days after you have been served with this Plaintiff's Claim, judgment may be obtained without notice and enforced against you. Forms and self-help materials are available at the Small Claims Court and on the following website: www.ontariocourtforms.on.ca.
CAUTION TO PARTIES:	Unless the court orders or the rules provide otherwise, **THIS ACTION WILL BE AUTOMATICALLY DISMISSED** if it has not been disposed of by order or otherwise two (2) years after it was commenced and a trial date or assessment under subrule 11.03(2) has not been requested.

FIGURE 9.9 **Additional Parties**

ONTARIO
Superior Court of Justice   PAGE 1A   **Additional Parties**
                                                                           Form 1A Ont. Reg. No.: 258/98

                                                                           _____
                                                                                    Claim No.

☐ **Plaintiff No.**   ☒ **Defendant No. 2**

Last name, or name of company **Gas Bar Limited**		
First name	Second name	Also known as
Address (street number, apt., unit) **111 Gasoline Alley West**		
City/Town **Toronto**	Province **ON**	Phone no. **647-788-3300**
Postal code **M5W 1A3**		Fax no.
Representative		LSUC #
Address (street number, apt., unit)		
City/Town	Province	Phone no.
Postal code		Fax no.

☐ **Plaintiff No.**   ☐ **Defendant No.**

Last name, or name of company		
First name	Second name	Also known as
Address (street number, apt., unit)		
City/Town	Province	Phone no.
Postal code		Fax no.
Representative		LSUC #
Address (street number, apt., unit)		
City/Town	Province	Phone no.
Postal code		Fax no.

☐ **Plaintiff No.**   ☐ **Defendant No.**

Last name, or name of company		
First name	Second name	Also known as
Address (street number, apt., unit)		
City/Town	Province	Phone no.
Postal code		Fax no.
Representative		LSUC #
Address (street number, apt., unit)		
City/Town	Province	Phone no.
Postal code		Fax no.

SCR 1.05-1A (January 23, 2014) CSD

FIGURE 9.10   Offer to Settle

ONTARIO
Superior Court of Justice

Offer to Settle
Form 14A Ont. Reg. No.: 258/98

Ontario
Small Claims Court

SC-17-2459
Claim No.

47 Sheppard Avenue East
Toronto, ON M2N 5N1
Address

416-326-3554
Phone number

BETWEEN

Danny Gill
Plaintiff(s)

and
99999 Ontairo Inc. carrying on business as My Gas Bar, and
Gas Bar Limited
Defendant(s)

My name is Danny Gill
(Full name)

1.   In this action, I am the

☒ Plaintiff

☐ Defendant

☐ representative of _____
(Name of party(ies))

the defendants, 99999 Ontario Inc. carrying on business as My Gas

2.   I offer to settle this action against **Bar, and Gas Bar Limited**
(Name of party(ies))

on the following terms: *(Set out terms in numbered paragraphs, or on an attached sheet.)*

1. The Defendants shall pay to the Plaintiff the sum of $18,000.00 for damages;

2. The Defendants will pay to the Plaintiff prejudgment interest on the aforesaid amount pursuant to the Courts of Justice Act, RSO 1990, c C.43, as amended;

3. The Defendants will pay special damages in the amount of $1,125.14, representing the amounts paid for treatment to the Ministry of Health under the Ontario Hospital Insurance Plan; and

4. The parties shall bear their own costs.

Les formules des tribunaux sont affichées en anglais et en français sur le site www.ontariocourtforms.on.ca. Visitez ce site pour des renseignements sur des formats accessibles.

SCR 14.01.1-14A (January 23, 2014) CSD

FIGURE 9.10   Continued

FORM 14A   PAGE 2   SC-17-2459
                                                                    ....
                                                                         Claim No.

3.   This offer to settle is available for acceptance until __October 1_____ , 20 __17__ .

This offer to settle may be accepted by serving an acceptance of offer to settle (Form 14B may be used) on the party who made it, at any time before it is withdrawn or before the court disposes of the claim to which the offer applies [R. 14.05(1)]. You can get forms at court offices or online at www.ontariocourtforms.on.ca.

__September 14_____ , 20 __17__   _____
                                              (Signature of party or representative making offer)

                                       ....
                                        (Name, address and phone number of party or representative)

NOTE:	**IF YOU ACCEPT AN OFFER TO SETTLE, THEN FAIL TO COMPLY WITH ITS TERMS,** judgment in the terms of the accepted offer may be obtained against you on motion to the court, or the action may continue as if there has been no offer to settle [R. 14.06].

NOTE:	**IF THIS OFFER TO SETTLE IS NOT ACCEPTED, IT SHALL NOT BE FILED WITH THE COURT OR DISCLOSED** to the trial judge until all questions of liability and relief (other than costs) have been determined [R. 14.04].

SCR 14.01.1-14A (January 23, 2014) CSD

FIGURE 9.11 **Affidavit of Service**

ONTARIO
Superior Court of Justice

Affidavit of Service
Form 8A Ont. Reg. No.: 258/98

_____
Small Claims Court

_____
Claim No.

_____
Address

_____
Phone number

BETWEEN

_____
Plaintiff(s)

and

_____
Defendant(s)

My name is _____
(Full name)

I live in _____
(Municipality & province)

and I swear/affirm that the following is true:

1. **I served** _____ , on _____ , 20 ____ ,
(Full name of person/corporation served)   (Date)

   at _____
   (Address (street and number, unit, municipality, province))

   which is ☐ the address of the person's home

   ☐ the address of the corporation's place of business

   ☐ the address of the person's or corporation's representative on record with the court

   ☐ the address on the document most recently filed in court by the party

   ☐ the address of the corporation's attorney for service in Ontario

   ☐ other address: _____
   (Specify.)

   with _____
   (Name(s) of document(s) served)

2. **I served the document(s) referred to in paragraph one by the following method:**
   (Tell how service took place by checking appropriate box(es).)

   Personal service ☐ leaving a copy with the person.

   ☐ leaving a copy with the _____ of the corporation.
   (Office or position)

   ☐ leaving a copy with: _____
   (Specify person's name and office/position.)

   at the place of business of the corporation who appeared to be in control or management of the place of business.

Les formules des tribunaux sont affichées en anglais et en français sur le site www.ontariocourtforms.on.ca. Visitez ce site pour des renseignements sur des formats accessibles.

SCR 8.06-8A (November 1, 2015) CSD

Continued on next page

FIGURE 9.11   **Continued**

FORM 8A	PAGE 2	
		_____
		Claim No.

Service at place of residence ☐ leaving a copy in a sealed envelope addressed to the person at the person's place of residence with a person who appeared to be an adult member of the same household, and sending another copy of the same document(s) to the person's place of residence on the same day or the following day by:

    ☐ regular lettermail.

    ☐ registered mail.

    ☐ courier.

Service by registered mail ☐ registered mail.
(If a copy of a plaintiff's claim or defendant's claim was served by registered mail, attach a copy of the Canada Post delivery confirmation, showing the signature verifying delivery, to this affidavit.)

Service by courier ☐ courier.
(If a copy of a plaintiff's claim or defendant's claim was served by courier, attach a copy of the courier's delivery confirmation, showing the signature verifying delivery, to this affidavit.)

Service on lawyer or paralegal ☐ leaving a copy with a lawyer or paralegal or an employee in the lawyer's or paralegal's office, who accepted service on the person's behalf.
(Attach a copy of the document endorsed with an acceptance of service.)

Service by regular lettermail ☐ regular lettermail.

Service by fax ☐ fax sent at _____ at the following fax number: _____
                    (Time)   (Fax number)

Service to last known address of corporation or attorney for service, and to the directors ☐ mail/courier to corporation or attorney for service at last known address recorded with the Ministry of Government Services, and

mail/courier to each director, as recorded with the Ministry of Government Services, as set out below:

Name of director	Director's address as recorded with the Ministry of Government Services (street & number, unit, municipality, province)
_____	_____
_____	_____
_____	_____
_____	_____
_____	_____

(Attach separate sheet for additional names if necessary.)

Substituted service ☐ substituted service as ordered by the court on _____ , 20 _____ ,
                                                      (Date)

as follows: (Give details.)

Sworn/Affirmed before me at _____
                                    (Municipality)

in _____
                (Province, state, or country)

on _____ , 20 _____

                Commissioner for taking affidavits
                (Type or print name below if signature
                is illegible.)

_____
Signature
(This form is to be signed in front of a lawyer, justice of the peace, notary public or commissioner for taking affidavits.)

SCR 8.06-8A (November 1, 2015) CSD

EXERCISE 9.4

Revise a Plaintiff's Claim

Review the Plaintiff's Claim shown in Figure 9.8. Revise the claim to improve the writing style based on the skills you learned in Chapter 3.

EXERCISE 9.5

Prepare an Affidavit of Service

Using the facts in Figure 9.7 and the completed Plaintiff's Claim in Figure 9.8, complete the Affidavit of Service in Figure 9.11 to indicate that the first defendant, 99999 Ontario Inc. carrying on business as My Gas Bar, was served with the Plaintiff's Claim. The relevant *Rules of the Small Claims Court* are:

Rules of the Small Claims Court, O Reg 258/98

RULE 8 SERVICE

Service of Particular Documents Plaintiff's or Defendant's Claim

   8.01   (1)   A plaintiff's claim or defendant's claim (Form 7A or 10A) shall be served personally as provided in rule 8.02 or by an alternative to personal service as provided in rule 8.03.

Personal Service

   8.02   If a document is to be served personally, service shall be made,

Individual

(a)   on an individual, other than a person under disability, by leaving a copy of the document with him or her;

Municipality

(b)   on a municipal corporation, by leaving a copy of the document with the chair, mayor, warden or reeve of the municipality, with the clerk or deputy clerk of the municipality or with a lawyer for the municipality;

Corporation

(c)   on any other corporation, by leaving a copy of the document with,

(i)   an officer, a director or another person authorized to act on behalf of the corporation, or

(ii)   a person at any place of business of the corporation who appears to be in control or management of the place of business;

Source: *Rules of the Small Claims Court,* O Reg 258/98, online: <https://www.canlii.org/en/on/laws/regu/o-reg-258-98/latest/#sec8.02>

Ontario Court of Justice: Provincial Offences

The Ontario Court of Justice is a provincial court. It is a division of the Court of Ontario and is authorized by the *Courts of Justice Act*.[10] The Ontario Court of Justice hears criminal, family, and provincial offences matters. Provincial offences are minor (non-criminal) offences set out in various Ontario statues and are governed by the *Provincial Offences Act*.[11] They include offences under the *Highway Traffic Act*,[12] the *Liquor Licence Act*,[13] and the *Dog Owners' Liability Act*.[14]

Figure 9.12 shows one form relevant to provincial offences matters. The Summons appears online.

FIGURE 9.12   Notice of Intention to Appear

---

10 RSO 1990, c C.43.
11 *Supra* note 3.
12 RSO 1990, c H.8.
13 RSO 1990, c L.19.
14 RSO 1990, c D.16.

EXERCISE 9.6

Prepare a Notice of Intention to Appear

You are a licensed paralegal defending clients charged for various offences under the *Highway Traffic Act*, RSO 1990, c H.8 (the "Act"). You meet Hugo Schmidt on October 27, 2017, to discuss his careless driving charge under section 130 of the Act. He presents you with the Offence Notice shown in Figure 9.13. Hugo retains you to defend him. He wants to plead not guilty. He instructs you to prepare a Notice of Intention to Appear. Using these facts and the Office Notice in Figure 9.13, prepare a Notice of Intention to Appear on behalf of Hugo. The form is found in Figure 9.12.

FIGURE 9.13 Offence Notice

ICON Location Code / *Code d'emplacement du RIII* 2930 | Offence number / *Numéro d'infraction* 4570087A

Form 4, *Provincial Offences Act*, Ontario Court of Justice, O. Reg. 108/11
Formulaire 4*, Loi sur les infractions provinciales, *Cour de justice de l'Ontario, Règl. de l'Ont. 108/11

Offence Notice
Avis d'infraction

MEGAN LAPOINTE
(print name / *nom en lettres moulées*)

believe and certifies that on the day of / *crois et atteste que le* Y/A 2017 M/M 10 D/J 20 Time / *Heure* 7:40 PM

Name / *Nom* SCHMIDT (family / *nom de famille*)
HUGO (given / *prénom*) (initials / *initiales*)

Address / *Adresse* 29 HUMBER ST., UNIT 209 (number and street / *numéro et nom de la rue*)
TORONTO (municipality / *municipalité*) (P.O. / C.P.) ON (province) M2N 3Y5 (postal code / *code postal*)

Driver's Licence no. / *Nº de permis de conduire* S1234 29779 10115 Juris / *Aut. Lég.* ON

Birth Date / *Date de naissance* Y/A M/M D/J	Sex / *Sexe*	Motor Vehicle Involved / *Véhicule impliqué*	Collision Involved / *Collision*	Witnesses / *Témoins*
1991 01 15	M	☐ N/N	☐ Y/O	☐ Y/O

At / *À* MOUNT PLEASANT AVE & DAVISVILLE AVE, TORONTO (municipality / *municipalité*)

Did commit the offence of / *A commis l'infraction de* CARELESS DRIVING

contrary to / *contrairement à* HIGHWAY TRAFFIC ACT sect. / *art.* 130

Plate no. / *Nº de la plaque d'immatriculation*	Juris / *Aut. Lég.*	Commercial / *Utilitaire*	CVOR / *IUVU*	NSC / *CNS*	Code
BXAN 299	ON	☐ Y/O	☐ Y/O	☐ Y/O	

CVOR No. - NSC No. / *Nº de l'IUVU - Nº du CNS*

And I further certify that I served an offence notice personally upon the person charged on the offence date.
J'atteste également qu'à la date de l'infraction, j'ai signifié, en mains propres, un avis d'infraction à la personne accusée.

☐ Or other service date of: / *Autre date de signification, le :*

Signature of issuing Provincial Offences Officer / *Signature de l'agent des infractions provinciale*	Officer No. / *Nº de l'agent*	Platoon / *Peloton*	Unit / *Unité*
[signature]	3584		14

Set fine of / *Amende fixée de*	Total payable / *Montant total exigible*	
$ 400.00	$ 485.00	Total payable includes set fine, applicable victim fine surcharge and costs. / *Le montant total exigible comprend l'amende fixée, la suramende compensatoire pour l'aide aux victimes applicable et les frais.*

Important:
You have 15 days from the day you receive this notice to choose one of the options on the back of the notice.

Important :
À compter de la réception du présent avis, vous avez 15 jours pour choisir une des options décrites au verso de l'avis.

POA-0849-E (2011/11) Page 1 of 2

EXERCISE 9.7

Edit an Offer to Settle

Review the draft Offer to Settle shown in Figure 9.14 and edit it for errors, including spelling mistakes, grammatical errors, and stylistic problems.

FIGURE 9.14   **Offer to Settle**

ONTARIO
Superior Court of Justice

Offer to Settle
Form 14A Ont. Reg. No.: 258/98

ontario
Small Claims Court

SC-17-2222
Claim No.

47 Sheppard Avenue East
Toronto, ON M2N 5N1
Address

416-326-3554
Phone number

BETWEEN

Monica Laundry
Plaintiff(s)

and

David Smith
Defendant(s)

My name is Dave Smith I
(Full name)

1.   In this action, I am the
   ☒ Plaintiff
   ☐ Defendant
   ☐ representative of _____
(Name of party(ies))

2.   I offer to settle this action against **Marie Laundry**
(Name of party(ies))

on the following terms: *(Set out terms in numbered paragraphs, or on an attached sheet.)*

1. The Defendant shall pay to the Plaintiff the total sum of 45,000.00 for damages

2. The defendant will pay to the plaintiff prejudgment interest on the aforesaid amount pursuant to the Courts of Justice Act, RSO 1990, c C.43, as amended.

3. The defendant will pay the total sum of $800.00 towards Monica's legal costs

Les formules des tribunaux sont affichées en anglais et en français sur le site www.ontariocourtforms.on.ca. Visitez ce site pour des renseignements sur des formats accessibles.

FORM 14A   PAGE 2   SC-17-2222
                                                               Claim No.

3. This offer to settle is available for acceptance until **dec 1**_____ , 20 **16** .

This offer to settle may be accepted by serving an acceptance of offer to settle (Form 14B may be used) on the party who made it, at any time before it is withdrawn or before the court disposes of the claim to which the offer applies [R. 14.05(1)]. You can get forms at court offices or online at www.ontariocourtforms.on.ca.

November 25_____ , 20 **17**   _____
                                               (Signature of party or representative making offer)
                                               Dave smith
                                               131 Fechlawn Avenue
                                               Toronto, ON, M4G 1L1
                                               Tel. 647-333-2900
                                               _____
                                               (Name, address and phone number of party or representative)

NOTE: **IF YOU ACCEPT AN OFFER TO SETTLE, THEN FAIL TO COMPLY WITH ITS TERMS,** judgment in the terms of the accepted offer may be obtained against you on motion to the court, or the action may continue as if there has been no offer to settle [R. 14.06].

NOTE: **IF THIS OFFER TO SETTLE IS NOT ACCEPTED, IT SHALL NOT BE FILED WITH THE COURT OR DISCLOSED** to the trial judge until all questions of liability and relief (other than costs) have been determined [R. 14.04].

SCR 14.01.1-14A (January 23, 2014) CSD

Summary

An essential part of working as a paralegal is the ability to complete legal forms on behalf of clients. This chapter introduced different kinds of legal forms you will encounter in practice. However, there are many more forms not covered here that you may deal with in practice. It is important to become familiar with these forms. You must complete legal forms accurately. Strive for clarity and consistency when completing legal forms, and always remember to edit your writing.

Appendixes

Appendices

Editing Checklist

Step 1: Revise

1. Format

☐ Have you used an acceptable font and type size that is compliant with the *Accessibility for Ontarians with Disabilities Act* (AODA)?

   If writing a letter:

   ☐ Have you included the date, delivery method, inside address, salutation, subject line, complimentary closing, enclosures, carbon copy, etc., as appropriate?

   ☐ Should you include any special notations (e.g., *personal and confidential*, *without prejudice*)?

   ☐ Does the body of your letter have a proper structure (introduction, middle, and close)?

   ☐ Have you inserted your signature?

   ☐ Have you identified yourself as a licensed paralegal?

   If writing a memorandum:

   ☐ Does your memo have an appropriate header that includes the recipient, sender, date, and subject line?

   ☐ If you are writing a memorandum of law or a case brief, does it follow an appropriate format and structure?

2. Organization

☐ Does each paragraph have a topic sentence?
☐ Do you use point-first writing?
☐ Do you use transitional words and phrases to help the reader understand the connections between various ideas and arguments?
☐ Have you considered using numbered lists?
☐ Have you considered using headings and sub-headings?

3.   Substance

☐ Have you achieved the purpose for which you are writing? For example, have you answered the question based on who your audience is (e.g., client, opposing advocate, judge)?

☐ Is the information correct and relevant?

☐ Do your references to case law and legislation follow the rules for legal citations?

☐ Do you deal with one issue at a time?

☐ Do you lead with your strongest argument first, if applicable?

☐ Do you address counter-arguments, if applicable?

☐ Do you identify any assumptions you are making?

Step 2: Edit For Grammar and Style

1.   Grammar

☐ Use complete sentences with subject, verb, and object.

☐ Use the correct verb tense.

☐ Ensure subject–verb agreement.

☐ Edit sentence fragments and run-on sentences.

☐ Ensure there are no misplaced or dangling modifiers.

☐ Use appropriate pronouns.

☐ Remove ambiguous and indefinite pronoun references.

☐ Use parallel sentence structure.

☐ Ensure proper use of capital letters.

☐ Change passive voice to active voice, where possible.

2.   Style

☐ Use abbreviations, acronyms, and other-short form references appropriately.

☐ Use short-form references and names consistently.

☐ Remove unnecessary legal jargon.

☐ Simplify complicated words, where possible.

☐ Remove expressions and contractions.

☐ Express numbers consistently and appropriately.

☐ Simplify writing by removing redundant synonyms and unnecessary words.

☐ Shorten long sentences, where possible.

☐ Change sentences from negative to affirmative form, where possible.

☐ Include strong action verbs, where possible.

☐ Have you used an appropriate tone? Is the tone of the document professional, civil, and respectful?

Step 3: Edit For Spelling, Punctuation, and Typing Errors

☐ Check for correct use of commas, apostrophes, periods, colons, semi-colons, and quotation marks.

☐ Review for spelling errors.

☐ Double-check titles, headings, and names for embarrassing spelling errors.

☐ Ensure proper Canadian spelling of words.

☐ Check that dates are correct.

Proofreading Techniques and Exercises

B

Proofreading Techniques

Following are some useful proofreading techniques:

- Read your work aloud, slowly. This will help you see errors you could easily miss if reading silently.
- Read one line at a time, and read each word in the line individually.
- If proofreading on a screen, temporarily increase the size of the font or zoom in closer to the material to make it easier to read.
- Personalize your proofreading. What mistakes do you, or the particular writer you are working with, usually make? Keep an eye out for those mistakes in particular.
- Read backwards. When we read in the normal way, we sometimes see what we expect to see, based on the context of the words, instead of what is actually there. If you read the material backwards, you will more easily spot any misspelled words.

Practise the above techniques, and look out for the following:

- transposed letters (e.g., *adn, htat, edlerly*).
- missing or extra letters (e.g., *repot, stilll*).
- missing words (e.g., *Please to page 10*).
- numbers (check against the numbers in the draft, and do the arithmetic to confirm amounts).
- dates on the calendar (e.g., Is the 15th really a Wednesday?).
- typos.
- wrong word in context (e.g., did you use *too* when you wanted *two* or *to*?).

When unsure of a word or a spelling, check your dictionary or thesaurus.

Exercise 1: Proofreading for Spelling

One or more words have been misspelled in each of the following sentences. (*Note:* Canadian spellings are not errors.)

1. Susie, anxious to secure an apartment, actualy included a charecter reference with her letter of application to the building superintendant.
2. She was determined to have a pleasent appearance on her first day of classses and so naturally wanted to buy some beautifull new clothes.
3. She had transferred money into a convinient chequing account, but every bank statement proved it was impossible for her to maintain even a minimum balance.
4. She usually was without transportation and therefor found it practicle to shop online.
5. She was obliged to make partial payments on her annual income, regretting the lack of assistence from her parents.
6. Although it was with some endevor that she read the instructions on the examination envalope, she finally understood them.
7. By Febuary her funds were extremaly low, and so, after some concideration, she made the decicion to accept a second position as a research asssistant.
8. An additional inquery was unnecessary as the description of the car left no dobt that it was a foreign model.
9. Evedently it is advisable to remember to ask for an undertaking.
10. She prefered to believe that the difference between succes and failure was all in the mind.

Exercise 2: Proofreading for Spelling

One or more words have been misspelled in each of the following sentences. (*Note:* Canadian spellings are not errors.)

1. We are planning to deliver the balance of the shippment either on Wednesday or on Saterday.
2. Many Canadiens are undoutedly begining to realise the value of traveling.
3. Imagine how greatfull I am for an opportunity to get expierience at this temprary job.
4. With only my business training certificait, I should have had difficulty in getting a permanant job.
5. In this office, a general knowlege of business practice is a neccessity.
6. Even though no definate length of time was specefied, in my opinon, the job will last approximetely three months.
7. Prehaps, if my work is satisfactary, the firm will allow me to use its name as a referance.
8. Every customer, without exception, knows that it is our policy to give promt and excellent service under all circumstances.
9. We ashure you that out association will make every effort to furnish various types of merchandize in accordance with your individual requirements.
10. They showed their appreceation of our curtesy and co-operation by replying immediately to our communication.

Exercise 3: Proofreading for Subject–Verb Agreement

Correct the mistakes in subject–verb agreement in the following sentences:

1. Across from the hospital are a collection of old homes.
2. Either Tom or Jerry have agreed to confess to the crime.
3. The entire briefcase, including my pens, cellphone, and address book, were taken from my car.
4. Some consideration for the needs of others are expected from the social worker.
5. All the members of the lacrosse team and the coach was given a rousing cheer.
6. Either Lee or his brothers is responsible for the damage.
7. In front of the house stand two oak trees.
8. One of the shoes have disappeared.
9. None of the dishes are of any value.
10. A package of toys were given to the boy.

Exercise 4: Proofreading for Comma Splices

Correct the comma-splice errors in the following sentences.

1. The instructor's late, let's go to the pub!
2. Just let me get out of here, I might say something that I will regret.
3. I keep buying Lotto 6/49 tickets, but I have never won anything.
4. My brother golfs and swims every day, he is quite healthy, he is only in his thirties.
5. As long as you use correct grammar, you can be accepted in any profession.
6. Montreal used to be called Ville Ste. Marie, I think, but before that it had another name.
7. Students today need summer jobs, tuition and living expenses are more than most families can afford.
8. Tam will be going to the University of Toronto if accepted, he will be trying to get a scholarship.
9. I am seeking a hero after whom I can model my life, so far I have rejected all Canadian politicians.

Exercise 5: Proofreading for Sentence Fragments

Identify the sentence-fragment errors in the following passage, then revise to correct them.

Going shopping with my sister is a waste of time. Because she never knows what she is looking for. After I have arrived home from work. My sister comes into the room. Gathers up her purse. And announces that she is going shopping. And would I like to come. It is a difficult situation to avoid. So off we go. When we get to the grocery store. She goes running up and down the aisles. Trying to remember what she needs. Finally, when we get to the check-out counter, she remembers a number of items that she forgot to pick up. So back she goes while I hold the place in line. And other shoppers glare at me. Finally, we get to the car. With me carrying all the groceries and her complaining. About the price of food. The next time. I must figure out a way to gracefully decline. A trip to the grocery store.

_____

_____

_____

_____

_____

_____

_____

_____

_____

_____

_____

_____

Exercise 6: Proofreading for Apostrophe Errors

Identify the apostrophe errors in the following sentences, then correct them.

1. Children find 9s hard to make.
2. Someone elses brothers car was stolen.
3. Bill picked up his friend's costs for them.
4. Childrens hands' have a way of getting dirty.
5. Lightning hit the Joneses house last night.
6. The cars horns beeped angrily as traffic backed up.
7. Dangers cousin is carelessness.
8. Developing the firms business plan was Peters favourite project.
9. The walkers feet were sore after the days hike.
10. The stones momentum grew as it rolled down the mountain.
11. Smiths car and Greens truck collided at Brantfords main intersection.
12. As the weeks slip by summers approach is felt.
13. It is not Jamess fault that Mike is away.
14. As she heard the stair's creak, she recognized her daughters footsteps.
15. Castles walls were built to withstand the enemies attack.

Exercise 7: Proofreading for Misplaced Modifiers

Rewrite the following sentences to eliminate misplaced modifiers.

1. We can only supply one of the items that you ordered with the blue trimming.

   _____

2. The little girl was balancing a basket on her head held down by a stone.

   _____

3. George lived with a friend he trusted in a small apartment.

   _____

4. Students who miss classes frequently fall behind in their studies.

   _____

5. Today I saw a woman whose car side-swiped yours in front of the hotel.

   _____

6. You should not keep a dog that is used to a warm apartment in a doghouse.

   _____

7. Most cars have sun visors above the windshield, which can be adjusted to shade the eyes.

   _____

8. Buried in an old trunk for half a century, the owner of the painting discovered that it was done by a famous artist.

   _____

9. The antique table was purchased by a blonde woman with Queen Anne legs.

   _____

10. The stadium nearly seated 40,000 people.

    _____

Exercise 8: Proofreading for Dangling Modifiers

Rewrite the following sentences to remove the dangling modifiers.

1. Driving through the mountains, several bears were seen.

   _____

2. Riding my bicycle, a dog chased me.

   _____

3. Working at my computer, the morning seemed endless.

   _____

4. Being made of glass, I did not expect the door to withstand abuse from children.

   _____

5. Spanning the river, I admired the bridge over the St. Lawrence.

   _____

6. Fearing cats, he noticed that the birds only came to the feeder early in the morning.

   _____

7. After putting a worm on my hook, the fish began to bite.

   _____

8. Before exploring Algonquin Park, our car was tuned up.

   _____

9. On opening the letter, a loonie fell out.

   _____

10. While rowing on the lake, the boat overturned.

    _____

Exercise 9: Proofreading for Ambiguous Pronoun References

Rewrite the following sentences to eliminate ambiguous pronoun references.

1. The farmer went to his neighbour and told him his cattle were in his field.

   _____

2. The clerk told his employer that whatever he did he could not please him.

   _____

3. Charles's guilt was revealed to James in a letter to his neighbour.

   _____

4. He sent the man to his neighbour with the money he wanted.

   _____

5. Dennis asked his cousin to bring his wallet, as he was going on an errand.

6. Alice promised Jane that she would pay her debt.

   _____

7. The lawyer had a disagreement with opposing counsel, and he won.

   _____

8. When David met Shawn, he shook his hand.

   _____

9. The girls asked the boys whether the books that they had in their hands were the ones they had seen on their desks.

   _____

Exercise 10: Proofreading for Pronoun Errors

Correct the faulty pronoun references in the following paragraph.

When a person does not know their way around a new town, you should always stop and ask for directions. If they do not do this, the person will waste a lot of their time driving their car around, searching for one's destination. If we would just take a few seconds to ask questions, we would save many minutes of one's valuable time. And no one will think you are stupid; they will think that person is just unfamiliar with their surroundings. One must overcome needless shyness if they want to use their time more efficiently. If a person is overly shy, I would force myself to go out more and talk to more people, if you are really serious about overcoming the problem. We must always think positively if you expect to solve a problem, no matter how difficult one may find it to do. It is just an attitude you must develop if one wants a more profitable future for themselves.

Exercise 11: Proofreading for Pronoun Case

Correct the errors in pronoun case in the following sentences.

1. Wait for Agnes and I.

   _____

2. Everybody was late except we.

   _____

3. Him and Gary played together.

   _____

4. Mother told you and she to stay here.

   _____

5. I never saw Wayne and they together before.

   _____

6. We expect you and they at the meeting.

   _____

7. You and me are both invited.

   _____

8. Father expects you or I to meet him at the airport.

   _____

9. The Smiths are going, and us too.

   _____

10. I initiated the lawsuit, but it was him who raised the money for the court costs.

    _____

Exercise 12: Proofreading for Consistent Use of Acronyms and Other Short-Form References

Correct the acronyms and other short-form references in the following paragraphs.

1. The Law Society of Ontario held its annual meeting on February 15, 2018. Many attendees discussed expanding the scope of paralegal practice. The Treasurer of the LSO advised that the Law Society has not taken a position on this issue.

   _____

2. The parties attended a hearing at the Human Rights Tribunal of Ontario. The Applicant called three witnesses to testify about the incident. The Tribunal released its decision within two months. The decision is available on the OHRT's website.

   _____

3. The SCC released its decision in *R v Whittaker* today. The Court ordered a new trial for the appellant ("A"). The Court heard from A and the respondent, as well as many interveners. The Supreme Court is the highest court in Canada.

   _____

4. The defendant is a valuable member of the community. She volunteers with MADD on a daily basis. On the day of the incident, she was on her way home from volunteering with MADD.

   _____

Exercise 13: Proofreading for Legal Jargon, Expressions, and Contractions

Revise the following paragraphs to correct any inappropriate use of legal jargon, expressions, and/or contractions.

1. The paralegal advised her client that she did not have a cause of action in order to successfully pursue her claim in a court of law. An analysis of case law revealed that the elements of negligence were not present.

    _____

2. The court order requires that the defendant pay the plaintiff $5,322.00 forthwith. At the end of the day, if the defendant does not pay forthwith, he will be in breach of a court order.

    _____

3. I wanna schedule you in for another meeting to chat about your upcoming settlement conference. It'd be great if you could call my office to book a time that works for you. I'm also attaching herewith a copy of your latest invoice. I'll grab you a receipt once you've paid.

    _____

4. I've requested on three different occasions now that your client provide the requisite disclosure. To date, I've received nil from you. If I don't receive the disclosure from you by November 15, 2017, I will bring a motion before the Court on the grounds that your client is in breach of the *Rules of the Small Claims Court*.

    _____

Exercise 14: Proofreading Letters

Turn the following text into a business letter that uses full block style with mixed punctuation. Correct all errors in grammar, spelling, punctuation, and style. Organize the text into paragraphs. The letter is to Kevin Muise, who is the president of Muise Brothers, 700 Bloor Street West, Toronto, Ontario M3T 4E8. You are a licensed paralegal who is writing the letter on behalf of your client, Karen Greene. Provide an appropriate date, salutation, and complimentary close. The letter is being sent by courier.

On December 17, 2017 my client wrote to the manager of the furniture department Andrew Lerner regarding a wall unit she had purchased during a recent sale celebrating the stores 75th anniversary. She paid $600 dollars. The unit arrived in damaged condition and she is still awaiting advise from Mr. Lerner regarding how he proposes to handle the matter. As I indicated in my client's letter to Mr. Lerner there are three major defects in the unit. The left cabinet door doesnt close the edge of the bottom shelf is rough and unfinished and the edge of the top shelf has nicks in it. Their are a number of minor defects beside the major ones and the overall effect is a unit that all ready looks like a much used poorly made peace of furniture. This is not the first time my client has purchased furniture from Muise Brothers however it is the first time that she has been so displeased. It is difficult to hide the fact that she is mad. If a manufacturer is lax about inspecting furniture before it leaves the factory Muise Brothers should inspect it before delivery is made to the customer. Mr. Lerner is taking all together to much time to reply to my client's first letter which was sent the same day the unit was received. Therefore I would appreciate your taking care of this matter and responding to my letter to advise how this matter is to be settled.

Exercise 15: Proofreading Letters

Turn the following text into a letter that uses full block style with mixed punctuation. Correct all errors in grammar, spelling, punctuation, and style. Organize the text into paragraphs. Address the letter to Grace Smith, Simpson Paralegal Services, 20 Bedford Road, Toronto, Ontario M2P 3L9. The letter is from you, a licensed paralegal, representing David King in a human rights matter. The letter is to the paralegal representing the respondent. The matter name is *King v Ari Brothers Inc*. The file number is 17-1514. Provide an appropriate date, salutation, and complimentary close. The letter is being sent by fax to 416-222-2222.

As you know, our clients hearing will be heard in 60 days time. Pursuant to Rule 16 of the Rules of Procedure for Applications under the Human Rights Code regarding diclosure, I've enclosed copies of docs that David intends to rely on at the upcumuing hearing which are an email dated March 17, 2017 an email dated March 18, 2017, a medical report dated January 15, 2017 by Dr. Karim Seaton and a e-mail dated April 1, 2017. Will I be receiving yours? I hope so considering I set my request to you over 5 weeks ago. Also, I am gonna provide you with David's list of witnesses shortly as per rule 17.

Exercise 16: Proofreading Letters

Turn the following text into a letter that uses full block style with mixed punctuation. Correct all errors in grammar, spelling, punctuation, and style. Revise as necessary. Organize the text into paragraphs. The letter is from a licensed paralegal to her client, Christopher Mendez. Christopher's address is 34 Brennon Avenue, Suite 1430, Toronto, Ontario M5S 2L2. The matter name is *R v Mendez*. The file number is 17-1517. Provide an appropriate date, salutation, and complimentary close. The letter is being sent by regular mail.

Hey Chris! I'm glad we had a chance to chat yesterday about your theft under charge. I wanted to write to you to confirm my explanation of things, particularly the possible penalties for your charge. As you know, you have been charged with the offence of theft under pursuant to the Criminal Code of Canada. The relevant provisions are sections 322, 334, and 484(1) of the CC. Section 334 of the CC sets out the possible penalties a person can face should the person be convicted of the offence. As explained, the Crown must prove the elements of the offence beyond a reasonable doubt. Section 334(b)(i) of the Criminal Code notes that everyone who commits theft (b) is guilty (i) of an indictable offence and is liable to imprisonment for a term not exceeding two years. However, Section 334(b)(ii) notes that …[E]very one who commits theft (b) is guilty (ii) of an offence punishable on summary conviction." Section 787(i) of the CC sets out the punishments and disincentives of being found guilty of a summary conviction. It says, "Unless otherwise provided by law, everyone who is convicted of an offence punishable on summary conviction is liable to a fine of not more than five thousand dollars or to a term of imprisonment not exceeding six months or to both." What you need to understand is that the offence of theft under is a hybrid offence which means that the Crown can decide to proceed with the charge as either an indictable offence or a summary conviction offence. Serious crimes are usually indictrable offences while summary offences are usually less serious crimes. Crown in your case has decided to proceed by way of summary conviction. This means that if the Crown proves the case, the worst case scenario for you in terms of your penalty would be a fine of up to $5,000 and jail time of up to, but not more than, six months or both. During our meeting, I advised that based on the disclosure that the Crown has provided to us, even if you were to be found guilty of the offence, the chances of receiving this maximum penalty for the summary conviction offence would be small. We'll discuss your case further next time we meet closer to the trial date. Let me know if you have any questions or concerns! Until next time!
Beth Hogarth

Exercise 17: Proofreading Memos

Correct all spelling, grammar and style errors in the following text, and put it into proper memorandum format. Divide it into paragraphs. The memo is from you to the file regarding your recent meeting with the firm's client Vincent Hothe, who is being sued by Alex Mille in small claims court. Use today's date. Include an appropriate subject line.

Met with Vince today. Told him I reviewed the Alex's Plaintiff's Claim. Explained that based on my reading of the clam, there is no reasonable cause of action and may be considered to be an abyse of the court's process under rule 12.02(1) of the Rules of the Small claims court. I suggested that he bring a motion before the court asking the court to dismiss the plaintiff's claim on the basis that it discloses no reasonable cause of Action and that it is an abuse of the courts process. I explained to him the rules about requests to dismiss and what this would require. Explained that if successful, plaintiff's application would be dismissed and he would be unable to continue the proceeding. Spoke about approximate costs to prepare a request to dismiss. Vince instructed me to prep necessary docs to request a dmissal of alex's claim. Will prep and send drafts to him for review in about a week.

Speaking Effectively

C

LEARNING OUTCOMES

After reading this appendix, you should be able to

- Speak effectively in front of an audience.
- Select a topic for an oral presentation.
- Organize an oral presentation.
- Understand the mechanics of oral presentations.
- Handle question-and-answer periods.
- Avoid nervousness and distracting gestures.
- Use audiovisual aids to enhance presentations.
- Understand nonverbal communication methods.
- Use influential language.
- Understand the SIR method of impromptu speaking.

Introduction

In order to be effective communicators, paralegals must understand and practise oral communications skills. Whether interviewing clients; advocating in front of a judge, adjudicator, or other decision maker; or speaking with colleagues and opposing legal representatives, effective speaking skills enhance effectiveness in the legal field. One way to improve oral communications skills is to prepare and deliver an oral presentation. Many of the skills learned and refined by giving oral presentations can be used in all communications situations, personal as well as professional. It is also important to learn about nonverbal communication skills, both to use them and to recognize their use by others.

When certain people speak, no matter what they say, it hardly seems worth the effort to listen; others speak with such authority that whatever they say seems worth listening to. Speaking in such a way as to be heard, to be influential, and to be an object of respect depends on three factors: *words*, *delivery and tone*, and *appearance*.

In other words, when you speak, your message is made up of what you say, how you say it, and how you look when you say it. For a spoken message to be effective, all three must concur. Learning to prepare an oral presentation will help you develop skills of permanent value in your professional and personal life.

Effective Oral Presentations

Purpose

Through an effective oral presentation, you can sway a group of people toward your point of view or inform them about something you think is important. You must ask yourself what you are trying to accomplish through any particular oral presentation. Are you aiming to inform (through exposition), to persuade, or to tell a story (through narration)? Decide on the subject of your presentation, and ask yourself what you expect from your audience after your presentation.

For example, do you want your audience to

- recognize the role of the paralegal?
- realize the complexity of the legal profession?
- understand the nature of criminal proceedings?
- agree to a recommended course of action on a client file?

Whatever your purpose, select and develop a topic that suits your interests and those of your audience.

Selecting a Topic

You may be in a position to select a topic that is of particular interest to you, or you may be assigned a topic by your instructor. Selecting your own topic can become one of the most difficult parts of the oral presentation. It is not easy to come up with a topic that is both interesting and manageable in the time allotted for your presentation. If you have the freedom to choose your own topic, here are a few guidelines that may be useful:

1. Draw on your own interests, experiences, and opinions.
2. Consider your audience.
3. Select a topic that is timely and of which your audience might already be aware.

As a student who is interested in the legal field and is giving a presentation to a class of paralegals, you have a wide range of topics to draw from that meet the criteria outlined above. Look in your local media for ideas: stories relating to the field of law are usually well covered. Appendix D offers a number of readings that might help get you started. If a topic is covered in the local media, it is usually timely and sufficiently important that most of your audience will be aware of it.

This appendix is designed to give you the opportunity to plan and organize an in-class oral presentation, after first developing various components of the presentation and perfecting them through practice and with help from your instructor. Exercises 1–3 contribute to the development of the major oral presentation, after which you will be asked to combine the various components into your presentation.

Exercise 1: Starting Research

In your school library or online, look in local and national media and find between five and ten stories likely to interest people in the paralegal profession. List their titles and briefly summarize them, making sure to include the thesis and main supporting points. For each article, answer the following questions:

1. Who is the intended audience for the article?
2. What do you yourself know about the topic covered in the article?
3. Do you hold any strong opinions about the topic?
4. What more would you like to know about the topic?
5. How would you obtain additional information about the topic?

Narrowing the Topic

Once you have chosen a topic, you should consider the following questions:

1. How much time is available for your presentation?
2. How many ideas can you cover in that time?
3. What are the most important parts of the topic, and how many of them will you have time for?
4. Which ideas will most interest your audience?

Exercise 2: Gathering Information

Using the articles you selected during Exercise 1, choose the one that you feel would be most interesting to an audience of paralegals. Assume that you have been assigned a five-minute oral presentation on the topic covered in this article. Within the time allotted to prepare your presentation, determine the following:

1. What is the purpose of your presentation (e.g., to inform, to teach, to entertain)?
2. What points to support your purpose can you cover within the allotted time? (Assume that the average speaker can deliver between 115 and 120 words per minute.)
3. What are some secondary issues you might want to cover? Are there issues related to the main topic that would help your audience understand your main point?
4. How much research will you need to do in order to make an effective presentation?
5. What thesis statement effectively defines the purpose of your presentation?
6. What is an appropriate title for your presentation?

Research

Having decided on your topic, you must begin researching it, compiling as much information as you can within the time you have. Summarize any information you find, noting the main points found in your sources. Keep a full bibliographic record of each source so that you can find it again if necessary. You may find it useful to record the following information in outline form:

1. A full citation of your source.
2. A summary of the article's contents.
3. The main ideas in the article.
4. Any direct quotations you will be using.
5. A paraphrased version of the ideas you will be using.
6. Any additional references indicated in your source that might provide further information about your topic.

Cite evidence accurately; do not distort data or take it out of context. Credit your source for any information and ideas you use, even when you paraphrase the material. Edit your notes, eliminating unnecessary material or material that will not fit into the time you have available.

Preparation

An oral presentation must be prepared, and prepared well. In this way, it is like any of the written material discussed in this book. Whether speaking to a colleague about a matter relating to your law firm, making a presentation to a superior, or composing a classroom presentation, you must be prepared. The following are some things to remember when preparing your oral presentation:

1. *Prepare an outline.* Include a topic and thesis statement, as you would for an essay or a paragraph. The topic is what you are speaking about; the thesis statement is your point of view, usually expressed at the beginning of your discussion.

2. *List your main points.*

3. *Revise your list.* Review your points, and omit those that are unnecessary.

4. *Arrange your remaining points in logical order.* Use the procedure you would use for writing an essay.

5. *Write your opening sentence.*

6. *Write your introduction and conclusion.*

7. *Prepare your final draft.* Do not write out your whole presentation or memorize it. Instead, write down your main points in outline form, as well as your topic, thesis, opening sentence, and conclusion. You should know your topic well enough that you only need to refer to your outline to jog your memory about the flow of your presentation. If you have audiovisual materials, you should indicate in your outline where these materials are to be used.

There are various ways to begin an oral presentation. Some of the more common are as follows:

- *Tell a story or an anecdote:* My only previous contact with the legal system occurred when I was volunteering at a community legal aid clinic. I saw many frightened people looking for help navigating the legal system because they could not afford to pay a lawyer or paralegal to assist them. After what I saw here, I decided to do what I could to help those who cannot afford legal assistance.

- *Read a quotation:* As I read in a recent newspaper report, "Judges in this country never cease to amaze me." I have the greatest respect for the Canadian judicial system and for the people who sit behind the bench. I would like to discuss several recent court decisions in the area of provincial offences that are relevant to paralegal practice.

- *Reveal an interesting fact:* The legal aid system is in turmoil. Too few lawyers want to take legal aid cases, because it is too expensive for them within the legal aid guidelines legislated by the province. At the same time, the number of people needing legal aid is exploding, and the system is not able to help all of these people.

- *Relate a new fact about the subject:* The federal Cabinet will be looking at new legislation that would give police and security agencies the right to intercept personal emails and text messages and to monitor password-secure websites without explicit court approval.

The conclusion of an oral presentation, like the introduction, may be approached in various ways, but try to ensure that you accomplish the following:

- *Restate your main topic:* As I said at the beginning of this discussion, the legal aid system is in turmoil, and I have given only a few examples to prove my point.

- *Summarize your main points*: Paralegal programs are now found in almost every provincial community college, as well as in private training institutions. If the Attorney General and the Law Society of Ontario are to accept Justice Bonkalo's recommendations in the Family Legal Services Report to allow paralegals to provide certain types of family legal services, proper education, training, and regulation must be developed. Consultation with lawyers, paralegals, colleges, and other organizations and institutions is needed.

- *End with whatever method you used to begin.*

- *Leave the audience with a challenge*: As citizens of this country, we must stand up and speak out against this contemplated invasion of our privacy.

- *Set an example for the audience to follow*: Here is what I intend to do.

Exercise 3: Preparing an Outline

Prepare an outline that is appropriate for the topic you have selected. In point form, list the following:

1. Topic
2. Thesis
3. Method of beginning (e.g., anecdote, interesting fact)
4. Main points to cover

After creating this broad outline, list any sub-points you wish to cover.

Organization

Many experts recommend a three-step method of organizing an oral presentation:

1. Tell the audience what you are going to say.

2. Say it.

3. Tell the audience what you have just said.

These steps can be expanded into the Six Ps of public speaking:

1. *Preface.* What in your background qualifies you to speak on the chosen topic?

2. *Position.* What is your thesis—the position you take on the topic?

3. *Problem.* Define the problem and give some background, including relevant issues and any terminology that the audience might need to know.

4. *Possibilities.* Be sure to explore all sides of the issue, and be respectful toward points of view different from your own.

5. *Proposal.* Once you have explored an issue, suggest some possible solutions. Are all solutions workable?

6. *Postscript.* Restate the issue you have discussed, pointing out that you have proved something, solved a dilemma, or in some other way accomplished what you set out to do in your introduction.

A presentation that lasts from five to ten minutes can easily be organized along these lines.

Exercise 4: Organizing an Oral Presentation

Using the principles of organizing an oral presentation, prepare an outline for one of the following topics:

- Paralegals should (or should not) be permitted to provide family legal services.
- Marijuana should (or should not) be legalized.
- Commercial surrogacy should (or should not) be legally permitted in Canada.
- Performing experiments on animals violates (or does not violate) their rights.

Write a sentence for each of the Six Ps.

Mechanics

When you have finished organizing your oral presentation, you should begin working on the mechanics of it, including the following:

1. *Volume.* Speak to people at the back of the room. If they can hear you, everyone can hear you.

2. *Rate.* People speak at 115 to 120 words per minute. Practise this. Nervous speakers speak too quickly.

3. *Pauses.* Pause between main ideas, and even slightly after sentences. This will give your audience time to consider what you have said.

4. *Stance.* Do not slouch; project confidence. If you use a lectern, stand behind it with your hands to either side of the lectern; do not lean on it for support. If you do not use a lectern, keep your hands out of your pockets, and do not jiggle your change. Use your hands to express yourself. If you cannot think of anything else to do with your hands, leave them at your sides.

5. *Personality.* Be sincere, and smile. Show your audience that you care about the topic you are presenting.

Tips for a Great Presentation

1. Give your audience what they want to hear; be relevant.
2. Know your audience.
3. Realize that humour can work for you or against you.
4. Dress appropriately.
5. Do not read your presentation.
6. Do not exceed your time limit.
7. Use visual aids.
8. Rehearse, but do not memorize.
9. Be aware of your vocabulary level.

Answering Questions

You may have a question-and-answer period after your presentation to allow your audience to learn more about your topic. Prepare for this beforehand, during the planning phase, by anticipating any questions that might be asked and preparing potential answers ahead of time. Know your topic well enough that you can expand on certain points if asked.

There are three common categories of questions that might be asked:

1. *Open questions* ask for your opinion about something.
2. *Closed questions* require a specific "yes" or "no" answer.
3. *Questions seeking clarification* invite you to expand on a point.

Here are some general guidelines for responding to all three categories of questions:

1. *Listen and respond.* Listen to the entire question, and think before you answer. Be objective in your response.
2. *Restate and respond.* Restate the question to the person who asked it. This allows your time to think and ensures that you have understood the question.
3. *Categorize and respond.* Be aware of the category of the question, and respond accordingly. If you have been asked for a factual answer, do not respond with an opinion.
4. *Retain your point of view.* Do not change your point of view from the position you adopted in your presentation.

If you do not know the answer to a question, say so. You can ask your audience for help, or refer the questioner to a source where the answer may be found, but trying to fake an answer ruins your credibility and the effectiveness of your presentation.

Nervousness

Many people are nervous about speaking in front of an audience, but there are ways to overcome this anxiety:

1. *Observe others.* Watch other speakers and pick up on their strengths.
2. *Lower your blood pressure.* Running cold water over your wrists before you begin your presentation helps lower your blood pressure.
3. *Try to relax.* Loosen tense muscles through stretching and self-massage.
4. *Move your body.* Relax by moving your body unhurriedly and deliberately when you present.
5. *Suck on a candy.* Suck on a small hard candy before your presentation to eliminate a dry mouth.
6. *Breathe.* Take deep, regular breaths.

Exercise 5: Exploring Phobia

Fear of speaking in front of an audience is a common phobia. What is a phobia, and why do so many people have this particular phobia? Suggest some ways, apart from the techniques described above, that people might overcome their fear of public speaking.

Visual Aids

Visual aids, when used effectively, can enhance any presentation. You should keep a few things in mind, however, when considering the use of visual aids.

1. *Use visuals to clarify or enhance.* Visual aids should be used judiciously. They should not be used excessively or without a specific reason.

2. *Keep visuals simple.* You do not want to give your audience so much visual information that they are too distracted to listen to your words.

3. *Make visuals large.* Visuals should be large and visible enough that all members of your audience can see them.

4. *Provide time to absorb the visuals.* After displaying a visual, give the audience a moment to absorb the information before you paraphrase it and incorporate it into your presentation.

5. *Practise using visuals.* Do not ignore your visuals when you practise your presentation. Be sure they go where they are supposed to go and work when they are supposed to work.

Well-chosen visual aids can help an audience understand your presentation and remember what you have said. It is important to use appropriate visuals for your presentation. Each kind of visual has particular advantages:

1. *Digital visuals.* Digital visuals or "slideshows," using software such as Power-Point, can create a professional effect with relatively little effort, can offer sound, movement, and colour, and can be used with a large monitor or a projector.

2. *Flip charts.* While somewhat old-fashioned, flip charts are easy to prepare and use, are portable, and allow you to create new visuals while the presentation is in progress.

3. *Videos.* Videos can be effective if properly cued up in advance. On the other hand, searching for the right spot in a video during your presentation is very distracting both for you and to your audience, and if your video is online, technical issues such as a slow network or insufficient bandwidth can delay or derail your presentation. It can also be difficult to find an alternative if the equipment you need is not available.

4. *Handouts.* Handouts are common in presentations, and can be as effective as other visuals. Audiences often like these souvenirs, and they do help retention, but to avoid having your audience focus on them rather than on what you are saying, always provide handouts *after* you have made your points.

Exercise 6: Speaking Skills for Paralegals

1. As a class, discuss ways in which effective oral presentation skills are valuable to paralegals. Be specific: what situations can paralegals encounter in which effective oral communications skills are valuable?

2. Research a software program used in legal offices, and report back to your class on how this software has increased efficiency in the office, has made the job of a paralegal, law clerk, or legal assistant easier, and, in general, has been a benefit to those people using it.

Nonverbal Communication

"Actions speak louder than words." This statement is certainly true in oral communication. The use of body language reveals a great deal about both the communicator and the person receiving the communication. Understanding nonverbal communication is essential for effective communication and, in many cases, for discovering the truth.

Approximately 65 percent of our face-to-face communication is nonverbal; many of our messages are transmitted through facial expressions, gestures, eye movements, and tone of voice. Many speakers are unaware of the nonverbal dimensions of their communications, and therefore send unintended messages. Frequently glancing at the clock while a client is speaking, for example, is clearly sending the message that you are impatient or bored or that you consider the speaker's words to be unimportant.

Nonverbal communication can be divided into *visual* elements and *vocal* elements.

Visual Elements

Eye Contact

People who fail to make or fail to maintain effective eye contact are not good communicators. They give the impression of being embarrassed, nervous, at a loss for words. Maintaining eye contact allows a paralegal to send the message that he or she is honest and concerned about the client. When meeting a client for the first time, for example, maintaining eye contact (without staring) allows the legal professional to send the message that the client is welcome, and that the client's needs are of prime importance. Be aware of cultural differences in nonverbal communication. In most Western cultures, eye contact indicates a desire to communicate and an interest in what is being said. In other cultures, eye contact may be seen as aggressive and disrespectful, and in some cases intimidating.

Facial Expression

Your facial expression, which is key to nonverbal communication, must match your message in order for you to be taken seriously. Scowling throughout your presentation will give the impression that you want to be anywhere but speaking in front of the class. A sea of bored faces in a classroom sends an effective message to the instructor, regardless of the verbal communication taking place.

Gestures and Posture

Using your hands during an oral presentation can be very effective. On the other hand, your gestures and posture can seriously detract from your message. Fidgeting, nervous hand gestures, shuffling from foot to foot: any of these may signal that a person is nervous. Exaggerated hand gestures, extreme body movements, or stabbing with the fingers to make a point often indicates a lack of confidence on the part of the speaker.

In one-on-one communications, the use of the hands can send mixed signals. A firm handshake, for instance, can be an appropriate gesture of greeting, but in some cultures—in the Middle East or parts of Asia, for example—a firm handshake is seen as aggressive. Some Asian cultures consider bowing, rather than shaking hands, an appropriate form of greeting.

Body Orientation

The position of a person's body during a conversation tells a great deal about his or her approach to the situation. If someone faces you head-on, with squared shoulders and feet, you may gather that he or she is being aggressive and confrontational.

Manner of Dress

How we dress sends a message about our professional and social standing. Well-groomed, well-dressed people convey a sense of professionalism and responsibility; they give the impression of taking their positions seriously.

Vocal Elements

Volume

Using a loud voice can indicate that you have control over a situation, but it can also convey the wrong message. A loud voice can indicate aggression toward the other party, and it may elicit a loud voice in response.

Saying "Please speak louder" in a firm, normal speaking voice asks for cooperation. Shouting "Speak louder!" might indicate that you are looking for, or even require, an aggressive response. Using *please* indicates a request for cooperation. The effect of emphasizing certain words in a spoken sentence is discussed below.

Speed

Speaking quickly can indicate nervousness. In addition, speaking quickly can make it difficult for others to understand you. Combine speaking quickly with a loud voice and aggressive tone and body language, and you have a potential confrontation.

Emphasis

The emphasis you put on certain words in a sentence can give that sentence completely different meanings.

> "*Are* you sure of your facts?" (You do not sound sure.)
> "Are you *sure* of your facts?" (It sounds like hearsay.)

Exercise 7: Practising Verbal and Nonverbal Communication

Role-play in a number of different situations involving both verbal and nonverbal communication. Assume that you are a practising paralegal and that you have to deal with each of the following:

- A senior paralegal who wants you to complete a 10-hour research project and prepare a memorandum of law within two days.
- A senior lawyer who wants you to come into the office during your week off.
- A client you are interviewing who is not sure of his facts.
- A lawyer for the opposing party who insults you and talks down to you on the telephone when trying to discuss the case.
- Someone in your office who likes to gossip.

Have someone in your class play the role of the person you have to deal with in each of the above situations. Ask this person questions, while he or she responds using different types of verbal and nonverbal communication. Discuss your responses to the different communication styles.

Spatial Elements

Most people "need their own space"—that area surrounding a person that others are not allowed to enter, or are allowed to enter only under certain circumstances. Someone who "gets in your face" is aggressively asserting him- or herself. There are different types of space or distance:

1. *Personal distance.* Usually between 1.5 and 4 feet (roughly 50–125 cm) from one's body, this "arm's-length" distance is where we allow friends and acquaintances. It is not an intimate distance.

2. *Social distance.* Usually between 4 and 12 feet (roughly 1.25–3.5 m) from one's body, this is the distance at which most of our social interactions occur.

3. *Public distance.* Usually 12 feet (roughly 3.5 m) or more, this is the preferred distance for meetings, classroom teaching, and interviews.

Cultural differences are a factor in personal space preferences. While North Americans usually prefer to communicate at arm's length, people from Asian cultures typically prefer a greater distance. On the other hand, some Middle Eastern and Latin American cultures traditionally communicate at much closer quarters, in some cases toe to toe. When speaking to a client, try to establish a distance that is comfortable for both of you.

Impromptu Speaking: Say What You Mean, SIR

Suppose a senior paralegal requests a memorandum of law for an upcoming client meeting, but you do not have it ready yet. Do not succumb to the stress of the moment and offer hesitant or garbled excuses. Instead, muster your resources, collect your thoughts, and offer an organized, cohesive response. In other words, follow a simple formula whose initials form the acronym *SIR*: statement—information—restatement.

According to the SIR formula, you would answer the lawyer as follows:

1. *Statement:* "I cannot complete the memo on punitive damages because I am still waiting for some information."
2. *Information:*
   (a) "The client has not submitted the information requested."
   (b) "There were ambiguities in the materials the client provided and I am waiting for the clarifications."
3. *Restatement:* "Although I still expect to complete the memo in time for your meeting with the client, I wanted you to know why it is not ready for your review yet."

The impression this message creates is of an organized, well-thought-out position. A closer look at the structure of the message reveals the following:

1. Your initial *statement* is your basic position. Take a moment to decide on this main point, then express it simply and clearly.
2. The *information* comes next. One of the key factors in this formula is the providing two to three pieces of information. You may need more than one sentence for each, but you should clearly enumerate two to three main points.
3. When you make your *restatement*, take the opportunity to add something. In our example, the senior paralegal is reassured that the memo will be ready, which conveys that the situation is under control.

The ability to think on your feet and convey a message succinctly with little or no preparation is a highly regarded skill, and one worth cultivating for the sake of your career.

Exercise 8: Impromptu Speaking

1. Use the SIR method to answer the following questions:

   a. Why were you late for work today?

   b. You did not return my call. Were you ill?

   c. Where have you been? I have been trying to phone you all morning.

2. Work with a classmate to perfect the SIR technique. Throw questions at each other concerning a variety of topics, and work on coming up with appropriate answers, giving three pieces of information with every answer.

A Last Word about Oral Presentations: Do Not Read

While it is fine to review your outline for directions, glance down and check a statistic, or read out a quotation you have copied from your notes, reading a written report or summary is not the same as giving an oral presentation. Without eye contact, gesture, and enthusiasm, without visuals and audience involvement, there is no oral presentation—only a reading. Watching someone read can be a miserable experience. When someone stands up and reads a presentation, the audience tends to become distracted and lose interest. In other words, *the presentation is a failure.* Do not read your notes word for word!

Workplace Communication

Among the challenges paralegals face is dealing with difficult people and with people severely stressed about their a legal situation—facing a lawsuit, for example. Another challenge is that of making oral presentations to peers within a firm or to members of the public as part of marketing legal services.

Dealing with a Difficult Client

In any situation that is confrontational or challenging, the most important thing you can do is be professional. Remember that you are dealing with an emotional person and that your best approach is to try to defuse the emotion and bring the conversation back to a practical level.

There are many ways of accomplishing this. Keep the following in mind:

1. *Adjust the behaviour.* Clients are emotional or difficult for a reason—they may be angry or fearful; they may feel threatened, or feel that they have been treated unjustly. Instead of responding to the emotion, try to determine what is making the client difficult or emotional, and then to remove whatever is

triggering that reaction. In other words, try to perceive and acknowledge what is at the root of the client's behaviour, then use the principles of active listening to adjust the behaviour.

2. *Be tolerant.* The client's difficult attitude is entirely justified as far as he or she is concerned. Perhaps this attitude has helped the client deal with problems in the past. For instance, a defensive attitude may stem from the client's past experiences of having to ward off outside interference. You are an outsider, even though you are there to help. The client is conscious that you will get paid, or keep your job, even if he or she goes to prison or goes bankrupt.

3. *Reward non-defensive behaviour* on the client's part by mirroring it when it occurs; keep the pace of your conversation slow, do not exhibit negative nonverbal communication, listen sympathetically, and bring a calming manner to the situation.

4. *Show that you are on the client's side* and want to help by using phrases such as "I see what you mean," "I understand what you are saying," and "I think I can help you." Do not make promises that you cannot keep.

5. *Give your clients options* and let them make decisions that will allow them to feel in control of their own lives. Clients often react negatively to feeling that their lives are in the hands of a legal professional.

6. *Reassure the client* with empathetic statements such as, "After all you have been through, I can understand why you are angry."

7. *Do not label your client* by saying things like, "Everyone who is in financial trouble has to fill out these forms." It is embarrassing for the client to be categorized this way.

8. If your client is abusive or non-responsive, *respond with verbal and nonverbal attention,* and encourage any part of the client's conversation that is appropriate and constructive. Avoid resistance. The following exchange shows a paralegal responding appropriately to an angry client:

> CLIENT: All you ever do is talk! I'm about to lose everything and all you can do is talk!
> PARALEGAL: I do talk a lot.
> CLIENT: If you were paying attention to what I have been saying, you might have some answers for me. That's what I'm paying you for!
> PARALEGAL: That may be true. I could be paying more attention.
> CLIENT: You're just like all the other people in these law offices. You take my money and use a lot of language that I don't understand, and I still have to face the consequences!
> PARALEGAL: So far there are no consequences. I talk a lot and ask questions because I'm trying to find the best way to help you.

In the end, you can maintain your professionalism by simply following good listening habits, responding when appropriate, and offering constructive advice when emotions have subsided.

Conferencing with Peers or Members of the Public

Small conferences, workshops, and discussions with your peers or members of the public must be structured in much the same way as formal presentations. A presentation to our peers is more than a conversation, and the fact that you might be seated does not mean that you can be offhand or casual. Your approach should be based on the following questions:

1. What is the purpose of your presentation?
2. Who is the audience, and how much do they know about your topic?
3. How much time will be allotted to your talk?
4. Will there be a question period?
5. Are other speakers involved?

After answering these questions, begin to prepare by

1. brushing up on your topic,
2. planning a general outline,
3. gathering key facts and statistics, and
4. preparing visual aids, diagrams, or handouts if necessary.

Following these suggestions and practising good speaking skills should allow you to make an effective presentation.

Exercise 9: Presenting to Small Groups of Peers

Your instructor will divide the class into small groups and assign topics to each member of each group. These topics will be either related to something taught in the course or subjects on which the participants have knowledge. Each member of the class will be responsible for preparing a presentation for his or her small group.

FIGURE 1 **Sample Rating Sheet for an Oral Presentation**

SAMPLE RATING SHEET FOR AN ORAL PRESENTATION

SPEAKER _____ DATE _____

DELIVERY	RATING	COMMENTS
General attitude	_____	_____
Use of voice	_____	_____
Quality	_____	_____
Pitch	_____	_____
Volume	_____	_____
Speed	_____	_____
Articulation & pronunciation	_____	_____
Body movements	_____	_____
• Posture	_____	_____
• Movement	_____	_____
• Gestures	_____	_____
• Facial expressions	_____	_____
• Eye contact	_____	_____
Use of language	_____	_____
Speaker's purpose	_____	_____
Theme	_____	_____
Desired audience response	_____	_____
Use of notes & reading	_____	_____

FIGURE 1 **Continued**

SAMPLE RATING SHEET FOR AN ORAL PRESENTATION (CONT'D)

CONTENT	RATING	COMMENTS
Introduction	_____	_____
Conclusion	_____	_____
Organization	_____	_____
Development and Support of Main Points	_____	_____

GENERAL COMMENTS

_____

_____

_____

_____

_____

_____

_____

_____

_____

_____

_____

_____

_____

_____

_____

_____

_____

Summary

Effective speaking skills can improve interpersonal communications and are a practical necessity for paralegals. Whether you are addressing a large group of legal professionals, advocating before a judge, adjudicator, or other decision maker, engaging in a small-group discussion, or simply speaking one-on-one with a client or a colleague, you will perform better if you have effective speaking skills.

Readings

D

Clients Without Lawyers Disturb Chief Justice

"Complex problem" due to lack of money, but money alone won't help

VANCOUVER—The increasing trend of Canadians representing themselves in court, despite their lack of legal knowledge, is causing "serious repercussions" for the justice system, Canada's top judge says.

"While we have a great justice system, increasing numbers of Canadians do not have access to it," Chief Justice Beverley McLachlin of the Supreme Court of Canada told the opening conference of the Canadian Bar Association here yesterday.

"This has serious repercussions for the justice system, which is based on litigants being represented by lawyers. Even more serious are the repercussions for the public." Pre-trial meetings and trials become longer as judges struggle to explain the process to unrepresented parties, all the while having to be careful they don't appear to favour one side, McLachlin said.

Ironically, say legal experts, those who go it alone for financial reasons often end up adding to the cost and complexity of court proceedings.

McLachlin said money is just one of the issues. "It would be facile and simplistic of me to attempt to tell you what I think the problems are," she told reporters at a news conference following her speech. "It's not just a money problem. It's a complex problem that requires more than just a simplistic solution."

The problem is particularly acute in family courts, where "the cost of litigation uses up precious resources that could better be used in providing housing and clothing for children and parents," the country's top judge said.

One possible solution being tried in the family courts of some provinces, McLachlin said, is to make mediation and counselling services available in order to resolve custody and property disputes more quickly, cheaply, and with the least rancour possible.

In her speech, McLachlin said part of the answer may lie with the country's richest law firms, which she suggested might do more to offer free legal services to those who can't afford a lawyer. "I wonder if some of our largest and most profitable law firms might be more active in constructively supporting their lawyers who would like to give more time to pro-bono work."

Government, judges and lawyers all have to do their part, McLachlin said.

That may be difficult for lawyers, who already feel they are on a "treadmill" and often face "serious pressures" to bill for 2,000 or more hours of work each year, which adds up to 65 or 70 hours in the office each week, she added.

Judges are so concerned about the problem that the Canadian Judicial Council has undertaken a study on unrepresented litigants, hoping to understand the dimensions of the problem, she said. But already judges across the country are reporting that the number of self-represented litigants is rising, she added.

McLachlin said she's also concerned about the process for naming federally appointed judges, who sit on the Supreme Court of Canada, provincial superior courts, and courts of appeal. A House of Commons standing committee on human rights and justice will hold hearings this fall on how the process can be improved … .

In contrast to the process underway for the confirmation of Justice John Roberts to the United States Supreme Court, Canada's newest Supreme Court appointees were not questioned. Instead, [Justice Minister Irwin] Cotler appeared before the justice committee to explain whom he consulted with and the personal and professional qualities that merited the appointments.

While from her vantage point, the Canadian judiciary already meets high standards of competence, impartiality, empathy and wisdom, McLachlin said it's legitimate for the public to seek the best process possible.

But, she stressed, it's "equally legitimate" to insist the process respect the independence of judges and all appointments be made on the basis of merit.

"I think this is a political matter, the appointment of judges. They're studying it and it's their job to find a good system. I'm not interested so much in the mechanics."

Tracey Tyler, "Clients without Lawyers Disturb Chief Justice," *Toronto Star* (14 August 2005). Torstar Syndication Services. Reprinted with permission.

Report Recommends Paralegals Provide Services in Some Family Law Matters

A much-anticipated report has recommended broadening the scope of family law to let paralegals provide legal services in some matters.

If implemented by the provincial government and the Law Society of Upper Canada, the report's recommendations would let paralegals represent clients in court in a number of family law areas, including custody, access and simple child support cases.

"I recognize that the issue of paralegals representing clients in court is one of considerable controversy," Justice Annemarie Bonkalo said in the report.

Bonkalo is a part-time judge and former chief justice of the Ontario Court of Justice, who was tasked with conducting a review of family law services to assess what can be done to boost access to justice. Among what are expected to be some of the more controversial recommendations is a call for the law society to create a specialized licence for paralegals to provide certain services in family law.

In 2014-15, more than 57 per cent of Ontarians who went through family court did not have legal representation.

"When I began this review, my own feeling, based on the written submissions I received, was that in-court assistance would not be appropriate and that a line could be reasonably drawn at the courtroom door," she added.

"As I continued to explore the issues and hear from different communities, it became clear to me that precluding paralegals from appearing in court would be a disservice to clients."

The report contends that paralegals should also be allowed to represent clients in matters concerning restraining orders, enforcement and simple and joint divorces without property, but draws the line at more complex proceedings.

The report recommends that paralegals should not be allowed to provide services that involve child protection, property, spousal support or relocation. They also would not be able to do anything that involves the Convention on the Civil Aspects of International Child Abduction or complex child support in which discretionary determinations are needed to arrive at an income amount.

Paralegals can currently appear in the Small Claims Court and the Ontario Court of Justice for Provincial Offences Act infractions.

Bonkalo has also recommended paralegals should not have to seek a judge's permission before entering court, as it would create uncertainty and would be a disincentive to hiring a paralegal.

"From a practical stand, it may discourage individuals from pursuing the specialized paralegal licence in family law, as it would be frustrating to not be able to provide continuous service to one's client," Bonkalo said.

"It would be difficult to explain to a client that one could assist the client with filling out forms and preparing for court but that, where the client perhaps most needed assistance, the paralegal could not enter the courtroom. Such a limitation could very well play into a person's decision on whether to hire a paralegal."

Family lawyers have voiced concerns that they could be pushed out of the market if paralegals are given the right to provide legal services in any part of family law. Opponents have also said that family law is a very complex area, in which even tasks that seem simple can have serious consequences and can lead to more complicated matters. Family lawyers have also said paralegals simply do not have the same training and called for the government to let other reforms play out before considering widening the scope of the area.

The report, which was commissioned by the provincial government and the law society, also recommends that the regulator take steps to facilitate collaboration between lawyers and paralegals to create referral networks and interdisciplinary teams.

"After reading all the written submissions and hearing the diverse views expressed, it is clear to me that unrepresented litigants in family law need more options in obtaining legal assistance to resolve their family disputes," she said in the report.

Bonkalo has submitted the report to MAG [the Ministry of the Attorney General] and the law society, who will now determine the next steps needed to implement its recommendations.

In statement responding to the report, Attorney General Yasir Naqvi said the provincial government will be working over the coming months with the law society and the federal government to create an action plan for the recommendations.

"Over half of Ontarians who use the family law system do not have legal representation, and the problem is growing," he said in the statement.

"It is more important than ever that we work to improve access to justice for families. Our government is ready to act. We are committed to working with our partners and the federal government to consider changes that will have a real, positive impact on people's lives, like allowing paralegals to be trained to provide family law services."

Alex Robinson, "Report Recommends Paralegals Provide Services in Some Family Law Matters," *Canadian Lawyer* (6 March 2017), online: <http://www.canadianlawyermag.com/legalfeeds/author/alex-robinson/report-recommends-paralegals-provide-services-in-some-family-law-matters-7329>. Reprinted with permission.

Glossary

abbreviation a shortened version of a longer word or phrase

acronym a word formed from the initial letters of other words

administrative tribunals independent quasi-judicial bodies established by legislation to implement legislative policy; they are specialized bodies that settle disputes involving government rules and regulations

affirmative sentence a sentence that is in positive form

appellate decision a decision of a court or tribunal having the jurisdiction to review and reverse the decision of an inferior court, tribunal, or other administrative decision-making authority

brainstorming a process for solving a problem or answering a question which involves gathering a list of all possible ideas spontaneously

case brief a concise summary of a court decision

cause of action a set of facts that support one party's legal right to sue another party

clause any group of words that contains a subject and a verb

client a person (or legal entity) who retains a paralegal or lawyer to provide legal services

comma splice occurs when two independent clauses are incorrectly connected by a comma

complete subject a subject that consists of more than one word

concurring decision a judicial opinion by one or more judges or decision-makers deciding a case in which they agree with the majority decision but for different reasons

contractions words that are formed by replacing a letter or group of letters with an apostrophe

dangling modifiers modifiers that do not logically modify anything in its sentence

defence a document in prescribed form setting out the facts that the defendant in a court proceeding intends to rely on to prove his or her defence

dependent clause a clause that contains a subject and a verb, but does not express a complete thought

disposition of the case a court's (or tribunal's) final decision in a case

dissenting opinion a judicial opinion by one or more judges or decision-makers deciding a case in which they disagree with the majority decision

independent clause a clause that contains a subject, a verb, and only one complete thought

infinitive the basic verb form, without inflections to show person, number, or tense

irregular verbs verbs that cannot be changed from present to past tense by adding –*ed* to the present form of the verb

judicial review a process which allows courts to review the decisions of administrative tribunals and administrative agencies

Law Society of Ontario a self-governing body that is authorized to educate, license, and regulate paralegals and lawyers in Ontario in accordance with the *Law Society Act*, RSO 1990, c. l.8; its regulations; its by-laws; and its rules of conduct

legal jargon specialized legal language that those who are not trained legal professionals find difficult to understand

linking verbs verbs that do not appear to be "action" verbs but link subjects to other parts of the sentence

majority decision the judicial opinion of more than half of the judges or decision-makers deciding a case

misplaced modifiers modifiers that are placed within a sentence in such a way that it is unclear what word they apply to

negative sentence a sentence that is in negative form

opposing advocate the lawyer or paralegal representing the other party (or parties) in a court proceeding

paraphrase restating another person's communication in your own words to demonstrate an understanding of that person's meaning

plaintiff a person (or legal entity) who starts a legal proceeding against another person (or legal entity) in a court

pleadings formal written statements by each party in a legal proceeding that contain the alleged facts each party relies on to support his or her claim or defence

point-first writing an approach to writing where the writer states the conclusion or point first, followed by an explanation or discussion of that point

point form using a few words or incomplete sentences to summarize a main idea

prescribed to set down as a law, rule, or direction that must be followed

process servers individuals who give legal notice to parties in a legal proceeding regarding commencement of a claim, response to a claim, etc. by presenting legal documents to the party; process servers are also used by lawyers and paralegals to file legal documents with various court and tribunal offices

proofreading a process in which the writer or another individual reads the text to identify and correct spelling and typing errors, as well as grammatical and stylistic mistakes

prospective client a potential client

ratio decidendi the principle of law for which the judicial decision stands for

redundant synonyms two or more words used together that mean the same thing

regular verbs verbs that can be changed from present to past tense by adding *–ed* to the present form of the verb

reporting letter a letter sent to a client that describes the steps the lawyer or paralegal has taken on behalf of the client, the results obtained, and any next steps

retain to hire or engage a lawyer or paralegal

run-on sentence two complete sentences or independent clauses that have been incorrectly joined together; it expresses more than one thought with no division between the thoughts

sentence fragment a group of words without a subject, verb, or a complete thought

simple subject in a sentence, a simple subject is a subject that is a noun, pronoun, or a word ending in *–ing*

slang words or phrases usually used in informal speech

strike out when a judge orders the removal of all or part of a party's pleading in a legal proceeding. as a result, the party cannot rely on or refer to the pleading that was struck out

subject in a sentence, the subject is the word or group of words that the sentence is about or that the sentence concerns

summary a concisely written overview of an original of text in your own words without changing the meaning of the original

tense indicates when the action (verb) took place (past), is taking place (present), or will take place (future)

thesis a statement or conclusion expressed as the main idea in a text or speech, which a person attempts to prove or support using logical arguments

title of proceeding the formal name of a court case which identifies the parties, the court level, and the year of the decision

tone the attitude conveyed by the writer in a document

topic sentence the sentence that introduces the reader to the substance of a paragraph by summarizing the main idea; usually the first sentence or two

verb the action word in a sentence

voice a type of sentence structure

Index

Note: Page numbers followed by *f* represent figures.

Credits

Chapter 2

All forms © Queen's Printer for Ontario, 2018. Reproduced with permission. The forms listed are subject to change without notice. The most current version can be found on the website of the Ministry of the Attorney General at <http://ontariocourtforms.on.ca/static/media/uploads/courtforms/scc/09a/rscc-9a-e.pdf>. The Government of Ontario and The Ministry of the Attorney General had no role in the creation of the publication.

Chapter 4

Tara Schauerte, "By the Book," *Campus Starter*. Reprinted by permission of the EI Group.

Chapter 9

All forms from the Social Justice Tribunal Ontario © Queen's Printer for Ontario, 2018. Reproduced with permission. The forms listed are subject to change without notice. The most current version can be found on the web site of the Social Justice Tribunal Ontario at . The Government of Ontario and the Social Justice Tribunal Ontario had no role in the creation of the publication.

All forms from the Safety, Licensing Appeals & Standards Tribunals Ontario © Queen's Printer for Ontario, 2018. Reproduced with permission. The forms listed are subject to change without notice. The most current version can be found on the web site of the Safety, Licensing Appeals & Standards Tribunals Ontario at The Government of Ontario and the Safety, Licensing Appeals & Standards Tribunals Ontario had no role in the creation of the publication.

All forms from the Ministry of the Attorney General © Queen's Printer for Ontario, 2018. Reproduced with permission. The forms listed are subject to change without notice. The most current version can be found on the web site of the Ministry of the Attorney General at . The Government of Ontario and The Ministry of the Attorney General had no role in the creation of the publication.

Appendix B

Alex Robinson, "Report recommends paralegals provide services in some family law matter," *Canadian Lawyer*, 6 March 2017.